Orpheus in Macedonia

Also available from Bloomsbury

Corinth in Late Antiquity by Amelia R. Brown
Funerary Epigrams of Ancient Greece by Marta González González
The Myth of Hero and Leander by Silvia Montiglio
The Religious Worlds of the Laity in Late Antique Gaul by Lisa Kaaren Bailey
The Roman Mithras Cult by Olympia Panagiotidou with Roger Beck

Orpheus in Macedonia

Myth, Cult and Ideology

Tomasz Mojsik

translated by Grzegorz Kulesza

BLOOMSBURY ACADEMIC
LONDON • NEW YORK • OXFORD • NEW DELHI • SYDNEY

BLOOMSBURY ACADEMIC
Bloomsbury Publishing Plc
50 Bedford Square, London, WC1B 3DP, UK
1385 Broadway, New York, NY 10018, USA
29 Earlsfort Terrace, Dublin 2, Ireland

BLOOMSBURY, BLOOMSBURY ACADEMIC and the Diana logo are trademarks
of Bloomsbury Publishing Plc

First published in Great Britain 2023
Paperback edition published 2024

Copyright © Tomasz Mojsik, 2023

Tomasz Mojsik has asserted his right under the Copyright, Designs and Patents Act,
1988, to be identified as Author of this work.

For legal purposes the Acknowledgements on p. viii constitute an
extension of this copyright page.

Cover design: Terry Woodley
Cover image © lfreytag/Getty

All rights reserved. No part of this publication may be reproduced or transmitted
in any form or by any means, electronic or mechanical, including photocopying,
recording, or any information storage or retrieval system, without prior permission
in writing from the publishers.

Bloomsbury Publishing Plc does not have any control over, or responsibility for, any
third-party websites referred to or in this book. All internet addresses given
in this book were correct at the time of going to press. The author and publisher
regret any inconvenience caused if addresses have changed or sites have
ceased to exist, but can accept no responsibility for any such changes.

A catalogue record for this book is available from the British Library.

Library of Congress Cataloging-in-Publication Data
Names: Mojsik, Tomasz, author.
Title: Orpheus in Macedonia : myth, cult and ideology / Tomasz Mojsik.
Description: London : Bloomsbury Academic, 2023. | Includes bibliographical
references and index.
Identifiers: LCCN 2022036221 | ISBN 9781350213180 (hardback) |
ISBN 9781350213227 (paperback) | ISBN 9781350213197 (ebook) |
ISBN 9781350213203 (epub)
Subjects: LCSH: Orpheus (Greek mythological character) | Orpheus (Greek
mythological character)–Homes and haunts–Greece–Pieria. | Orpheus (Greek
mythological character)–Homes and haunts–Macedonia. | Mythology, Greek.
Classification: LCC BL820.O7 M58 2023 | DDC 292.1/3–dc23/eng20221024
LC record available at https://lccn.loc.gov/2022036221

ISBN:	HB:	978-1-3502-1318-0
	PB:	978-1-3502-1322-7
	ePDF:	978-1-3502-1319-7
	eBook:	978-1-3502-1320-3

Typeset by RefineCatch Limited, Bungay, Suffolk

To find out more about our authors and books visit www.bloomsbury.com
and sign up for our newsletters.

Contents

List of Illustrations	vii
Preface and Acknowledgement	viii
Abbreviations	xi
Introduction	1
1 Orpheus and the Mythical Tradition	11
Orpheus as a mythical hero	13
Orpheus and mythical tradition: Sources	14
Stories, variants, local contexts	21
2 Orpheus, Oeagrus and Thracians in Early Testimonies	29
Early iconography	29
Orpheus on stage	33
Fourth century and beyond	34
Oeagrus	35
Why Thrace? Contexts and explanations	37
3 Leibethra, Pimpleia and Mythical Geography	43
Leibethra and Pimpleia: What do we know?	47
Leibethra and Pimpleia: Changes in mythical geography	49
Contexts and explanations	56
Leibethra, Pimpleia and Thracia	61
Orpheus and Thracian tribes	63
Summary, Nysa and scholiasts	67
4 Thracians, Pieria and Music	69
Strabo I: Leibethra and Boeotia	70
Strabo II: Ephorus, Leibethra and Thracians	73
Thucydides 2,99: Pieres are not Pierians	77
Thracians and *mousikē*	85
Conclusions	88

5	Orpheus in Pieria	89
	Birth, life and music in Pieria	90
	Orpheus' death in Pieria	94
	The proverb about Leibethrians	98
	Genealogies of Orpheus: Pierus and Methone	100
	Pierian toponyms and the Muses	104
	Conclusions	107
6	Orpheus' Tomb in Pieria	109
	Lesbos and Kitharodia	110
	Pieria: Tomb, statues and cult	114
	Contexts	123
	Summary	132
	Coda: The two graves of Saint Adalbert	134
7	*Mousikē*, Identity and Ideology	135
	Orpheus and the Pierian tradition: A recapitulation	136
	Macedon: *Mousikē* and Orphics	138
	Macedon in context: Identity and ideology	146
Epilogue: Orpheuses, not Orpheus		151
Notes		155
Bibliography		179
Index		199

Illustrations

Figures

1 Orpheus playing lyra and singing, between two standing Thracians xiv
2 Orpheus' death xiv
3 Orpheus amongst the Thracians xv
4 Orpheus' head xv

Maps

1 Map of the Greek world and Thracian tribes xiii
2 Map of the Macedonian Kingdom xiii

Preface and Acknowledgement

This book was originally published in Polish in 2019 under the title *Orfeusz między Tracją a Pierią. Mit, kult i tożsamość macedońska* ('Orpheus between Pieria and Thrace: Myth, Cult, and Macedonian Identity'). In 2021, having read Polish reviews and remarks from the reviewers at Bloomsbury, I took the difficult decision of rearranging the contents and sequence of chapters, resulting in a major overhaul. For this reason, about 85 per cent of the book has been rewritten on its way to the final version. This took twice as long as creating the original text, but I am hoping it was worth it. Certainly, if the option existed, I would still be looking for the optimal arrangement of the material and writing the book for another ten years, or perhaps more.

I was aided in formulating some of the conclusions by my parallel work on translating Apollodorus' *Library*. In preparing that text, the commentary, and especially the introduction about Ancient mythography, I could rethink Ancient mythical tradition and examine it as part of a bigger picture. Naturally, the choice of Orpheus as the main subject of the work was related to his musical skill and his being the son of a Muse. Moreover, in recent years, I have been intensively researching the literary careers of places connected to the divine keepers of poetic inspiration. What we might call the 'landscape of the Muses' deserves a book of its own, which I am hoping to see soon. The sources of fascination with Pierian toponyms must, however, be seen elsewhere. Its origins should be linked to the difficult passage in the longest surviving poem of Poseidippus (118 A–B) and the interpretation of the enigmatic phrase 'Pi(m)pleian Thebes'. It is the reading of that phrase that directed me to Macedon, its mythical tradition, and to its royal propaganda, as well as the role of toponyms in historical and literary analyses.

Some of the conclusions featured in the book were also presented at various gatherings over the past few years, especially at a conference in Montpellier ('Devenir un dieu, devenir un héros en Grèce ancienne') and during scholarly meetings in Warsaw, Cracow and Poznań. The early proposed interpretations were presented in 2020 in an article in *Mythos. Rivista di Storia delle Religioni*, in the aftermath of the Montpellier conference. One of the important interpretative concepts appeared to me during a train ride to Poznań, where I was supposed to speak about Poseidippus and 'Pimpleian Thebes'. Instead, I spent the entire journey thinking about Lycophron and his riddle about the nymphs of Bephyros (*Alex.* 274–6). It appears the Muses have adjusted to the rapid world we live in and provide inspiration even in the trains of the Polish State Railways. As for the geographical aspects of the myth of Orpheus, I presented them at a geography and cartography conference in Supraśl, which resulted in the inclusion of prototype theory in the new version of the book.

This book would not have been written without the support of many people and help in accessing latest publications. I owe much to discussions at conferences, seminars and over e-mail, which allowed me to rethink and better describe the interpretations of numerous testimonies cited in the book. Special thanks go to Bartłomiej Bednarek, Robert Cowan, Barbara Graziosi, Mathias Haake, Alex Hardie, Greta Hawes, Flore Kimmel-Clauzet, Jan Kwapisz, Pauline LeVen, Karol Łopatecki, Federicomaria Muccioli, Francis Pownall, Sławomir Sprawski, Susan A. Stephens, Mikołaj Szymański and Elżbieta Wesołowska. I would like to thank the Polish reviewers of the book, Marek Węcowski, Sławomir Sprawski and Krzysztof Nawotka, and the anonymous review staff of Bloomsbury, for their remarks upon the text. However, the key role in the critical assessment of the entire text and its numerous revisions belongs to Bogdan Burliga, whom I would hereby like to offer heartfelt thanks for his time, patience and friendship. Any mistakes that remain are, of course, solely my own.

This book would also never have happened without the support from the University of Białystok, especially its kind Rector Robert Ciborowski, and Dean Joanna Sadowska. Separate thanks go to my friends and colleagues from the Chair of History of Demographic, Economic, and Religious Structures: Cezary Kuklo, Marzena Liedke, Radek Poniat, and especially Piotr Guzowski, who knows how to motivate me not just on the football pitch, but also in writing.

Finally, some technical remarks. It was impossible to maintain complete consistency in proper names, and so I am following the established custom: place names are given in commonly accepted English transcription, if one exists, and in a Hellenised form if one does not. In both situations, this serves to prioritise the comfort of the reader. Ancient sources (names of authors and titles of works) are cited as per the *Oxford Classical Dictionary* (OCD) that is, in their Latinised forms. Where there are citations from sources translated into English, I attempt to present a version available to the audience, especially from the Loeb Classical Library, *Brill's New Jacoby* (BNJ, online) or another esteemed edition. I only translate personally passages like scholia, commentaries or proverbs that are not available in English.

This book is dedicated to my niece Martha in recognition of her support and unwavering faith in my work, and as gratitude for the many sage conversations. May the Muses ever be in your favour.

Abbreviations

BNJ	*Brill's New Jacoby* (online).
CMG	*Corpus Medicorum Graecorum* (1908–).
DK	*Die Fragmente der Vorsokratiker*, griechisch und deutsch, von H. Diels, sechste verbesserte Auflage, herausg. von W. Kranz, vols I–III; Berlin-Grunewald, 1951–1952.
Gow-Page	A. S. F. Gow and D. L. Page, *The Greek Anthology: Hellenistic Epigrams* vols 1–2, Cambridge: Cambridge University Press, 1965.
LIMC	*Lexicon Iconographicum Mythologiae Classicae*, vols 1–8, Zürich, München: Artemis Verlag, 1981–1999.
LSJ	*Greek-English Lexicon*, Ninth Edition with a Revised Supplement, ed. H. G. Liddell, R. Scott, H. S. Jones and R. McKenzie, Oxford: Oxford University Press, 1996.
Montanari	Montanari F. (ed.) 2015, *The Brill Dictionary of Ancient Greek*, Leiden: Brill.
OCD	*Oxford Classical Dictionary*, S. Hornblower and A. Spawforth (eds), 3rd ed., Oxford and New York: Oxford University Press 1996.
OF	*Orphicorum Fragmenta*: Bernabé A. 2004–2007, *Poetae epici Graeci. Testimonia et fragmenta*, vol. 2.1–3, Leiden: Brill.
OGIS	*Orientis Graeci Inscriptiones Selectae*.
PCG	R. Kassel and C. Austin (eds), *Poetae Comici Graeci*, (1983–).
PMG	*Poetae melici Graeci*, edited by D. L. Page, Oxford: Oxford University Press, 1962.

Powell	*Collectanea Alexandrina. Reliquiae minores poetarum Graecorum aetatis Ptolemaicae 323–146 A.C.: epicorum, elegiacorum, lyricorum, ethicorum, cum epimetris et indice nominum*, ed. I. U. Powell, Oxford 1925 (2nd edition: 1970; reprint: Chicago 1981).
RE	A. Pauly, G. Wissowa, W. Kroll, K. Witte, K. Mittelhaus, K. Ziegler (eds), *Paulys Realencyclopädie der classischen Altertumswissenschaft*, Stuttgart, 1894–1980.
SEG	*Supplementum epigraphicum Graecum* (1923–).
SH	*Supplementum Hellenisticum*, H. Lloyd-Jones and P. Parsons (eds), indices in hoc *Supplementum necnon in Powellii Collectanea Alexandrina confecit H.-G. Nesselrath*, Berolini et Novi Eboraci [New York], 1983.
TGrF	*Tragicorum Graecorum Fragmenta*, vols 1–5, ed. B. Snell (vol. 1), S. Radt (vols 3–4) and R. Kannicht (vols 2 and 5), Göttingen: Vandenhoeck & Ruprecht, 1971–2004.

Map 1 Map of the Greek world and Thracian tribes. © Bloomsbury Academic.

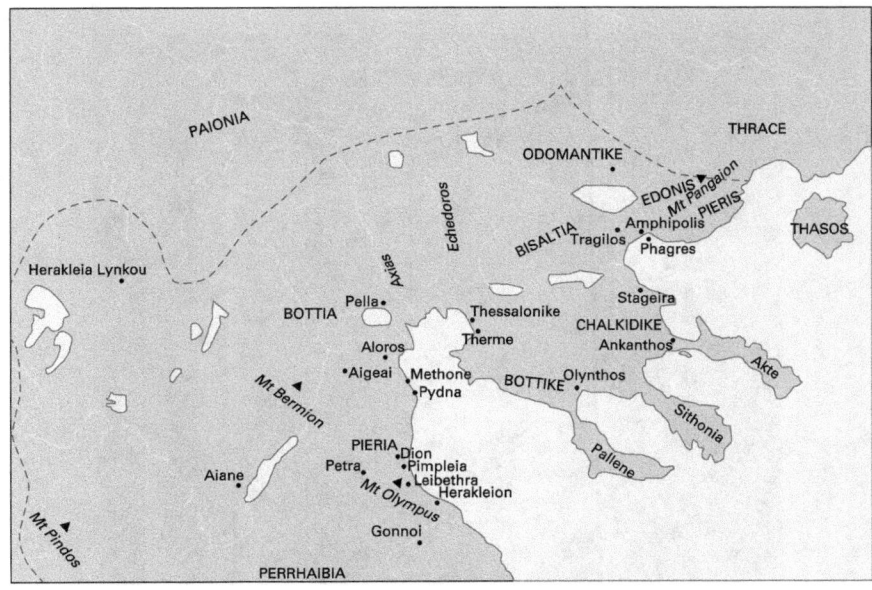

Map 2 Map of the Macedonian Kingdom. © Wikimedia/ drawing by Marsyas. Redrawn by Tomasz Mojsik.

Figure 1 Orpheus playing lyra and singing, between two standing Thracians. Attic red figure pelike, manner of the Kleophon Painter, *c.* 430 BC; ARV 1148 7; London, British Museum 1846,0925.10 Cat. Vases E 390. © Wikimedia/ ArchaiOptix.

Figure 2 Orpheus' death. Attic red-figure stamnos, *c.* 470 BC; Louvre, Department of Greek, Etruscan and Roman Antiquities. © Wikimedia/ Collection of Giampietro Campana di Cavelli.

Figure 3 Orpheus amongst the Thracians. Side A of an Attic red-figure bell-krater; c. 440 BC; Attributed to the Painter of London E 497. Metropolitan Museum of Art. © Wikimedia/ Fletcher Fund, 1924.

Figure 4 Orpheus' head. Attic red-figure hydria, Inv. BS 481. © Antikenmuseum Basel und Sammlung Ludwig. Photograph by Claire Niggli, courtesy of Antikenmuseum Basel.

Introduction

Apollodorus' *Library*, an Imperial Roman-era compendium of Greek myths, describes Orpheus as follows (1,14–15):[1]

> Calliope and Oiagros (though really Apollo) had Linos, whom Heracles killed, and Orpheus, who was trained to sing to the cithara and moved stones and trees by his singing. When his wife, Eurydice, died after being bitten by a snake, he went down to the house of Hades, wishing to bring her back, and persuaded Plouton to send her up. Plouton promised to do this if Orpheus would not turn around as he made his way until he arrived at his own house. But Orpheus, in doubt, turned around and looked at his wife, and she returned to the underworld. Orpheus also discovered the mysteries of Dionysos, and he was buried near Pieria after he was torn apart by Mainads.
>
> Translated by R.S. Smith and S.M. Trzaskoma

This passage is interesting, as despite its brevity it manages to include nearly all stories associated with Orpheus. The lack of references to his participation in the expedition of the Argonauts is symptomatic as well, rather than proof of the author's absent-mindedness or ignorance. Apollodorus simply mentions the expedition elsewhere (1,111), alongside the story of the quest for the Golden Fleece. Another interesting feature of this typical mythographical précis is the focus it places on the tragic death of Eurydice.

But it would be wrong to declare Apollodorus' account representative for all versions of the myth. It is so because by its nature, a summary gathers threads that do not necessarily function together in the literature into a cohesive whole. The Argonauts' expedition had no connection to Eurydice's death or the hero's role in establishing mysteries. Some local traditions focused more on the circumstances and causes of Orpheus' death, or the fate of his remains – to which Apollodorus allots only half a sentence. Moreover, the myth changed over time and varied geographically. For many years, Orpheus' wife was a nameless, unimportant character (with the interesting exception of the poet Hermesianax calling her Agriope); the name Eurydice first appears in *The Lament for Bion* from the first century BC. The tragic love and Orpheus' adventures in Hades are a late addition, characteristic of Hellenistic and especially Roman poetry's interests. Apollodorus' version is therefore the result of his choices, as well as systematisation and reduction of the narrative to a necessary minimum. It does not reflect the changes in the image of the hero or local or authorial particularities.

Modern mythology textbooks follow Apollodorus in attempting to present Greek stories in a uniform, cohesive way. Thus, the commonly known myth of Orpheus is a smoother, unitary version, more characteristic of later writing.[2] *Orpheus in Macedon* focuses on one of those less known, but no less fascinating faces of Greek mythology: Orpheus' ties to Pieria, a region of Macedonia. This provides us with a unique opportunity to examine a regional, non-canonical version of the myth, and to discover an early mythical tradition.

But why is the issue of Orpheus' ties to Pieria or Macedonia so interesting? Traditionally, the hero is presented as a 'Thracian musician'.[3] While Apollodorus' summary never mentions the word 'Thracian,' the intended recipients of his work definitely found the origin obvious (OF 919–22T). Fritz Graf (1987, 86) summarised this in an oft-repeated phrase: 'Orpheus is always a Thracian.'

Orpheus' Thracian ties are also perceived as crucial to understanding his musical ability, which, despite the popularity of the tragic love plot in Roman poetry, was always the unifying element of the myth. The role of music can be seen in Apollodorus' story, in Roman mosaics, in Christian 'Good Shepherd' imagery, and in Renaissance depictions of the hero.[4] It also inspired Jacopo Peri and Claudio Monteverdi to compose operas about Orpheus. In European culture, he is the archetypical artist: the first musician, the poet personifying the power of song and music and their helplessness in the face of death. A divine, immortal and very human dimension of art – in a single image.[5] As Rilke said in a sonnet: '*Ein für alle Male / ists Orpheus, wenn es singt*'.[6] Orpheus' music was viewed as a primal phenomenon, at the frontier between nature and culture, a gift from beyond 'our' world, one that we have lost. And presenting Orpheus as Thracian seemed to properly express that primacy and otherness, as well as the social ambiguity of music. Hence, already in Strabo (C 471 [10,3,17]) we find it said that: 'Those who devoted their attention to the music of early times are called Thracians, I mean Orpheus, Musaeus, and Thamyris'. Does that mean the Greeks believed Thracians to be the originators of their music and culture?

In the ancient mythical tradition, particularly in the early depictions of Orpheus, there is a contradiction between two groups of spatial references: some point to Thrace, others to Pieria/Macedonia.[7] This tension is particularly visible in the context of the birth, death and grave of the hero. A good illustration of the issues of Orpheus' ethnic and geographic background is a passage from a Hellenistic poet, Apollonius of Rhodes. He begins his *Argonautica* by describing the participants of the famous expedition. Although the journey to world's end attracted great warriors, such as Heracles, Apollonius begins his roster with the musician Orpheus (1,23–34):[8]

> First then let us name Orpheus whom once Calliope bare, it is said, wedded to Thracian Oeagrus, near the Pimpleian height. Men say that he by the music of his songs charmed the stubborn rocks upon the mountains and the course of rivers. And the wild oak-trees to this day, tokens of that magic strain, that grow at Zone on the Thracian shore, stand in ordered ranks close together, the same which under the charm of his lyre he led down from Pieria. Such then was Orpheus whom Aeson's son welcomed to share his toils, in obedience to the behest of Cheiron, Orpheus ruler of Bistonian Pieria.
>
> Translated by R. C. Seaton

Born in Pierian Pimpleia, the son of the Muse Calliope and the Thracian Oeagrus travels (alongside Pierian oaks) to Thrace, where he would rule 'Bistonian Pieria' – a sort of new Pieria in the land of Bistonians, a Thracian tribe. Both his parents and the merging of distant toponyms seem an attempt to connect opposites and link culturally and spatially distant phenomena. Calliope, the daughter of Zeus, first among the Muses (goddesses personifying civilisation), communes with the savage Thracian to birth the first musician, a predecessor to Homer and Hesiod.[9] The mythical musician is born in Pieria, but travels to 'Bistonian Pieria', a land absent from ancient maps. Was this how Apollonius envisioned music and song at the dawn of existence? A merging of opposites, fundamentally ambiguous, equal parts Greek and barbarian? How should we understand Orpheus being born in Macedonian Pieria? Does it mean he was not Thracian, or, at least, not entirely? What value did the poet assign to the hero's journey to Thracian Bistonia and to leaving Macedonian

Pieria behind? Why was it Bistonia, rather than the environs of the Thracian River Strymon, towards the Pangaion, as the better-known versions of the myth claim? How did others in the Alexandrian literary circles interpret the motif of leaving Pieria (understood to be the birthplace of the Muses and, as such, the cradle of Greek culture) to search for a 'new home'? A great majority of them, including Apollonius himself, had abandoned their home cities to move to Alexandria, or, as the contemporary poet Posidippus put it, 'Pimpleian Thebes'.[10] The Pierian Pimpleia, where Orpheus was born according to Apollonius (1,24), appears roughly contemporaneously in a work by Apollonius' rival, Callimachus of Cyrene. In his hymn to Apollo (4,7-8), this Alexandrian poet and scholar suggests that it was there that the Muses were born, and that the site is as important as Delos was for Apollo. Choosing Pimpleia, an insignificant village in Pieria, as the birthplace of the Muses and Orpheus and the repetition of the toponym in two different literary texts from the period, was not accidental. The decision granted us a back door into the debate over the origins of poetry and music in the Greek world.

The tales of Orpheus, the son of a Muse, thus highlights another important question, one which Greeks had been asking since the Archaic period: Where and how was *mousikē*, understood as 'the domain of Muses and any human activity overseen by these goddesses', born (or invented)? And, by extension, what makes Greeks Greek, as *mousikē* was also an equivalent of our notions of 'culture' or 'civilisation'?[11] In his great antiquarian work *The Learned Banqueters*, Athenaeus argues that music had been the foundation of Greek wisdom since the beginning, and also adds (14,632c [OF 960T]): 'This is why they regarded Apollo and Orpheus as the most musical and the wisest of the gods and demigods, respectively' [tr. S. Douglas Olson]. When this sentence mentions μουσικώτατον καὶ σοφώτατον ('most musical and the wisest'), the author highlight not their narrow musical proficiency, but rather a supreme culture and the associated wisdom.

What did the Greeks understand as 'the origins of *mousikē*'? Certainly the birth of Muses from Mnemosyne, their immanent existence, or their birth from primordial deities, like Ouranos and Gaia. Some tales, including their birth from Zeus, highlight the central role of music and *choreia* in Greek life. Others, meanwhile, such as the narrative from Pindar's Theban hymn (fr. 29–35), present the birth of the Muses as the emergence of memory and song, which become the ultimate complement to the world of men and gods.[12]

The origins of *mousikē* were also associated with the first instrument, invented by Hermes or Apollo and placed in the sky, or its significance for the flourishing of musical talent on Lesbos.[13] Occasionally, stories highlight places sanctified by the Muses' presence or by the instrument. The nature of Greek myth was such that every local version was true for the inhabitants of the given city without necessarily being viewed as contradictory with Panhellenic versions found in celebrated literary works. Thus, Thespians mentioned the Aloadae as the first to sacrifice to the Muses, Troezenians claimed it was Ardalus, and elsewhere, Pieros, eponym of Pieria.[14] In Plato's *Phaedrus* (259b–d), Socrates regales the titular character with a tale of ancient people who, charmed by music, forgot about nourishment and were turned into cicadas, insects who thereafter served the Muses as their representatives in the human and natural world.

Greeks presented the birth of *mousikē* also as the moment of emergence of *protoi heuretai*, the 'inventors', the first to use an instrument, establish a genre, or win a musical agon. As described in *On Music* (5, o. 1132f [OF 884T]), attributed to Plutarch and based on Classical-era sources:[15]

> Olympus first brought the music of the auloi to the Greeks, but that the Idaean Dactyls did so too; that Hyagnis was the first to play the auloi and that his son Marsyas came next, and after him Olympus; and that Terpander took as his models the hexameters of Homer and the music of Orpheus. But Orpheus evidently imitated no predecessor, as there were none as yet, unless it was composers of songs for the auloi, and Orpheus' work resembles theirs in no way.[16]

The references to mythical predecessors reigned in the chronology, explained the origins of historical performers, and indicated the source of their skill. This image of Orpheus as a musician *par excellence* was already present in Polygnotos' fresco in Delphi (in the Lesche of the Cnidians; c. 450 BC), where the hero is shown in Hades alongside other musicians, including Thamyris and the aulos players Olympus and Marsyas (Paus. 10,30,6–8).

A lesser-known effect of the Greek debate over the origins of *mousikē* was the Ancient interest in the graves of musicians and poets, especially mythical. The tomb of Linus was associated with Euboea and Thebes, and his cult emerged in the Valley of the Muses at the foot of Mount Helicon, near Thespiae, as well as in Epidauros, in the sacred precinct of Asclepius. The place of death and burial of Mousaios, the 'Muses' Musician', as his name would imply, was linked to either Piraeus or the Mouseion Hill in central Athens.[17] The 'discoveries' of graves of great individuals, particularly poets or mythical musicians, began in the late fifth century, coinciding with the first histories of literature and music, works of literary criticism, biographies and collections of mementos of celebrated figures.[18] The story of Orpheus' grave, believed to be in Macedonian Leibethra, is discussed extensively in Pausanias' *Periegesis*, while his cult at the site is described by Conon in his *Narratives*.[19] The city also appears in the proverb about 'less educated/civilized than Leibethrians'. Zenobius, a rhetorician from the Roman era who included the saying in his collection, explains it as follows: 'Leibethrians are Pierian *ethnos*, mentioned [by Aristotle] in the *Constitution of Methone*; it is said that Leibethrians are very uncivilized, as it was among them that Orpheus' death happened.'[20] Those who enabled the killing, or even caused the death of Orpheus, were revealed as uncivilised – either misunderstanding the gifts of the Muses, or out of favour with the goddesses after the hero's death. In the latter case, their *amousia* (hostility towards or ignorance of the Muses) meant they were stripped of culture (*mousikē*), of what made them human and civilised. Leibethra is the second Pierian site associated with the myth of Orpheus, after Pimpleia. Both toponyms represent the physical extremes of his life: from birth in Pimpleia to death or burial in Leibethra.

Does Orpheus' birthplace and grave being in Pieria mean that the hero, commonly regarded as Thracian, was Macedonian? If so, when was that connection made? In the Classical period? And, crucially, why was he associated specifically with Macedonia? In his edition of accounts of Orpheus, Alberto Bernabé explains (p. 416) that 'duae traditiones de Orphei patria narrabantur: Orpheus in Thracia vel in Pieria natus est (vel in Pieria vitam egit); saepe mixtae inveniuntur'.[21] It is this duality of tradition, tying Orpheus to Thrace and/or Pieria, and its background that will comprise the main subject of interest to the present book. It will attempt to demonstrate that current scholarship excessively highlights Orpheus' Thracian identity over his ties to Pieria.

The goal of this study shall be to reinterpret the origins, extent, meaning and context of Orpheus' Pierian ties in the early stories about the hero.[22] This analysis fits naturally into an investigation into the so-called Hellenisation of Macedonia in the Classical period and into the role of myth and religious gesture in the ideological practices of the era. Ideological functions of myth are better known from Athenian material, while Macedonia remains relatively poorly researched.[23] Tying Orpheus to Pieria may therefore allow us to restart the discussion on the role and extent of propaganda in Classical Macedonia.

As shown by the above quote from Bernabé, the Pierian tradition is not a novel interpretation. This work is not the first in the field; the research herein stems from important analyses by Linforth, Graf, Bremmer, Bernabé, and a host of other scholars intrigued by Orpheus over the centuries.[24] However, until now, no attempt has been made at a detailed analysis of this Macedonian tradition, in particular the meaning and reasons for Pierian toponym references in the myth (placing the birth, death and grave of Orpheus in Pieria). The main obstacle may have been the fragmentary and dispersed sources, as well as the late origins of scholia and commentaries, which tend to obfuscate rather than explain. Only by dividing the tradition into layers, particularly through the analysis of spatial references in the myth as well as the contextualisation of variants and later versions of the story, is it possible to re-examine and reorganise the entire picture.

The analyses below aim to include all heretofore disregarded and scattered accounts, reinterpret some known testimonies, link them to information about the grave and cult of Orpheus in Pieria, as well as demonstrate the appropriate historical and cultural context for the rise of the fundamentals of the so-called Pierian tradition and of Orpheus' grave in Macedonia. All other aspects either result from the above or are somehow linked with them.

The matter of Orpheus' presence in and ties to Macedonian Pieria is interesting because at no point in its existence was that ancient realm a place we could link to the origins of Greek culture or to mythological novelties. Militarily outstanding, politically important, but developing at its own pace, Macedon was typically considered a culturally poor cousin of the Greek world. Most myths known to us today have origins in literature and are tied to places like Athens, Thebes, Argos or Corinth. It is therefore rare that we notice and investigate local traditions, especially ones linked to Macedon, and even more so that we may connect them to religious gestures or local cultural politics.

The Macedonian case is all the more interesting in that this area is nearly absent from mythical geography, aside from the royal family's reputed ties to Heracles or Paris.[25] In this context, identifying the Pierian tradition of Orpheus and dating it offers a unique opportunity for insight into local mythographic practices and their ideological background. The present work will demonstrate that known accounts can be linked in particular to Archelaus I, king of Macedon between 415 and 399. The author considers the ideological dimension of Macedonian activities and the role of cult and narrative of the Pierian hero Orpheus in contemporary politics critical to the research. The main thesis of the work is therefore demonstrating the existence of a Pierian tradition in the sources, and portraying Macedonian changes to the image of the hero arising probably in the late fifth century and likely responsible for the rise of that tradition. In Greek mythical stories, choosing a musician or poet to be linked to a location is not an insignificant phenomenon, but an expression of ideological activity related to the creation of local identities or wider-reaching cultural capital.

Our focus on Pieria does not mean abandoning the question of Orpheus' Thracian background, as these two matters are tightly interconnected. A serious approach to the Thracian roots of Orpheus is necessary due to ancient explanations and to the role of that ancestry in mythology textbooks or scholarship. Many works claim that the figure of Orpheus was directly borrowed from Thracian religions.[26] However, accounts appear to indicate that it is only a loose hypothesis based on frail premises and late testimonies. And so, what does it mean today when we declare Orpheus 'a Thracian musician'? Why is this an interpretation problem worth tackling? Most importantly, why and how did this image spread?

These aspects shall be the starting point of the first part of the book (Chapters 2–4), which will focus on the significance of the Thracian component in the source base. The goal is to discover its possible roots and how it changed between the Classical and the Hellenistic eras. An important part of this analysis will also be the examination of the particularities of Orpheus as a mythical figure (Chapter 1), including the readings of variants, lesser-known stories, plots, modifications and non-standard explanations, or local versions present in the mythical tradition of Orpheus. Completing this task will give us the tools to evaluate ethnic and spatial choices seen in the stories of the mythical musician.

The second part of the book will be dedicated to an analysis of literary and mythographic accounts of Orpheus' links to Pieria (Chapter 5) and information about his grave, statues and cult (Chapter 6). To verify the source material, we shall call back on the broader knowledge of the worship of poets and 'spatial appropriation' of intellectuals. Chapter 7 will recapitulate the conclusions of previous analyses while investigating the dating of the Pierian tradition and Orpheus' grave and cult in Pieria. Its search for the appropriate context for innovations in this field points to the likely involvement of Archelaus I and the ideological functions of the cult of the Muses and Orpheus in contemporaneous Macedon. The work ends in an Epilogue, which will bring to the fore the heterogeneity of the portrayal of the hero in ancient sources and attempt to link the select versions and plots of the myth to Macedon.

Finally, two notes about matters outside the scope of this book. Firstly, despite references to Macedonian identity and the ongoing debate on Macedon's place within the Hellenic world,[27] the work does not discuss if the Macedonians were Greek. The author otherwise believes that the 'if' question is difficult to analyse or answer. Far more interesting and concrete is the 'how' question: How was the Hellenicity of Macedonians created and negotiated, both within and outside Macedon? In this aspect, the book offers solutions that may inform further discussion.

Secondly, due to the specifics of the subject, the examinations of Orpheus' links to Orphic literature and to so-called Orphism as a socioreligious phenomenon are limited within the book. This matter has inspired several interesting monographs in recent years.[28] Moreover, 'Orphic' accounts, while few, cause intense debate.[29] Thus, the book also does not discuss the matter of how Orpheus the mythical figure was tied to Orphic philosophical, religious, ritualistic and eschatological writings. So few accounts exist for the early period that drawing conclusions in the matter appears risky. The author also believes that before approaching that question, it is necessary to first meticulously research the mythical tradition itself and its evolution. It is there (Orpheus' descent to Hades, his refusal to kill animals, ties to Dionysus and the natural world) that we seek the reasons for the hero's linking to knowledge of the soul's fate after death. Our sources survive only in fragments, while early Attic iconography focuses almost exclusively on Orpheus' ignominious slaying by women, not the 'Orphic' aspects of his image. The problem clearly calls for separate analyses and is intentionally left at the fringe of the present disquisition. Nevertheless, the author is aware that the paths of mythical tradition and Orphic texts meet frequently and separating them might seem artificial.[30] The reader shall thus find here some attempts at linking myth to Orphic literature, with the caveat that such proposals have inherent defects and the author does not currently claim a part in the broader discussion of Orphism.

1

Orpheus and the Mythical Tradition

When thinking about the beginnings of opera, the first work that comes to mind is Claudio Monteverdi's *L'Orfeo*.[1] However, the first famous opera was actually Jacopo Peri's *Daphne*, and the oldest surviving *favole in musica* is his *Euridice*. The latter work, dedicated to the story of Orpheus' wife, was officially staged on 6 October 1600 as part of the wedding festivities of Marie de' Medici and Henri IV of France. The mythical musician was played by the composer himself, reputedly bringing the audience to tears singing Orpheus' plea at the gates of Hades.

The circumstances may appear surprising, considering that all known versions of the myth ended with the death of the young wife and her irrevocable loss. Such a story would be an extravagant choice for a wedding. However, Ottavio Rinuccini's libretto has Orfeo descend into Hades and persuade its ruler to bend its laws so that Euridice may safely return to earth. The opera concludes with an unexpected happy ending. The musical story portrayed the triumph of music over sorrow and death; such a version of the myth would soon become a thesis statement of opera as a genre.[2] In the history of European culture, Greek myth has two important variables: the endurance of the core narrative, with the associated ossification of the tradition focusing on the most popular plot threads and devices; and simultaneously the malleability of the story, allowing it to be modified and adjusted to fit audience needs or the circumstances. These seemingly contradictory tendencies are actually complementary, making myth a particularly vivacious narrative material.

The myth of Orpheus is a good example of this phenomenon. Since the Roman Empire, its core plot is the narrative of Virgil and Ovid, which focused on the tragic love of the hero, the descent into Hades, his attempt to rescue his wife, and death. These late versions have become so popular that they overshadowed narrative threads known from earlier sources. This in no way limited the creative possibilities, as evidenced by the libretto of Peri's opera, or, to cite phenomena closer to us, the plot of the film *Black Orpheus*, set in a Brazilian favela. Every tradition results from the ossification of earlier innovation, but simultaneously in almost all cases they become a basis for further creative changes and alterations.

Modern encyclopaedias and textbooks tend to show Greek myths as colourful, cohesive stories. We must, however, be aware that mythical narrations only reached that cohesion at the point in their transmission when they were compiled, particularly as collections of myths started appearing in the Imperial period (Apollodorus' *Library*) and later in the Middle Ages (e.g. *Mythographus Vaticanus*) and the Renaissance. Greek mythology assumed its final shape, the one we know today, in modern textbooks. In ancient culture, myth was mostly a multitext: it had no original version, especially one we could access, and every version known to us is a result of recomposition and reperformance. This presents a dilemma: how to outline, and, crucially, how to research such a protean phenomenon?

Helpful for an analysis of this fluid mythical tradition is Albert Henrichs' (1987) model of 'applied mythography'. The advantage of 'mythographic analysis' is that it is agnostic of the quality and state of preservation of literary *testimonia*. 'Applied mythography' focuses not on distinguished, longer narratives, but rather on the analysis of chronology, story patterns, narrative changes, and their contextualisation. Thus, it highlights lesser-known, marginal traditions, arranges them chronologically, and contextualises specific plots and motifs, demonstrating relationships between versions, as well as innovations and errors of ancient interpretations.[3] In this approach, a myth is viewed as a network of interconnected stories which generated diverse realisations and readings in different periods.

The objective of our study will not be a complete analysis of the mythical tradition of Orpheus; that would go beyond the scope of the present monograph. Instead, it focuses on select aspects of the myth present in Classical and Hellenistic accounts, particularly genealogy, information about the hero's birth and death (also his tomb and worship), and toponyms or ethnonyms linking him to Macedonia and Thrace. However, first we will examine the peculiarities of Orpheus as a mythical figure. This chapter will present the sources of specific narrative threads, since, as we shall see, the roots of the hero's story reach far beyond poetry. We will also be interested in variants, lesser-known stories, plots, modifications and non-standard explanations, local versions and poetic innovations.[4] This broader perspective will allow us for a better assessment of the parts of the myth of Orpheus that interest us, including in particular his ethnicity and the role of Thrace and Pieria in his story.

Orpheus as a mythical hero

Orpheus is a complex figure, and his mythical image contains many contradictions. Although Homer does not list him among mythical heroes, and Aristotle (fr. 7 Rose = OF 889T) claimed that he never existed, Orpheus became one of the most recognisable figures in European culture. Moreover, he did not fit into the usual mould of a mythical hero, like Achilles, Heracles or Theseus: he was not a warrior, conqueror, ruler or hunter, but a musician killed by women. Early fifth-century iconography has him use his instrument to protect himself from their attack, suggesting a role reversal and lack of masculinity.[5] Perhaps that is why some would doubt his participation in the journey of the Argonauts.[6] Orpheus' unheroic nature is stressed by Phaedrus in Plato's *Symposion* (179d): '[H]e was accounted to have gone upon a coward's quest, too like the minstrel that he was, and to have lacked the spirit to die as Alcestis did for the sake of love, when he contrived the means of entering Hades alive' [tr. H. N. Fowler].

In the Panhellenic tradition, Orpheus is not associated with a specific part of the Greek world – see below for some exceptions – even though other heroes tend to be tied to places or cities, and their actions have a 'political' dimension. According to surviving stories, Orpheus founded no cities, ruled no place in particular, conquered nothing. He is linked very broadly to Thrace or Pieria, and most of his actions take place on the fringes of the Greek world. Aside from the journey of the Argonauts, he takes no part in important mythical events.

This lack of ties to sociopolitical realities, which always envelop a myth, is visible in his genealogy as well.[7] Orpheus has a wife, but no progeny, since, as most versions claim, his spouse died on their wedding day. Occasionally, we learn of his descendants, but the known sources say nothing of how and with whom they were begotten; however, they certainly were not children of his beloved Eurydice.[8] Orpheus' father was either Apollo, which would not link him to any mythical line, or the otherwise unknown Thracian Oeagrus, placing him at the global fringe (OF 890–901T). Orpheus is, in a sense, a foreign body within mythology; his familial links only indicate inherited musical skill (Apollo and a Muse as parents, Homer/Hesiod as descendants). In this aspect, he is similar to other hero musicians: Linus, Thamyris or Musaeus.

Finally, Orpheus is also an exceptional figure due to the diversity of sources discussing him and of socioreligious contexts in which his story played a major part. Most mythical figures are known either from poetic narrations or from mythographic works that ultimately also cite literary accounts. In Orpheus' case, the situation is more complex, which had so far eluded our attention.

Orpheus and mythical tradition: Sources

In the beginning of his book (1988, 1–2), Charles Segal notes that he will deal not with Orpheus as the 'founder of Orphism', but rather the 'Orpheus of poetic tradition'. Although in our case it would be convenient to echo those sentiments, the reality of our sources does not present a simple dichotomy. What Segal calls 'poetic tradition' is actually a complex entity, and the adjective 'poetic' does not reflect the nature of many accounts.

In discussions of Greek mythology there is a tendency to focus on *testimonia* of exceptional literary value, extant in full, and long. Thus, we use especially the poetic texts from Classical, Hellenistic and above all the Roman era, as well as late but extensive commentaries and scholia. To state the obvious, only written, typically Athenian, Alexandrian or Roman versions are available, at the expense of oral or less widespread accounts and local points of view. For example, the 'Sources and Interpretations' section of *The Cambridge Companion to Greek Mythology* includes chapters on Homer, Hesiod, lyric, tragedy, Aristophanes, Plato, and Hellenistic Mythography. Similarly, an analysis of Theban myths in a splendid work by Berman (2015) consists of chapters discussing the portrayals of the city in epic, lyric, drama or in the erudite literature. It is also undeniable that there is no trace of any religious or professional groups influencing the depictions of Oedipus. For Orpheus, this situation is far more complex, as the sources of the stories about him far exceed the typical canon of poetic *testimonia*. A more thorough analysis also demonstrates that each of these groups of sources may have had a large influence on how his story was shaped, on the narrative choices of poets, and on the survival or disappearance of specific plot threads.

First, a brief description of Orpheus' presence in poetic and literary traditions. As indicated before, the hero is absent from the histories of Homer and Hesiod and it is doubtful if he appeared in Pseudo-Hesiod's *Catalogue of Women*. He is conspicuously not mentioned in known fragments of the *Catalogue*, even though a reference to Linus, another musician, has survived (fr. 305 M.-W.). Perhaps this means, as some scholars maintain, that at first he was only an obscure Argonaut.[9] The hero first appears in works of Ibycus (fr. 306 PMG) and Simonides (fr. 567 PMG), written in the late sixth or early fifth century, and in early fifth-century iconography. Orpheus is thus not only the sole Argonaut so poorly mentioned by early sources, but in fact the only such case of all main Greek mythological heroes.

Although his role began to grow in the second half of the fifth century, most accounts that form the basis for the reconstruction of the myth come from the late Hellenistic or early Roman period.[10] Key here are especially long passages from Virgil's *Georgics* (4,450–527) and Ovid's *Metamorphoses* (10,1–85; 11,1–66).[11] The depiction of Orpheus in these texts is the basis for the general idea of his character in European culture, and in this form it formed the starting point for the description of his life in all mythology textbooks. Referencing this late form of the myth has some advantages, but mostly drawbacks. The former include the cohesiveness of the portrayal and the continuity of the story in Virgil's and Ovid's poetry, which mean we do not need to infer the direction of the plot or parcel and question its lesser-known threads. As for the drawbacks, it has to be stressed that the late, Roman-era image does not reflect early Greek notions, as it results mostly from later decisions and changes to the myth. Thus, when investigating what Classical Greece said and thought of Orpheus, those accounts should be filtered out and set aside.

Second, we must note local stories of Orpheus and their significance. The phrase 'local mythical stories' is usually meant here to imply stories relayed locally, associated with the territory of a given polis or region, and serving to describe and explain the world around it. Such stories can be encountered in local histories, but also in Pausanias' *Periegesis*.[12] Some local myths may also have commented on or complemented religious gestures of a community so as to create and reinforce its identity.[13] Of course, it is frequently difficult for a modern researcher to differentiate between local versions and the inventions of poets or mythographers, who remain our principal source of information about myths. Therefore, it is crucial to track the relationship between the story on one hand and the area of the polis or region as well as the monuments or religious gestures of the community on the other.

As for Orpheus, he was linked to the musically-gifted Euneid family of Athens (Eur. *Hypsipyle*), as well as to traditions from Antissa on Lesbos, where the burial site of his head was presented since the third century (OF 1065T), and from Aornum in Thesprotia, where it was claimed that it was in that region that Orpheus left the underworld and committed suicide (Paus. 9,30,6); these are just a handful of examples. Each of these tales demonstrates the vitality of the myth through the involvement of the hero into political, religious and cultural explanations, even if they are less well-known and only have local reach. However, the most important case here is the situation of Thesprotia and Orpheus' association with the local environment, namely a cave called Charonium, considered an entrance to the underworld.

The next group of sources consists of mythography.[14] In the fifth and fourth centuries, entire works or significant passages were written about the hero by Pherecydes of Athens, Epigenes, Herodorus, Nicomedes of Acanthus, and other mythographers (OF 1127–39T). He was certainly discussed by Hellanicus and Damastes (Procl. *Vit. Hom.* 5,4), to name only the earliest writers. Some remarks we know from this period tied into discussions on Orpheus' participation in the journey of the Argonauts, the origins of Orphic texts (Hdt. 2,53), or his links to Homer, Hesiod and Musaeus.[15] Mythographers searched the mythical tradition (usually poetry) for elements shared between many versions of the story, selected and merged plots, smoothed out incongruities, or, to the contrary, divided them into narratives of homonymous characters. Moreover, they homogenised the chronology, creating an acceptable, complete tale, which may have never have existed in that form before.

A few examples: the Suda lexicon (*o* 654–6, s.v. Ὀρφεύς) lists seven characters named Orpheus in an attempt to clarify the divergent mythical sources, particularly the answer to the question whether Orpheus came before

Homer and when the so-called Orphic texts were written. Herodorus (BNJ 31 F42) originally only listed two Orpheuses, with the junior being probably the author of the Orphics. The same problem also led to other practices and solutions characteristic of mythography: Hellanicus, Damastes and Pherecydes linked the hero into a precise genealogy with Homer and Hesiod, arguing for his seniority among them (Procl. *Vit. Hom.* 5.4). This lineage displays connections to local mythical traditions of Cyme; thus, it is believed that it was invented by Hellanicus of Lesbos, an island opposite Aeolian Cyme.[16]

Another side effect of the debate over the origins of Orphic texts and dating of Orpheus was the questioning of his participation in the journey of the Argonauts (BNJ 3 T2: 'Pherekydes in Book Six says that Philammon and not Orpheus sailed with them') or justifying his presence on the Argo and tying him to Chiron (BNJ 31 F43a: 'Herodoros says that Chiron admonished Jason to take Orpheus in this way along with the Argonauts'). In all these situations, mythographic practice caused a visible and significant modification of the mythical tradition and had impact on later literary accounts (Ap. Rhod. 1,33–4).

The question of whether Orphic texts were original or derivative of Homer and Hesiod draws attention to Orpheus' presence in Orphic (and Neopythagorean) theogonic, ritual and general religious or philosophical texts.[17] These are particularly important when considering the reported popularity of those writings in Classical-era Athens (Eur. *Hipp.* 953–4; Pl. *Resp.* 364 e3), and so we may expect that works like *Katabasis*, *Lyra*, *Krater*, or the later *Hieros Logos*, as well as oral traditions, also included some elements of Orpheus' 'mythical biography'.[18]

In the fifth century, the hero was linked in various sources to eschatology, mysteries, and dietary and religious practices; these were important parts of his image.[19] However, Orphic texts must have included information on his genealogy, the chronology of mythical events, and spatial references, even if it was marginal. It may have been important, for example, to link Orpheus to the north, particularly Thrace, a land significant in Dionysian mythology.[20] Orphic imaginings may also have been the source of the story of the hero's head, while his descent into Hades has many commonalities with the myth, even if it would later become a romantic, rather than eschatological, narrative.[21] Perhaps the Orphics' reputed aversion to bloodshed may be linked to the motif of Orpheus' weakness and un-masculinity, and to the discussion over his involvement with the Argonauts.²² It seems, in any event, that with some mythical story threads various types of sources may have mutually supported some particular plot devices.

Orphic texts are not the last source for Orpheus' mythical 'biography'. Another is the role of kitharodes, singers accompanied by kitharas, a group responsible for shaping the idea of the hero. In the Classical period, there were many festivals featuring musical competitions, and kitharodia was very popular there.²³ Orpheus' early linking to the kitharodes might be already demonstrated on a mid-sixth-century Attic black-figure oinochoe decorated with the image of a musician ascending a platform with a kithara (CVA 303344). The figure bears an inscription saying *XAIPE ΟΡΦΕΥ* ('rejoice, Orpheus'). Furthermore, Timotheos' *Persians* (OF 883+902T) lists Orpheus as the first musician and a predecessor of the kitharodes. These accounts point to the general importance of the hero, but do not prove any vision of him was specific to the kitharodes. However, at this point it is worth citing the account from Plato's *Ion* (533). Socrates tests Ion's knowledge:

> But further, I expect you have also failed to find one in fluting or harping or minstrelsy or rhapsodizing who is skilled in expounding the art of Olympus or Thamyras, or Orpheus, or Phemius, the rhapsode of Ithaca, but is at a loss and has no remark to offer on the successes or failures in rhapsody of Ion of Ephesus.
>
> Translated by W. R. M. Lamb

According to Power (2010, 350), the formulation and context of Socrates' pronouncement, as well as Ion's answer, suggest that kitharodes 'perform explanations about Orpheus' (ἐξηγεῖσθαι ... περὶ Ὀρφέως). This would imply that a kitharode performance (during a public festival, such as the *Asclepieia* at Epidaurus) included statements on the mythical predecessor of the genre and profession. It is also likely that their declarations were less exegesis than biography. Based on the few available accounts, we may suppose that they may have referenced the genealogy, instrument, musical skill, or geographic ties of the hero. Considering the remarkable increase in the number of musical agons in the Classical period and their importance, this may have been one of the main sources of information about Orpheus for the average Greek. In a parallel development, kitharists appropriated Thamyris as their predecessor.²⁴

There is one more interesting aspect of Orpheus' ties to the kitharodes. It is possible to posit a correlation between some features of his portrayal (particularly the effeminacy and weakness, Pl. *Symp.* 179d; schol. Apollon. 1,23) and the perception of musicians in Classical sources.[25] Earlier, it has been mentioned that in the fifth century there were ongoing debates about Orpheus' presence on the *Argo*, his unheroicness, and on the role of Orphic attitude towards killing. These aspects converge in the image of kitharodes and musicians in general as weak, effeminate and hedonistic.

To name just two examples, in Euripides' *Suppliants* (881–3), one of the seven leaders, Hippomedon, is presented by Adrastus as someone who had the strength to reject the pleasures of the Muses and an easy life since childhood, placing a poet in opposition to 'masculine' occupations, such as hunting or horse breeding. Meanwhile, one of the known fragments of the tragedy *Antiope* has Zethus accusing his brother Amphion of effeminacy, related to his lifestyle as a poet and musician.[26] Thus, the passage from *Symposion* quoted above (179d) explains the weakness of Orpheus: 'like the kitharodos that he was'. Even if these portrayals of Orpheus do not follow the Athenian opinion of musicians in the late fifth century, it certainly may have impacted his mythical 'biography'.

Another source category consists of Classical and Hellenistic scholarship dealing with the origins of culture, music, literature, and criticism.[27] In the sixth and fifth-centuries, the Greeks began to analyse the origins of human activity in general, including their own mythographic, literary and musical output. This tied in with the attempts to find and describe the first musicians and poets, as well as the clean-up of chronology. Echoes of this activity in relation to Orpheus can be seen in Herodotus (2,53), Aristophanes (*Ran.* 1030–6), or Hippias (BNJ 6 F4). In literature and music history specifically it is worth pointing out the works of Glaucus of Rhegium (*On Poets*), Hellanicus of Lesbos (work on the Spartan festival *Carneia*), Damastes of Sigeum (*On Ancient Poets and Wise Men*), and scholars such as Metrodorus of Lampsacus or Stesimbrotos of Thasos, to name only the earliest.[28] In the fourth century, the volume of such works and their thematic range were immense, probably best seen in Aristotle's school.[29]

Some of these authors also attempted to find and describe the 'first inventors' (*protoi heuretai*) in various fields of social life, and Orpheus appeared on such lists frequently, at or near the top.³⁰ He was usually presented as the first mortal musician, heir to Apollo, inventor of kitharodia and *mousikē* in general, ancestor of Homer and Hesiod. Such texts contributed to reinforcing the vision of Orpheus as the first mythical musician and influenced his genealogies, lists of his students, and his musical accomplishments. We may infer that it was also important in tying him to Terpander, and thus possibly influenced the narrative of Lesbos as the resting place of his head.³¹

Orpheus was also credited with other cultural innovations, such as the invention of *sophia* (wisdom), letters, epic poetry, hexameter, or elegy (OF 1024–30T, beginning with Critias), which was possibly indirectly tied to Orphic literature. One of the early accounts of this aspect of his image was the *testimonium* of the rhetor and sophist Alcidamas (*Ulix*. 24), which also demonstrates the freedom enjoyed by creators of such lists of inventions, as they could be reinterpreted and adjusted to the needs of the author and his audience.³²

Finally, there is iconography, mentioned above.³³ Graphic depictions of myths not only reproduced literary texts, but engaged with them and inspired new ones. In the case of Orpheus, iconography opens the collection of extant sources (a metope from the Sicyonian Treasury), is key for the hero's early image (depictions of his death on early fifth-century pottery) and Orphic portrayals (pottery with the prophesying head motif – see Figure 4), but also closes out the Antiquity with hundreds of mosaics depicting the musician surrounded by animals. Particularly notable is the fact that these portrayals focus on select aspects of the hero and occasionally present him entirely differently than surviving contemporaneous literature.

In analysing the mythical portrayal of Orpheus, we are actually researching a multidimensional phenomenon with roots far beyond the types of sources typical of Greek mythology (poetry, mythography, occasionally iconography). This is undoubtedly related to the unique nature of the mythical musician, teacher, and mystagogue, and his multifaceted role in Greek culture and religion.

What does that imply for research into Orpheus? All the aforementioned areas of Greek intellectual and religious activity had a greater or smaller influence on the story of Orpheus and could have been the source of later versions, narrative threads, plot devices, or at least allusions. Additionally, every type of source, due to its specifics and immediate audience (e.g. Orphics), focused on slightly different elements of the hero's image and proposed different narrative solutions. Furthermore, the portrayals and descriptions of Orpheus did not function in isolation. We are justified to assume they cross-pollinated, freely interacted, or borrowed plots and reinterpreted them. In some instances we may even suppose that known details of Orpheus' 'biography' may be a reaction to an 'Orphic' or 'kitharode' version (OF 1028T). The addition and cross-pollination of new versions of the myth was reinforced with the spread of literacy in the fifth and fourth century, and of libraries in the fourth and third century. Thus, in the first century, when Conon wrote down Orpheus' story for King Archelaus Philopator of Cappadocia, he could create an erudite version, based on his readings and own invention.

Stories, variants, local contexts

Let us now examine a different part of the same mythical tradition: not the source types, but rather the specifics of the story tradition. We shall focus not on the so-called 'canon' version or the 'mythographic mainstream', as most analyses do, but on variants, modifications and marginal threads within the tradition.[34]

It is commonly believed that the myth of Orpheus consists of five main stories. The first is about his participation in the journey of the Argonauts; second is about the loss of his wife and the journey to Hades to rescue her; third is about his exceptional musical skill allowing him to tame animals (or barbarian Thracians) and move trees and rocks; the last two stories discuss the circumstances of his death at the hands of women/maenads/Thracians and the tales about his remains, particularly the severed head and the lyre, and thus also his grave and subsequent worship.[35]

This is a good overview of what is considered 'canon' today. However, it is also a simplification, based on the choices of an 'ethnographer' looking for a cohesive story about the object of his research. The idea of five main plots is correct from the point of view of Apollodorus the mythographer and a diachronic, unifying framing, but not necessarily from the standpoint of iconography, or local Thesprotian audiences. It is also clearly a product of the development of the myth's story, the state of sources, and text transmission. It stems from mythographic decisions made on the basis of a far broader narrative inventory. We must be aware that some periods and places had a completely different set of narrative devices used for Orpheus. In versions from Syracusae, Olbia or Cyrene, the geographic realities and circumstances of death of the musician would certainly be entirely different. Of course, the five basic plots are a conscious simplification, necessary for historical analysis, but it is important to remember how flawed modern reconstructions are.

There are several examples of lesser-known plot threads that were not developed in literature later. For instance, there was Euripides' story, known from the fragments of *Hypsipyle*, of Orpheus' guardianship of Thoas and Euneus, sons of Theseus. After the death of the Athenian hero, Orpheus took the boys to Thrace (fr. 759), where he taught them how to play instruments and fight. Euneus was the progenitor of the Athenian Euneid family, whose members were musicians and bore responsibility for the worship of Dionysus Melpomenus.[36] Making Orpheus, the first musician, a guardian of Euneus served to justify the position of the family and tie their musical skill into a mythical context.[37] The position of the Athenian Eumolpid family was justified very similarly, i.e. by referring to mythical tradition and ties of the house's founder to Musaeus.[38]

Another relatively obscure plot element was Orpheus' journey from Pieria, where he was born, to the land of his father (OF 928–9T). We find such a story in Apollonius' *Argonautica* (1,23–34). It demonstrated the musician's magical abilities (he is followed by Pierian oaks) and explained his links to a specific region of Thrace. This form of the story also explained the natural features of Pieria (dense woods: Livy 44,6) and parts of Thrace. When the destination was Bistonia, it probably also commented on the name of the town of Drys on the Thracian coast.[39] The story of Orpheus' journey and his Thracian kingdom was enduring, as evidenced by Nonnus' passages on Oeagrus' and Orpheus' rule over the Cicones in Bistonia (e.g. *Dion.* 13,428) and by topographic details of *Orphic Argonautica* (1373–6). The 'oaks of the son of Oeagrus' (δρύες Οἰαγρίδαο) mentioned by Nicander (OF 952T; see 930T) suggest that a Hellenistic-period reader knew a longer account of the trees' miraculous journey (see Pomp. Mela 2,28). We may perhaps also include the mysterious 'Oeagrian maidens' (κοῦραι Οἰαγρίδες) from the *Lament for Bion* (17) in this group, as they also tie Orpheus to Bistonia's landscape.

Another example is the story by the poet Phanocles about Orpheus' love for Calaïs, one of the Boreads (F1 Powell). The name of the beloved suggests that the poet tied the episode to the journey of the Argonauts, which the Boreads took part in. Further on, the narrative mentions that the hero had introduced homoerotic practices to Thrace, which, in turn, explained why he was attacked by women. Although the story of Orpheus' love for Calaïs is otherwise absent from our sources, allusions to his homoerotic proclivities can be found in later texts as well (OF 1004T). However, in those cases they are only introduced to explain the circumstances and reasons of his death.

Now, we shall examine the degree of modifications within a single narrative thread of the mythical tradition, using Orpheus' journey among the Argonauts as an example.[40] A sixth-century metope from the Sicyonian Treasury depicts Orpheus on the *Argo* alongside another musician, perhaps Philammon.[41] We do not know this version from written accounts, but it appears that originally Orpheus was not the only musician pursuing the Golden Fleece. It bears noting that Homer's *Iliad* does not feature a songsmith at Troy, which suggests that, despite appearances, the Argonauts need not have had a bard in the beginning.

In the fifth century, we encounter further controversy, as the mythographers began debating if Orpheus took part in the journey, and if so, which one. Pherecydes supposedly claimed that it was not Orpheus who went to Colchis (OF 1010T), but Philammon. Meanwhile, Herodorus (OF 1010T) analysed the reasons why the musician was admitted to the crew, despite lacking combat skills. He concluded that Jason took Orpheus on advice of Chiron, who warned him about the threat posed by the Sirens.

Orpheus' role as an Argonaut changes greatly in surviving literary texts. Pindar has him as just one of the participants, listed sixth. In Apollonius' *Argonautica*, he is the first invited to the journey, and serves as the author's alter ego. The most interesting version is presented in *Orphic Argonautica*, where Orpheus is crucial to the success of the expedition and narrates the story from his point of view, directing it at his student Musaeus. The core of the story remains the same, but highlighting select elements changes its narrative and influences how it is received.

A similar case of changes and modifications to the myth is connected to the motifs of Orpheus' head and lyre (OF 1052–61T; 1074–5T). To start with, the motif of the head was part of a broader narrative of his death and dismemberment, which first appears in fifth-century Athenian iconography and in Aeschylus (see Eratosth. *Catast.* 24), although we cannot tell if his play mentioned the head. In late fifth-century iconography, meanwhile, the head appears to reflect Orphic ideas of it and serves to explain the late origin of texts attributed to Orpheus (Graf 1987; Burges Watson 2013; see Figure 4): since it continues to sing, it may legitimise theological and ritual teachings. In the third century, after the tomb of Orpheus' head starts being presented in Antissa, where 'nightingales sing more sweetly than elsewhere' (OF 1065T), the head becomes an important element of Lesbian local tradition. On one hand, its burial on the island is clearly a local tradition; on the other, linking Terpander to Orpheus was caused by kitharode activity and literary critiques depicting the hero as the inventor of *mousikē*.

In this context, it is worth mentioning Orpheus' lyre as well, which, according to late accounts, was hung in the temple or placed in the hero's tomb on Lesbos (OF 1052T). However, in Hellenistic accounts, Orpheus' lyre was first and foremost an important part of the story of the origins of *mousikē* and the development of kitharodia. The narratives thus focused on the invention of the instrument, usually by Hermes, and then its transfer to Apollo and Orpheus (OF 1074–5T). After Orpheus' death, the instrument was usually placed in the sky in an example of catasterism (OF 1074–5T). This version contradicts the Lesbian tradition, although there were attempts to merge them by having the divine lyre pass to Terpander earlier (OF 1099T). Considering these transformations and recontextualisations of the motif, claims of a single, simple narrative about the head and lyre on Lesbos are untenable.

Another detail of Orpheus' story to be examined is his wife, and her name in particular. First, we must note that her character, so famous in late versions of the myth, is almost absent in the Classical period. Whenever she appears at all, she is anonymous. The name Eurydice is first attested in the early first century, in Pseudo-Moschus' *Lament for Bion*. Earlier, in the early Hellenistic period, there are mentions of another name, Agriope (Hermesianax fr. 3). Not much can be said about it, other than it resembles that of Thamyris' mother, Argiope.[42] Recently, however, Martine Cuypers remarked that the name used by Hermesianax 'seems to combine the names of Orpheus' father (Oi-agr-os) and mother (Call-iope)', which, as she notes, 'produces a not unhermesianactic jingle after Οἰάγροιο'.[43]

This provides an interesting example of the creation of new details in a myth. Additionally, the name Eurydice was probably a local invention, a tribute of the unknown writer to some member of the Macedonian or Ptolemaic royal family, as Bremmer (1991) attempted to prove. Eurydice may have become known due to the popularity of the *Lament for Bion* among Roman poets.

Aside from the aforementioned rarer plot devices, we also know of variants of plots that, in Graf's words (1987), deviate from the vulgate. For example, in the Thesprotian local version Orpheus was linked to an oracle of the dead and the exit from the underworld displayed in that land, alongside explanations that the hero committed suicide in that region after losing his wife (Paus. 9,30,6). Notably, this variant assigns no role to women and gives them no part in Orpheus' death. However, it is tightly bound to local terrain (the Acheron River).

We know of other versions of Orpheus' death, as his killing by women/maenads/Thracians was only one of several narrative solutions functioning in Antiquity. Already in the fourth century we can find proof of a version that has Orpheus struck by Zeus' lightning.[44] Presented reasons for it include divulging secrets of the gods or spreading scandalous stories about them.[45] This is a common motif in mythography; many other mythical heroes died in similar circumstances for similar reasons (Pentheus, Sisyphus, Asclepius).[46] However, in Orpheus' case this solution contributes to his perception as a founder of mysteries and author of theosophic texts. Moreover, this information first appears in relation to the epitaph on the hero's tomb, potentially implying that it was a local version, perhaps related to a legend of his cult.[47]

Strabo (7, fr. 10), meanwhile, relates a story of a political coup which causes the death of Orpheus. The hero is shown as a careerist and a wizard, profiting from music, oracles, and induction into mysteries. In this framing, his portrayal was, as Graf (1987, 89–90) notes, modelled after the descriptions of the death of Pythagoras. Such a rationalising version of the myth owes its existence to Late Hellenistic Neopythagorean texts and also presumes women played no part in the hero's demise. The existence of diverse narratives of the death of Orpheus confirms that the mythical story was adapted to local (Thesprotian, Pierian, Lesbian) or group (Orphic, Neopythagorean) needs and modified according to some narrative precepts (lightning strike). Assuming, after Virgil and Ovid, that Orpheus died at the hands of women, is a major simplification.

Greeks living in various places and periods knew a slightly different mythical story and pushing them out of the canon would be historically inappropriate.

The reasoning behind the protagonists' motivations within well-known mythical plot lines does not always fit in the 'mythographic mainstream' either. But does that necessarily imply any poetic extravagance, or merely result from the normal human need to transform a story, typical not only of the Greeks, but of *homo narrans* in general?

And so, according to Hyginus' story (*Poet. astr.* 2,7, with sources reaching back to Eratosthenes),[48] Orpheus' dismemberment was a side effect of extreme emotions of the women overcome with love for the hero, which, in turn, was provoked by Aphrodite as revenge on the Muse Calliope, Orpheus' mother, for her decision in the argument over Adonis.[49] Graf summarizes the story as follows (1987, 86): 'explanation offered by Hyginus (...) looks rather like a bad joke based on a well-known myth'. Of course, the description of the circumstances of the assault was an attractive part of Orpheus' story and many authors attempted to contribute to it. The most frequently cited version – the hero's distaste for women after losing his wife – is only one of many. Hyginus himself brings up another version later on (*Poet. astr.* 2,7,5): 'Some say that because Orpheus first favoured love for youths, he seemed to insult women, and for this reason they killed him'. Aphrodite's wrath has to be assessed in the context of the history of the entire plot line and as a product of the search for novel narratives. In this form, it is in any event a frequent theme in mythical stories and may be considered a typical mythographic tool.[50]

Considering that most known explanations for the circumstances of Orpheus' death have traits of literary interventions into a mythical tradition, there are no grounds to assume that Aeschylus', Virgil', or Hyginus' justifications are somehow superior. Motivations of protagonists were freely modified to fit a communicative context or the needs of the audience.

All the aforementioned examples of lesser-known stories, plots, modifications and non-standard explanations illustrate the difficulty of the task facing a researcher analysing stories of Orpheus or another mythical character. The knowledge of the contexts in which myths functioned in Greek culture is also a warning against rushing to conclusions based on select accounts from various periods. Mythical stories were modified so frequently and to so large an extent, and the earlier versions were so often misinterpreted due to a misunderstanding of the text and distance from the original cultural context, that the risk of distorting research results is immense.

The conclusions from the review of the specificities of the mythical tradition of Orpheus are of particular importance for the evaluation of his 'ethnicity'. This aspect of his presentation, much like spatial relationships, could not be a constant part of the myth, as it depended on the political situation, the context of performance, the audience, and the knowledge and intentions of the author. Therefore, we cannot attempt to answer the question of if Orpheus was a Thracian, but rather where, when and why he would be one.

2

Orpheus, Oeagrus and Thracians in Early Testimonies

Orpheus' 'Thracianness' is an important and lasting element of his portrayal. This aspect of the hero has always maintained a large influence over how the stories of him are interpreted.[1] In the mythical narrative, the Thracian identity of the hero has three main roots: his father was the Thracian Oeagrus; Orpheus lived in Thrace; Orpheus lived in Pieria, which was Thracian at the time.[2] There is also a fourth assumption: that he was based on a Thracian deity or hero.[3] However, it has no reasonable source foundation and in this form is redundant with one of the first three.

The focus on Orpheus' ties to Thracia (and the Thracian origins of music), visible in many ancient sources, contributed significantly to the gradual diminishing of the status of his other ethnic and geographic identities, including his links to Pieria. A tendency to accept a straightforward Thracian ethnicity in a way similar to that of a historical figure can also be found in modern texts. For this reason, a reconstruction of the Macedonian tradition of Orpheus must begin with an analysis of the development, changes and functions of the Thracian elements of the hero's story. This chapter will focus on early (Classical and Hellenistic) accounts and on the characteristics of his portrayal in early iconography and Chapters 3 and 4 will attempt to list the circumstances responsible for the gradual marginalisation of the Pierian tradition.

Early iconography

Orpheus is first connected to the Thracians in early fifth-century vase iconography. In *c.* 490–440, depictions of the hero charming them with his music and his death at the hands of their women became popular before slowly disappearing from vase art.[4] It is worth noting here that in the earliest depictions, Orpheus did not wear Thracian clothes, which has been explained in various ways.[5] Staying within the bounds of what is not disputed, we can state that in the iconography Thracians were originally his audience, while he himself was portrayed as Greek with a Greek instrument.[6]

Most depictions from this period focus on the scenes of the charming of Thracians (LIMC 7,1,7–15 – see Figure 1) and Orpheus' violent murder by women (LIMC 7,1,28–51 – see Figure 2). In some vessels, we can clearly see that the attacking women are marked with tattoos, identifying them as Thracians. A few examples link both episodes together (LIMC 7,1,28–31 – see Figure 3).[7] This may suggest a plot connection and a sequence of events: the attack is somehow related to the music bewitching the men.

It is worth bringing up F. Lissarague's (1994; 2002) opinion that considering the entirety of the depiction, particularly random objects wielded by the women, one may surmise that '[T]he women's violence is not arbitrary, but seems to be carried out to defend the survival of the *oikos* connoted by the implements with which they are armed' (2002, 121). Lissarague believes that in effect, the artist presents not the Thracian world, but rather the masculine–feminine opposition, expressed here by the contrast between the Thracian men and women's reactions to Orpheus' music.

Similar conclusions can be drawn from A. M. Desbals' (1997) analyses of the image of Thracians in the Archaic and Classical periods. She remarks that in those vessel paintings the supposed reasons for the hero's death mattered less than what the images revealed about Athenian values. According to her, the depictions clearly show that '[W]omen are capable of threatening the order of men' (1997, 186). Meanwhile, Isler-Kerenyi (2009) highlighted that the depictions focus on the image of Orpheus as a poet and musician – he usually has his instrument even when attacked. This might imply the attack is really connected to music or, more broadly, *mousikē*.[8]

The common denominator for these interpretations is the focus on the sociocultural context surrounding the creation and circulation of these portrayals, as well as the crucial role of women and music in iconography. Orpheus' death scene must therefore be interpreted in relation to the development of *mousikē* in Athenian culture of the fifth century. Pottery scenes would thus show the power of Orpheus' music, which can charm even the barbarian Thracians, who were included in the world of wild nature alongside trees and animals, which also listened to Orpheus.[9] On the other hand, the behaviour of women would express the incompatibility between *mousikē*/culture and the feminine.[10]

Why *mousikē*?

This aspect is obvious in the context of the first musician and son of a Muse, and emphasised on the vessels by the presence of an instrument he uses to defend himself. In fifth-century culture, participation in *mousikē* was an expression of the degree of civilisation and the place in the natural order (humans–animals–plants/rocks). A parallel for resistance to *mousikē* is offered by Pindar's (*Pyth.* 1,1–28) first Pythian ode: the monstrous children of Gaea fear and hate the music of the Muses. The 'golden lyre, rightful (. . .) possession of Apollo and the violet-haired Muses' can soothe even Zeus and Ares, charming the minds of deities. But there are creatures hostile to Zeus, like Typhon and other children of Gaea, who 'are stunned with terror when they hear the cry of the Pierian Muses'. Music enrages them and drives them mad. This creates an opposition between the wild/chthonic and civilisation, defining the latter as tied to *mousikē*. Whatever does not take part in *mousikē* or is hostile to it is as monstrous as the children of Gaea.

Why (Thracian) women?

In Orpheus' iconography, women take the place of Typhon, place themselves outside civilisation and are shown as hostile to *mousikē*. This brings to mind words attributed to Thales (Diog. Laert. 1,33) that he was thankful to fate for three things: that he was born a man and not an animal; that he was born a man and not a woman, and that he was born Greek and not barbarian. In that context (Pl. *Theaet.* 174a), we can cite an anecdote about how the philosopher fell into a hole in the ground and was mocked by a Thracian slave woman. Notably, the protagonist of that story is a figure from the lowest rung of the social hierarchy: a barbarian slave woman. It appears that the choice of Thracian women for Orpheus' death happened for similar reasons: they are female barbarians behaving worse than animals. Their attack could therefore be seen as a representation of female savagery immune to *mousikē*. This is also a better explanation for the duality of vessel scenes showing entranced Thracians and aggressive women. Social functions are transgressed against here twice: by attacking Orpheus, women usurp the role of men, and do so driven by emotion not soothed by his music, although even wild animals listened to it.

Seen in this light, rather than through the lens of later literary accounts, the iconography matches our knowledge of how women were perceived in the sixth and fifth centuries and how they were excluded from education (*mousikē*).[11] The pottery scenes may also be perceived as commentary for the dynamic development of schools in Greek cities during that period, i.e. an ideological statement to justify social inequality between the sexes.

Another notable aspect of Orpheus' depiction is how unheroic his death is. That is why it was possible that in the fifth century, the scenes of charming the Thracians and dismemberment were seen as a commentary on the ambiguous status of music and the kitharodes' social position. As mentioned before (Chapter 1, 'Orpheus and mythical tradition'), there is ample evidence from the fifth century that music was tied to effeminacy, inordinate emotionality and unmasculine social attitudes.[12] It is therefore possible that the portrayal of the unique musician Orpheus was indirectly an expression of the social reserve towards travelling musicians through contrasting his magical skill with unheroic death to (weak) women. The usage of house tools, as noted by Lissarague, would additionally highlight the hero's paradox: he does not die in combat, he cannot protect himself, he can only take cover behind an instrument. This message would suggest that music, while important, is too weak to protect a polis even from women.

Regardless of any differences in interpretation of Orpheus' portrayals (we assume the scenes could be read in multiple ways in the fifth century), one of the conclusions from the analysis of iconography is that Thracian men and women are there randomly.[13] We may also be dealing with a kind of 'dramatic gap' (Zeitlin 1996, 341–74), with Thracians being used to facilitate expressing an opinion about women as a social group. It is the women, in the end, that the painters focus on, rather than seemingly extraneous Thracian identity. It means that the earliest depictions of Orpheus as a musician playing to the Thracians do not indicate Thracian origins of music; the foreigners are merely a passive audience, which appears congruent with Classical accounts of Thracian feasts, where superficially Hellenised elites were surrounded by Greek (not Thracian) musicians and poets.

Orpheus on stage

Other than iconography, surviving fifth-century sources featuring Orpheus were mostly Athenian theatre plays: first Aeschylus' *Bassarids* in the 460s, then especially the works of Euripides.[14] Aeschylus' account is of great importance, but also a great challenge in terms of source critique, as the plot of the play is reconstructed from fragments surviving in late sources and from Eratosthenes' description of the catasterism of the lyre (*Catast.* 24).[15] The Hellenistic geographer's text – which will be investigated further in the following chapters – tells us Orpheus died on Mount Pangaion and was buried in Pieria, but never calls him a Thracian (which, in itself, is not meaningful). We do not know how he was portrayed by Aeschylus and whom did he claim as his parents. We can only say that there is a correlation between siting the events near Strymon and Pangaion and the Athenian interest in the area, and also that selecting Thrace may have tied into its links to Dionysus, who was crucial to Aeschylus' trilogy. Finally, note that while the setting of a play does not determine the ethnicity of its characters, it may influence it over time, particularly in the case of literary works that became popular, entered the Alexandrian canon, and were read in schools.

It is not until Euripides that we receive two more accounts connecting the hero to Thrace. Fragments of *Hypsipyle* indicate that after his return from the Argonauts' journey, Orpheus took the sons of Theseus and Hypsipyle to Thrace as his wards (fr. 759a). One of the fragments speaks of Edoni women and Mount Pangaion, situating Orpheus in the same area as Aeschylus' play.

Alcestis, meanwhile, includes the enigmatic 'voice of Orpheus', written down on 'Thracian tablets' (969–71: Θρήισσαις ἐν σανίσιν, τὰς / Ὀρφεία κατέγραψεν / γῆρυς). This suggests a link between the hero and the northern land and possibly that his death was tied to the area. The phrasing places sources of magical or healing knowledge in Thrace, and is also interpreted as an allusion to Orphic texts. Thus, as in Aeschylus, perhaps the crucial element was the mythical Thrace's connection to Dionysus. No other account from Euripides, although they are numerous, mentions the role of Thrace to the portrayal of Orpheus. In one case, as we shall see later, there are ties to Pieria and Olympus (*Bacch.* 560).

Fourth century and beyond

Notable among the fourth-century *testimonia* is the work of Alcidamas. This rhetorician and sophist wrote a fictional speech delivered by Odysseus, proving that the portrayal of Palamedes as an innovator was falsified. The hero enumerates inventions attributed to Palamedes and shows how they were actually discovered by other 'wise men'. His list includes Orpheus as the true inventor of wisdom and letters/writing. Odysseus/Alcidamas mentions as proof the epitaph from the grave of the poet, built by Thracians:[16]

> The Thracians buried Orpheus here, the minister of the Muses
> Whom lofty-ruling Zeus slew with the smoking thunderbolt
> The dear son of Oeagrus, who taught Heracles
> Having discovered writing and wisdom for mankind. [tr. J. V. Muir]

Remarkably, many events in the epitaph contradict the 'canon', from his teaching of Heracles, which was usually attributed to Linus, to the death at the hand of Zeus rather than Thracian women. It is very likely that the grave inscription served mostly to reinforce Alcidamas' argument and was invented by the author. We must note that the presence of Thracians in this narrative is limited exclusively to burying the hero. This, again, only points to his death in Thrace and little else.

It is commonly believed that Alcidamas' text, or other similar remarks on Orpheus as a cultural innovator, prompted a reaction by the attidographer Androtion of Athens. This student of Isocrates concluded in his work *Atthis* (OF 1028T = BNJ 324 F54a) that Thracians were illiterate, and so Orpheus could not be a wise man. This statement, if we believe Aelian, who quoted him, would mean that Orpheus was identified as Thracian at the time.

Another interpretation of the passage from Androtion assumes, however, that proclaiming Orpheus as Thracian was less an element of his polemic with

Alcidamas and more a critique of Homer's and Hesiod's genealogies as postulated by Hellanicus.[17] If Orpheus was an illiterate Thracian, as Androtion explained, he could not be the 'inventor' of wisdom, but also should not be the mythical predecessor of Homer and Hesiod (see BNJ 324 F54b). Importantly, this portrayal of Orpheus should be considered not in the context of late accounts, but of our knowledge of the Athenians' contacts with Thrace in the fourth century. During this period, *testimonia* depict Thracians as drunks who feasted with their wives, barbarian dancers, or rapacious and uncivilised warriors. Calling Orpheus Thracian would put him outside of the civilised world, thus making him an inappropriate ancestor for the two great poets. Moreover, the discussion involved the dating of Orphic texts, which, as explained for example in the scholia to Aelius Aristides (p. 544, 33 [BD]), were believed to be created after Homer.

The criticism of Orpheus and Orphics additionally served to strengthen the standing of Attica's mythical musician, Musaeus.[18] Androtion may have written about him in the part of his work covering the mythical history of Attica. In any event, Orpheus' ties to Thrace become more tangible in Alcidamas' and Androtion's writings than in earlier texts, where the hero was generally located in Thrace, tied to Thracians, or died in their lands. However, let us note that this link was usually quite clearly tied into contemporary ideological and political debates.

We also know of another epitaph from the grave of Orpheus, originating from Ps.-Aristotle's third-century collection known as *Peplos*. The work included a list of epitaphs for mythical heroes, including an inscription from Orpheus' grave, which informed the reader that the Thracian, son of Oeagrus, was buried by Cicones.[19] Orpheus is Thracian in later Hellenistic sources as well: in Phanocles (fr. 1 Powell) or Hermesianax, who also makes Orpheus' wife Agriope Thracian (fr. 3). In Apollonius, the hero is the son of Oeagrus the Thracian (1,23–4). Of particular note here is that all these Hellenistic *testimonia* highlight the Thracian origins of Orpheus' father, Oeagrus, whom we shall now discuss further.

Oeagrus

First, let us remember Cuypers' remark that the defining trait of Oeagrus' name is the root – *agr* (as in *agrios*, 'wild'). His name suggested savage, wild and barbarian connotations of Orpheus himself. This interpretation includes both the stories of the magical influence of music on wild animals (Simon. 567 PMG) and, more generally, the natural world, and the iconography placing the hero among the enraptured (and savage) Thracians. Giving Oeagrus a Muse for a wife may have indicated the merging of savagery and civilisation at the beginning of human 'musical' activity. The dual origins of *mousikē* would also explain its paradoxical ability to soothe and arouse emotions. In contrast, when Apollo was considered father to Orpheus instead, the genealogy appeared to highlight the hero's strong connection to music.[20]

Considering all the known accounts, we may conclude that Oeagrus was simply the hero's father, with his origins more of a commentary to his son's musical ability than some reflection over Thracian musicality.[21] Firstly, Oeagrus does not appear in iconography, and before the Roman period literature only mentions him as the father of Orpheus and nothing besides. Any more developed stories only appear after the Hellenistic period and seem to be the invention of poets and mythographers, not the results of late sources discovering some ancient versions of the myth of Oeagrus the Thracian.

Late stories of note include the mentions of Oeagrus as the king of Bistones (Nonnus *Dion.* 13,428–31) or son of Thracian king Charops (Diod. Sic. 3,65,6). The latter version certainly originated from the ties between Orpheus, Orphic literature and Dionysian mysteries.[22] The whole should be perceived as a rationalisation of the myth, in the vein of Dionysius Scytobrachion, who was Diodorus' main source for this part of his work (3,65,5–6).

However, modern analyses most frequently cite Servius' claim that Oeagrus was a Thracian river god.[23] This late information appears to stem entirely from a push to make Oeagrus and Orpheus more similar to Strymon and Rhesus.[24] The roots of the phenomenon can also be seen in the emergence of the Hebrus River as an important element of the new scenery of Orpheus' death, alternative for Strymon, during the Hellenistic period. Roman poetry from Virgil onward provides Hebrus with the epithet 'Oeagrium',[25] which originally had to express Oeagrus' rule over the Bistonia area. The adjective did not identify him with the river or suggest a lineage. Nevertheless, Servius, perhaps by analogy to Rhesus as the son of Strymon, read the poetic phrase as such.

Finally, there is also another, early genealogy of Orpheus, which will be examined closely in Chapter 5. In it, Oeagrus was the son of Methone and

Pierus, two of the Pierian eponyms (OF 872T). It clearly demonstrates that Oeagrus was a mythical figure and his story could be adapted to the needs of the author and audience, e.g. Macedonian in this case. Thus, if asked whether Oeagrus was Thracian, the answer is yes, inasmuch as that was relevant for the story's author and his audience.

Why Thrace? Contexts and explanations

Accounts after the Hellenistic period strengthen the image of Orpheus and Oeagrus as Thracians and add nothing new to our analysis; they will no longer be discussed. In most cases they are a product of a developed literary culture with an ossified mythical tradition. Instead, we shall assess the early accounts, particularly the circumstances of linking Orpheus to Thrace. Early iconography does not argue for the hero's Thracian ethnicity, but rather uses a Thracian context to make statements on the role of *mousikē* and on women's lack of culture. Orpheus as a resident of Thrace first appears in Euripides' *Hypsipyle*, and Androtion provides the first instance of describing him as Thracian outright. It appears paradoxical, since Androtion attempted to discredit Orpheus as a sage and predecessor of Homer and Hesiod. In pre-Roman times, Orpheus' connection to Thrace was explored in many ways, but did not constitute an indispensable feature of his depiction. One of the more interesting examples here is Apollonius' description (1,23–34), according to which Orpheus was born in Macedonian Pieria and then travelled to Thrace to take rulership of the otherwise unknown 'Bistonian Pieria'.

Sources also present indications that Classical-era Greeks did not perceive Orpheus exclusively through his connections to Thracians and Thrace. This includes genealogies suggesting he was the son of Apollo and a Muse or that his father, Oeagrus, was born to Pieros and descended from Apollo. These explain the role of Orpheus as the first musician, also confirmed by the instrument he would have received from his father (Eratosth. *Catast.* 24; Hyg. *Poet. astr.* 2,7). The Lesbian version of the myth presents that instrument as the cause of the local musicality (Hyg. *Poet. astr.* 2,7; Himerios *or.* 26). Orpheus was also placed at the beginning of the Greek literary and musical tradition, or presented as an ancestor of Homer and Hesiod (OF 871T). This distinctly

Greek aspect of his portrayal in some sources behoves us to reconsider the hero's widely presumed Thracian identity.

Divergent versions of the myth, its local variants, and poetic interpretations clearly prove that the mythical story cannot be read like a historical description. The Orpheus who commits suicide in Thesprotia (Paus. 9,30) does not appear particularly Thracian. The story of his killing by Zeus' lightning leaves no room for Thracian women. Thrace was an important option in Orpheus' mythical geography since the fifth century, but not the only one, and it carried various meanings.

What could Orpheus' connection to Thrace express and what experiences could it reflect? Firstly, the name of his father Oeagrus suggests savagery and the natural world, and Thracians fit the perception of those concepts in the fifth and fourth centuries well.[26] Perhaps these aspects of his portrayal arise from Orpheus' musical ability, which gives him the power to tame the wild and to civilise through *mousikē*. In this sense, a Thracian father would say more about Orpheus' music and the origins of music in general than of his ancestry.

Moreover, the ethnicity of mythical figures may change according to the needs of the audience. In Classical Athens, this usually manifested in links to the North, including Thrace.[27] The most famous example is the case of Tereus, a Phocian hero who, through coincidence and the similarity of his name to that of King Teres, father of Sitalces, is transformed on an Athenian stage into a savage Thracian.[28] Similarly, Eumolpus turns from an autochthon into a Thracian who invades Attica, which expresses, among other notions, the perception of mysteries as something foreign, arriving from Thrace or Egypt.[29] Such changes (barbarisation, and in Athens especially Thracisation) resulted from the peculiarities of the period, and reflected specific local experiences. Greek residents of Olbia, Syracusae, Megara or Cyrene treated the same questions (Where was music born? What was it at its origins? What is its role in human life?) in the context of their own geography, politics and religion.[30]

One of the arguments in favour of the Thracian origins of Orpheus, usually supported with Strabo (C 471 [10,3,17], see Chapter 4), is the Thracian lineage of other mythical musicians.[31] However, this proposal cuts both ways: origins of Linus, Musaeus or Thamyris were freely modified in mythology.[32] This is clear in Fritz Graf's description of Musaeus for the *Oxford Classical Dictionary* (s.v.): 'his life is a blank. He is nothing but a source of verses. Even his name, (belonging to the Muse), is a patent artificiality. His parentage and land of birth vary according to the use being made of him.'

Many mythical narratives reference Thracian lineages of famous musicians, but not as an inherent trait. Connections to Thrace are sometimes an imitation of other musicians (Thamyris/Orpheus), a commentary on the origins of music (from outside, from before), or an expression of its lost primal power. They do not, however, express facts about the origins of mythical figures. Thracianness is, in the case of mythical musicians, always a construct bestowed with specific values within a given context; it has undoubtedly gained much popularity, particularly in the Roman period and in mythography textbooks, but largely due to quasi-historical explanations, evidenced by Strabo (C 410 [9,2,25]), Pausanias (9,29,3), or Themistius (*or.* 16,209c), that included suggestions of an aboriginal musicality of Thracians.

At this point, it is reasonable to briefly examine the matter of ethnicity in Greek myth. Mythical heroes could not have an ethnicity as it is understood today.[33] The adventures and behaviour of mythical protagonists are typically an expression of Greek preconceptions about people from a given area (savagery, brutality, love of horse breeding, natural situation, specific method of fighting, religious observances etc.) rather than of a simple ethnic relationship.[34] In most cases, Greek heroes are 'outsiders', or their status as such expresses ideas important to a story or its significance. It is true many of them are eponyms and kings of other nations; in fact, a distinguishing feature of Greek mythology is that it reaches far outside its own world and touches on much of the *oikoumene*; this does not, however, mean that a hero's association with an area is tribal in nature. In most cases, heroes rule ethnic groups that neighbour Greeks, but they themselves are not descended from those groups. They are sons of gods, chthonic deities (nymphs, river gods), or, most frequently, heroic lineages. Thus, if any ethnicity can be proposed for them, it would be along the lines of a great 'heroic family'. Its representatives constantly travel to find land, power and fame, and through these travels become Thracians, Persians, Phoenicians or Lydians. It is no different when a narrative makes Orpheus the leader of Thracians, enthroned through his skill (Strabo, Conon) or by inheritance (Diodorus). A simple diachronic analysis shows that Greeks linked Orpheus to various Thracian groups, often for political reasons (Chapter 3).

Thus, 'why Thrace?' becomes a valid question. Why is Orpheus linked to Thracians, rather than Pelasgians or Scythians? Firstly, considering the earliest attested mythical plot involving Orpheus was the journey of the Argonauts, it is reasonable to consider that the iconographic scene of singing to Thracians and death by their women may have originated from the story of the quest for the Golden Fleece. The *Argo*'s route to Colchis originally ran along the Thracian coast and it is conceivable that story may have had a side narrative of the songsmith soothing savage Thracians, e.g. Homer's Cicones, particularly considering one of the earliest literary accounts of the hero (a fragment from Simonides) describes him charming fish, which suggests a sea journey.[35]

Secondly, nearly all known fifth- and fourth-century accounts were written in Athens or by authors closely associated with the city (Aeschylus, Euripides, Alcidamas, Androtion). Choosing Thracians and placing Orpheus' activity and death near Strymon and Mount Pangaion (Aeschylus, Euripides) thus had to tie into Athenian interest in that area, which began in the mid-sixth century.[36] In particular, colonisation attempts at the Strymon (460s) should inform us that mythical geography is not accidental or simply an enduring memory of ancient events. A myth is not a history, but it is told and processed in a historical context that may influence it to a certain degree. Thus, the founding of Brea around 440 BC, of Amphipolis in 437, the bestowing of Athenian citizenship on Sitalces' son Sadocus in 431, or the introduction of the cult of Bendis to Athens in 429 constitute important background information for the portrayal of Orpheus.[37] This obviously does not imply that the Athenians invented the Thracian context for the hero; however, it is possible that what was merely potential in the earlier realisations of the myth (Orpheus singing to Thracians or murdered by Thracian women) may have become a very concrete link because of Athenian fascination with the area.[38]

Another possibility is to assume that Thrace was chosen because of its links to Dionysus and Orphic literature, which also featured Dionysus prominently, and because of the perception of mysteries as something foreign. Orpheus as the author of Orphic texts was a better fit for a character from the fringes of the Greek world, and Thrace was a splendid choice for his homeland, particularly with its earlier ties to Dionysus.[39] Perhaps the key role was played by Aeschylus, who featured Orpheus in *Bassarids*, a play from his tetralogy about Dionysus and Lycurgus, in which the hero's home was Mount Pangaion. This variant would both be very Athenian (Strymon/Pangaion) and appropriate for the imagined origins of mysteries and arcane lore.[40] Such explanations are later found in Neopythagorean texts as well, and although those are late, they may reflect Orphic perceptions from the Classical period.[41]

How, then, should *testimonia* written between the fifth and third centuries be interpreted? First, they do not suggest the simple conclusion we know from mythology textbooks and collections that Orpheus was originally Thracian, a Thracian hero or a Thracian god. Accounts from that period simply do not substantiate it unequivocally. That depiction comes from late works, which in turn merely reflect Classical-era information through creative readings and modifications.[42] However, even the later realisations offer diverse explanations for Orpheus' connections to Thrace, not a coherent image. Many of them suggest that his rule over Thracians was not inherited, but, for example, assumed thanks to his musical prowess. One of the writers to suggest it was Conon (*Diegeseis* 45; see 7 [*Thamyris*]), who also pointed to an exceptional *philomousia* (proclivity for music) of the Thracians (and Macedonians).[43] This beautiful image of a people so enamoured with music and song that it crowns the greatest musician its king stands in stark contrast to the accounts of Thracian 'musicality' or the Greek perception of those tribes in the Classical period. In this form, it is, at best, a vision of the origins of *mousikē* and an expression of nostalgia for a mythical prehistory embodied in the vision of Thracians as 'noble savages'.

And so, was Orpheus Thracian? Yes and no. Yes, as he was described as such by Virgil and Ovid, the most widely read Roman poets since Antiquity. This tells us nothing of his ethnicity as a mythical figure, but very much about Roman writers' erudition and geographic horizons, and about their cultural specificities. No, because early accounts present a more subtle framing, usually connecting the hero to Thrace spatially and genealogically, but without drawing quasi-historical conclusions. Surviving texts depict the hero's links to Thrace in many different ways, creating an entire spectrum of possibilities. No, because in Antiquity such an ethnic descriptor, especially used for a mythical figure, was not straightforward and unambiguous. Classical-era Greeks called Orpheus 'Thracian' primarily to describe his spatial relationship with the northern fringes of the Greek world and with that area's many connotations, not ethnicity as understood through modern categories. Thus, of importance were the connotations of Thrace, its ties to Dionysus, arcane lore, savagery and nature. Ethnic and spatial references in myth were not inherent, instead depending on performative context and modified to fit the political situation, or the author's knowledge and inventiveness.

Orpheus was sometimes proclaimed a Thracian, if that feature was interesting; before that, we only see him among them, which is not the same. This is true in the case of his killing by Thracian women or maenads as well. This element of his portrayal is part of the characteristic of a mythical figure. It was occasionally used, developed and became more common, but it was never a dominant or constant aspect of Orpheus' depictions before Roman times. The same phenomenon of adapting the story to the circumstances of the presentation and the needs of an audience happened to Jacopo Peri's opera *Euridice*.

This analysis began with a note that Orpheus' 'Thracianness' could be based on a few simple assumptions: his father was Oeagrus, a Thracian; the hero lived in Thrace; or he lived in then-Thracian Pieria. This chapter has reviewed the various dimensions of the first two rationalisations, setting the third aside. It is worth investigating it, as tying Thracians to Pieria is still common in scholarly literature. But was Pieria originally inhabited by Thracians? As has been said in the Introduction, the toponyms visible in literary sources represent the physical extremes of his life: from birth in Pimpleia (Apollonius) to death or burial in Leibethra (proverb). It raises a question: are those locations actually Pierian? And how are they related to Thracians? The next two chapters will explore the answers. Until the matter is fully explained, the possibility of tying the hero to Thrace, and therefore to doubt his links to Macedonia in the Classical period, will remain.

3

Leibethra, Pimpleia and Mythical Geography

In the third book of his *Library*, Apollodorus (3,27–8) presents the circumstances surrounding the birth of Dionysus. After saving the newborn from a fire, Zeus sewed him in his thigh to bear him until the time was right. The child was sent, as a girl, first to Athamas and Ino, and after angry Hera punished them with madness, Zeus turned Dionysus into a boy to deceive his wife. However, as the son required care, Hermes brought him to the nymphs who dwelt at Nysa in Asia.

The oronym Nysa appears as early as Euripides' *Bacchae* (556–7) and is the most frequently presented place of birth or raising of Dionysus in Greek tradition. However, it is not the mountain's links to child Dionysus that attract attention (Greek gods were frequently associated with natural sites[1]), but rather its 'mobility' in our sources: ancient authors place it in nearly every corner of the contemporary world. Herodotus (2,146) located Nysa in Ethiopia, Diodorus (3,59,2) in Arabia, while Hesychius' lexicon lists fifteen possible placements (nu 742): 'Nysa and Nyseion: a mountain not confined to any one place; as it lies and in Arabia, in Ethiopia, Egypt, Babylon, Erythrai, Thrace, Thessaly, Cilicia, Indiae, Libya, Lydia, Macedon, on Naxos, around Pangaion, place in Syria.'

The mythical nature of the site is suggested in the lexicographer's first remark, which, if read literally, becomes emblematic: 'a mountain not confined to any one place' (οὐ καθ' ἕνα τόπον). Nysa is not a unique case, but rather the most famous example of a change in geographical coordinates and descriptions of locations in mythical narratives. We infer that the mountain being situated in lands as various as Thrace, Syria, Thessaly or Cilicia may have been a result of local ideas of the story, of audience expectations, the author's geographical knowledge, their inventiveness, and in some cases a specific reading of earlier authors.

Some mythical toponyms were seen as placed outside the geographic reality of the Greeks and were thus hard to mark on a map. But a great majority of mythical spatial references are real locations, well founded in ancient geography. The historical reality of the toponyms does not mean the authors knew and could precisely point to those sites. Some changes to mythical geography may have stemmed from a lack of maps and geographical literature the authors and audiences could consult.[2] New versions of a myth may have included incorrect or creative interpretations of positions or toponyms found in earlier poetic or mythographic works. Consequently, Greek myth became a space not only for creative narrative solutions, but also innovative geographical details. Thus, even if all variants of a story refer to the same name (e.g. Nysa), they may understand it differently (as a mountain, a city, a spring) and place it in a fantastical area or one known to the audience.

The deliberations over spatial references in poetry and mythography present us with two conclusions: one, geography, while often seemingly secondary in myth, is very important for the mythical story.[3] Secondly, the choice of toponyms and their portrayal depends on historical circumstance and may change, just like the names of characters, genealogies or motivations of heroes, or the sequences of events. A correct analysis of spatial references may therefore tell us much about how the narratives transformed over time and how the geographical knowledge and perceptions of given authors and audiences in the given period would change.

A special case of spatial innovations in myth are the changes in geographical meaning attributed to toponyms. The example of the 'travelling' Mount Nysa is one of the more pronounced of these. However, sometimes changes go much further than simply moving a toponym from one area to another and result in the appearance of completely new geographic content. A proper name might be tied to any terrain, e.g. a toponym of a settlement is extended to a mountain, a cave or a spring. Such modifications may result from the writer's creativity, but also from changes to geographical horizons, or they may respond to the needs of the audience. We may surmise that it was the expansion of the Greco-Roman world that caused Nysa to be placed in Arabia or Babylon. Changes to locales or values attributed to places important for the story have a major influence on the plot and the actions of the heroes.

The spatial references in the stories of Orpheus are some of the more interesting cases researched in the scholarship of the many aspects of mythical geography. On one hand, the story ties the mythical musician to Thracians and places him somewhere on the northern coast of the Aegean Sea – over Strymon, Hebrus, on Pangaion or Haemus. On the other hand, however, the great majority of contemporaneous Ancient accounts link him to the region of Pieria in Macedonia. Looking at just the early accounts, we can see that the Pierian city of Leibethra is his burial site in Aeschylus' tragedy, while the village of Pimpleia near Dion is his birthplace in Apollonius' *Argonautica*. Moreover, the reading of the myth is further complicated by the strong interconnectedness of the two ethnic and geographic areas (Thrace and Pieria) in the sources. And so, Leibethra, Pimpleia and Pieria itself laid within Thrace, were inhabited by Thracians, or were linked to them in some other way. A meticulous diachronic analysis shows, however, that the ties between Thrace and Pieria are known from late sources and only appear in late Hellenistic literature, where Pierian toponyms accrue new geographical values while also being linked to spaces typical of Muse epiphany sites. Hence, Late Ancient descriptions of Leibethra and Pimpleia include a mountain, a cave, or a spring of inspiration: places appropriate for the son of a Muse and the first musician or poet.

Modern descriptions occasionally accept such late, literary interpretations as historical or geographical information. The scholarly approach is well illustrated by entries from dictionaries which state that Leibethrion is a 'mountain district of Thrace inhabited by Orpheus' (LSJ s.v.) or a 'region of Thrace' (Montanari s.v.), while Pimpleia is a 'mountain in Pieria' (Montanari). Some works include more nuanced conclusions, but eventually we are left with questions regarding the credibility of late accounts and geographic content attributed to Pierian toponyms in scholia and lexicons.[4] At the root of the issue lies the paucity of information from earlier periods and an abundance of detail in later texts, as well as a lack of an accurate assessment of sources.

The objective in this chapter will therefore be to reassess available *testimonia* and investigate the degree of changes in the location and geographical meaning assigned to Leibethra and Pimpleia. These locations, key to the myth of Orpheus, are described in the sources as towns, mountains, rivers or springs, and placed in various areas. An analysis will show how they gradually lost their Macedonian connotations. Meanwhile, situating them in Thrace, as can be seen in late sources, reinforced the notion of a non-Greek background of Orpheus. A precise description, chronology, and explanation for the changes in the depictions of Leibethra and Pimpleia in later versions of the Orpheus myth is necessary for the research, since without it a reconstruction of the early traditions about the hero or an explanation of his ties to Pieria would be virtually impossible.

Three concepts shall be especially useful in researching Orpheus' mythical geography in chapters 3 and 4. The first is 'imaginary geography'/'imaginative geographies'. The creator of that notion is Edward Said, author of *Orientalism*, who used it to describe the portrayal of the East in Western culture.[5] The concept as formulated is not restricted to fiction, since 'all geographies are imaginative: even the most formal, geometric lattices of spatial science or the most up-to-date and accurate maps are at once abstractions and cultural constructions, and as such open to critical readings'.[6]

The second will be Lévi-Strauss's concept of *bricolage*, helpful to evaluate the methods of modifying the myth, especially the geographical details of a story.[7] Mainstreamed by the French anthropologist, this process of creating new meanings in a mythical story is tied to thinking and creation through a patchwork of a culture's collection of stories, which serves as a reservoir of plots, motives, characters or narrative models. Further permutations of the myth (as isolated by 'mythographical analysis') may therefore be a narrative replete with geographical references, characters or plots less or more loosely borrowed from other tales. Such new versions are easier to interpret as part of a collection (mythographic, for instance) than in isolation. What seems to us a quirk of an author or source (e.g. while reading one of Conon's tales) becomes understandable and acceptable in the context of a collection or of the typical practices of the genre.

The third concept will be the prototype theory, originating from cognitive psychology. Eleanor Rosch, the creator of the theory, noticed during an experiment that humans appear to have a tendency for remembering the most typical instances of a concept and assign atypical members to the group based on their basic traits.[8] For instance, if we decide that the defining trait of fish is that they live in water, we would automatically add dolphins to that group as well. Meanwhile, if the prototypical feature of birds are the wings allowing them to fly, then penguins, who fulfil only one of these conditions, become problematic. Rosch's research topics included arguments in favour of the concept of 'cognitive scripts', which allow for a rapid classification of any experience and operative use of the knowledge gained from it. In this chapter, the prototype model will be used to explain changes in the geographic concepts within the myth, pointing to a psychological background of the modification.

Leibethra and Pimpleia: What do we know?

We shall begin the analysis by evaluating formerly unknown topographic references in the vision of Leibethra and Pimpleia (as a mountain, a cave or a spring) and will attempt to explain how these elements entered the analysis and how they are related to Orpheus. But, before moving on to interpreting new geographical meanings of Leibethra and Pimpleia, we shall dedicate a moment to the state of our knowledge of both those places in epigraphical, archaeological and early literary sources. Let us begin with Leibethra. Currently, we have three epigraphic accounts of either the ethnicon *Leibethrioi* or the city of Leibethra. The former is first mentioned in an early third century BC honorific inscription from the city of Gonnoi in Thessalian Perrhaibia (*Gonnoi* 2,2):

μέχρι τῶν ὀρῶν τῶν Λειβ[ηθρίων]

up to the mountains of the Leib[ethrians]

The name of the city, meanwhile, appears in a *c.* 230 BC inscription from Delphi, containing a long list of *theorodokoi* (sacred envoy-receivers).[9] It lists a Nikostratos and a Nikonos from Leibethra. Before them are listed some citizens of Heracleion, and next on the list are people from Dion and Pydna. Considering that the Heracleion in question is a town in the Vale of Tempe, on the northeastern frontier of Thessaly, we may infer that Leibethra was located between Heracleion and Dion. The location of the city is best evidenced by an inconspicuous bronze weight of one mina (SEG 27,283) from southern Pieria with the inscription Λειβη[θρίων] – 'of the Leibethrians'. Taken together, these three sources point to the existence of a city named Leibethra, sited in the south of Pieria, near the borders with Magnesia and Thessaly, and to its inhabitants being called Leibethrioi.[10]

This data is corroborated by Greek archaeologists, who excavated part of the city's acropolis in the twentieth century.[11] The identification of the settlement appears decisive, and its location matches other accounts. The acropolis of Leibethra (modern Leivithra) rose on an isolated, fortified hill at the foot of Olympus, by the river now known as Ziliana and identified (after Pausanias) with the ancient River Sys. This location justifies Hellenistic accounts referring to Leibethra (and occasionally Pimpleia) as a *skopiē* ('height'). Archaeological data (in both cases) suggests that the term should not be understood as 'mountain top' or 'peak', but rather 'highland' or 'height'. We will return to this point later.

The city's location in this part of Pieria is also confirmed by various literary, historical and geographical sources. The earliest instance of the name may have been Aeschylus' play *Bassarids*, mentioned by Erathostenes (*Catast.* 24) in his description of the catasterism[12] of the lyre. Another account of the location of Leibethra is provided in Lycophron's *Alexandra*. Verse 410 speaks of 'Leibethrian gates of Dotion', a plain in northeastern Thessaly, south of Mount Ossa. This phrase informs us that the city was a kind of stronghold along the route from Thessaly to Pieria and Macedon, as confirmed in a passage from Livy (44,5,12) describing a Roman army camp on the Macedonian frontier in 169 BC. The historian mentions that Leibethra was in Pieria and bordered Thessalian Heracleion to the south. The Delphi inscription also placed Leibethrians between Heracleians and men of Dion.

The two largest accounts of the location of Leibethra survive in Pausanias' *Description of Greece* and in Strabo's *Geography*. The seventh book of Strabo's work, surviving in minor fragments, includes a partial description of Macedonia. Fragment 10 presents Dion, the region's largest city. Strabo thus mentions Pimpleia, which he calls a village (κώμη) within the territory of Dion, and describes the site's association with Orpheus, whom he calls a 'sorcerer'. At the end of this digression, he adds: 'and near here, also, is Leibethra'. Strabo mentions the city on two more occasions: C 471 [10,3,17] and C 410 [9,2,25]. Pausanias, meanwhile, refers (9,30,9–11) to the 'city of Libethra' (πόλις Λίβηθρα), where Orpheus had his tomb. The city was supposedly destroyed by the River Sys, and the grave was moved to nearby Dion. This is indirectly corroborated by archaeologists, as the Leibethra site has not revealed any indication of settlement activity in the Imperial period.

As for Pimpleia, we have no epigraphic testimony or physical findings. The settlement has still not been archaeologically identified; however, unlike Leibethra, it was not a city, but merely a village or hamlet in Dion's territory, according to Strabo (7, fr. 10, see above).[13] An early allusion to the toponym could be present in Epicharmus (fr. 39 PCG), who makes Pimpleis and Pierus the parents of the Muses in one of his comedies. This would suggest some links between the settlement and the Muses were already present in literature in the early fifth century. However, it is impossible to rule out that these names were a poet's invention, since both only point to Pieria and the fertility of the earth (Fat and Fullness).[14]

In summary, information on Leibethra and Pimpleia as settlements in Pieria dates back to the Classical period. Based on it, we can state with relative certainty that Pimpleia was a village in the territory of the polis of Dion, and Leibethra was a city in southern Pieria. Both places were at the foot or on the slopes of the Olympus range, but they were not mountains, peaks or rivers/springs; neither Strabo nor Pausanias suggest that and they are trustworthy in this regard. Leibethra's hilltop position allowed for it to be referred to as *skopiē*, meaning highland or height. The above conclusions are similar to historical and geographical analyses by Hammond (1972, 136–7), Papazoglou (1988, 113) and Hatzopoulos and Paschidis (2004).

Leibethra and Pimpleia: Changes in mythical geography

All accounts referenced so far are early or based on early sources. However, texts written after the Hellenistic period assign new meanings, usually incongruent with earlier works, to the toponyms of Leibethra and Pimpleia. These new interpretations fall into one of three groups: first, ones that identify Leibethra and Pimpleia with a mountain or a spring or add such significance to them; second, ones that tie the sites to Thracians or locate them (as town, mountain or spring) in Thrace; third, ones that link the Pierian city of Leibethra with Mount Libethrion in Boeotia. All these interpretations are present to some extent in modern historiography, complicating the assessment of Orpheus' mythical tradition.[15]

We shall begin by examining the first category (spring/mountain) before moving on to the Thracian component and Boeotian links, starting with the works of Roman writers. The 'Libethra spring' is mentioned, for example, in Pliny (*NH* 4,16): 'Adjoining Thessaly is Magnesia, to which belong the spring Libethra, the towns of Iolcus, Ormenium, Pyrrha, Methone and Olizon etc.' [tr. H. Rackham]. Obviously, Pliny confuses Magnesia with the nearby Pieria, which may tie in to Pierus' ancestry as a son of Magnes (Apollod. 1,16) or result from the mental deformation of the Greek geography by a writer in distant Rome. Nevertheless, the crucial information here is the existence of a spring named Libethra. We do not know where the first-century encyclopaedist sourced his knowledge from, but situating Leibethra in Magnesia rather than southern Pieria suggests it came from his reading.

Another suggestion tying Leibethra to the spring can be found in a work by Pomponius Mela (2,36): 'Here is Pieria, both the mother of the Muses and their home. (...) Here is Tempe, well known for its sacred grove, and Libethra, the fountain of songs' [tr. F. E. Romer]. The phrase *carminum fontes* ('fountain of songs') is a poetic periphrasis and metaphor, but it implies an association between Leibethra and water or a spring. Perhaps it is an attempt to link the two aspects of the location: a fountain that was placed there in some texts (as in Pliny, and see below) and the literary role tied to the Muses and Orpheus (Varro *Ling.* 7,20: *Libethrides* as an epithet of the Muses).

A third example of a clear entanglement between mythical spatial references and literary associations is found in Virgil's *Eclogue* 7 (v.21). At the beginning of his literary confrontation with Thyrsis, Corydon invokes the Leibethrian nymphs:

> *Nymphae noster amor Libethrides, aut mihi carmen,*
> *quale meo Codro, concedite (proxima Phoebi*
> *uersibus ille facit) aut, si non possumus omnes,*
> *hic arguta sacra pendebit fistula pinu.*

> Nymphs, our belov'd, Libethrians, either grant me song
> Such as you grant my Codrus (he is second best
> At verse to Phoebus), or, if we can't all succeed,
> Here on the sacred pine shall hang a tuneful pipe. [tr. G. Lee]

Such an apostrophe was debated even in antiquity, as Corydon asks for inspiration from nymphs, goddesses linked to nature, particularly water and springs, rather than the Muses. He also associates them with a location apparently missing from the metapoetic repertoire. But of even greater interest are the later explanations of the phrase 'nymphae Libethrides', as ancient commentators introduce a whole range of new meanings that the toponym Leibethra certainly did not have before. Servius interpreted that passage from Virgil as follows (schol. Danielis 21): 'from the Boeotian spring [Libethrus, or from] the poet Libethrus, who first passed on harmony and dedicated an altar to the Muses. Some say that it is the place called Libethron, where Hesiod was born, others still that it is the temple of the Libethrian Muses consecrated by Pierus, son of Apollo.' Similar explanation we find in the so-called *Scholia Bernensia*: 'Libethrian nymphs, from Mount Libethron in Boeotia, dedicated to the Muses, or river Libethrus in Thrace, where Orpheus was torn apart and where Muses bathed. Others say [it is] a spring in Boeotia.'[16]

Modern researchers are not as creative in their explanations, but they do consider this passage in *Eclogue 7* problematic. Some choose to identify 'Libethrian nymphs' with the Muses, others find the phrase *Nymphae Libethrides* neutral and ambiguous, but pointing towards the nymphs for the most part.[17] Magnelli (2010, 174, n. 1), attempting to bridge the two interpretations, indicated the Camenae, nymphs of springs and Roman counterparts of the Muses, as a possible solution. Meanwhile, Lipka (2001, 100–1, n. 346) insightfully remarked that the phrase *Nymphae Libethrides* refers us principally to Orpheus. The problem with explaining this phrase – are they Muses or not and why Libethrian? – is less in the reading than in its justification. The work in question is poetry, not a history or a geography; thus, the ambiguity may have been intentional. That may be the source of the broad range of ancient explanations (Pieria–Boeotia–Thrace) and of linking the adjective Libethrian to a spring or river in Boeotia or Thrace or a mountain.

As for Pimpleia, a suggestion that it was a site linked to a spring and water appears clearly in Statius' *Silvae* (2,2,37): 'Not if Helicon were to grant me all his streams or Piplea quench my thirst or the hoof of the flying horse etc.'[18] But the crucial information is available in scholia and lexicons from Late Antiquity. Hesychius (s.v. *Pipleiai*) explains the toponym Pimpleia as follows: 'Pipleiae: Muses [living] on Macedonian Olympus, after the spring Pipleia.'

This passage from the ancient lexicographer is frequently cited as proof that Pi(m)pleia was a spring associated with the Muses.[19] Similar explanations can also be found in scholia, commentaries and dictionaries.[20]

How can this new information about Leibethra and Pimpleia be interpreted? First, it bears repeating that geographic connotations are absent in accounts older than the first century, and they appear, as with the explanation for Virgil's *nymphae Libethrides*, more a result of creative reading than proof of some previously unheard of geographic details. Leibethra's name itself points to a general association with water (the verb λείβω meaning 'to pour'), Pieria's to the fertility of the land (from πῖαρ, 'fat'), and the toponym Pimpleia (from πιμπλάω/ πίμπλημι) suggests 'filling'. Both settlements are located on the slopes of the Olympus range, rich in streams flowing down to the sea. Such relationships between Pieria or Pimpleia and water may be suggested even in the oldest account by Epicharmus (fr. 39 PCG), who names the Muses, daughters of Pierus and the nymph Pimpleis, after rivers (although from various parts of the world).

Moreover, incidentally to the aforementioned fragment from Epicharmus, we note that ancient explanations are linked to the use of the epithet Pi(m)pleides as a title of the Muses and result from tying Pi(m)pleia to the goddesses. The wide spread of these connotations in the Roman period is evidenced by the account of Varro, who, explaining the title *Olympiades*, concluded (*Ling.* 7,20):

> Olympus is the name which the Greeks give to the sky, and all peoples give to a mountain in Macedonia; it is the latter, I am inclined to think, that the Muses are spoken of as the Olympiads: for they are called in the same way from other places on earth the Libethrids, the Pipleids, the Thespiads, the Heliconiads.
>
> Translated by R. G. Kent

This account also proves that Pierian toponyms had to be tied to the Muses at least in the Hellenistic period. This is corroborated by unrelated accounts, most famously Callimachus (*h.* 4,7–8).

These additional explanations help understand the relationship between the two places (Pimpleia and Leibethra) and the Muses, but do not explain the appearance and role of a spring in the popular concept of the toponyms, as well as them being placed in various locations (Boeotia, Thrace, Macedon). As said before, none of the pre-first-century accounts mention springs associated with the Muses in Leibethra or Pimpleia, and neither do Strabo or Pausanias. Such information is missing from Callimachus, although the poet writing about the birth of the Muses could mention an important, inspiration-giving spring. The passages from Lycophron (*Alex.* 275) and Apollonius (1,25) do not indicate any springs in either location. All this suggests that the 'spring' came from an interpretation of ambiguous Hellenistic or Roman poetry. More complete conclusions will appear at the end of the analysis; for now, we focus on mountains and caverns in the depictions of Leibethra and Pimpleia.

Mount Libethrum (in Boeotia) appears in the aforementioned *scholia Bernensia* (*a monte Boeotiae Libethro qui est Musis sacer*). Moreover, the manuscript version of the proverb about Leibethrians (see Introduction and 'The proverb about Leibethrians' in Chapter 5) from the compilation by Diogenianus (2,26) lacks the reference to the Pierian *ethnos*, as seen in Zenobius, and instead explains it as follows: Λειβήθριον γὰρ ὄρος Πιερικόν ('Leibethrion is a Pierian mountain'). Romero (2011: 341, n. 8) believed that replacing ἔθνος with ὄρος ('mountain') in some manuscripts was a copyist error. In light of the accounts above, it is more likely to be an alternative explanation, perhaps resulting from the use of additional literary or lexicographic sources. In addition, this version of the proverb replaces the ethnonym Leibethrioi with the toponym Leibethrion. A typical error would result in leaving the ethnonym and a logical error in the sentence.

Information tying Leibethra to a mountain of a similar name in Boeotia also appears in the scholia to Lycophron's *Alexandra* (ad 275): Λείβηθρα δὲ [....] ὄρος ἐν Ἑλικῶνι ('Leibethra [...] mountain on Helicon'). Notably, verses 274–5 of the poem include three toponyms: Leibethra, Pimpleia and Bephyra – all clearly tied to Pieria and Orpheus, not to Boeotia, making the scholia explanation surprising.[21] A relationship between Leibethra and the mountains is also implied by the *Orphic Argonautica* (v. 50-1):

Ὥς ποτε Πιερίην Λειβήθρων τ' ἄκρα κάρηνα

Once, in Pieria and the highest peaks of Libethra [tr. J. Colavito]

The ending of the epic, describing Orpheus' return home, also mentions the hero's home in a cave in Leibethra (1373–6). On both occasions, the text refers to a place linked to mountains, but, unlike the scholia, not a mountain of that name.

Even more examples related to mountains can be listed for Pimpleia. Despite Strabo's statements (7, fr. 10a), contemporary explanations for the location and geographic nature of the site are similarly confusing here.[22] The analysis begins with the account by Catullus, the first known source to mention a 'Pi(m)pleian mount'. In a short piece mocking (probably) the literary ambitions of Ceasar's subordinate Mamurrus, the poet uses climbing the mountain of the Muses as a metaphor for literary effort (105):

Mentula conatur Pipleium scandere montem:
Musae furcilis praecipitem eiciunt.

Cock strives to climb the Piplean mount:
the Muses with pitchforks drive him out headlong. [tr. F. W. Cornish]

Catullus speaks here of a metapoetic mountain of the Muses, located in Pi(m)pleia and apparently parallel to Helicon. This brings to mind the aforementioned account of Varro, listing Pipleides alongside Heliconiades and Thespiades as epithets of the Muses. But Pimpleia has no such association with mountains in texts before Catullus or contemporary to him, for example in Callimachus (*h.* 4,7), or in the slightly later Strabo (7, fr. 10a).

The only pre-Roman accounts notable in this context are passages from *Argonautica* by Apollonius of Rhodes and Lycophron's *Alexandra*. In both instances, Pimpleia and Libethra are associated with the noun *skopiē*, meaning 'a vantage point, a height, a highland', but also 'peak', or, consequently, 'watchtower'. In *Argonautica* (1,25), Apollonius says that Calliope bore Orpheus to Oeagrus σκοπιῆς Πιμπληίδος ἄγχι – 'near the Pimpleian height', or, in W. H. Race's translation, 'near the peak of Pimpleia'. The text does not imply that Pimpleia is a mountain, the poet only uses the periphrasis 'Pimpleian height'.[23] The further description of Orpheus' travel to Bistonia and the description of his kingdom as 'Bistonian Pieria' (1,34) indicates that Pimpleia is a Pierian toponym referring to a site located at the foot of Olympus. Similar, but somewhat more problematic, are the verses in Lycophron's *Alexandra*, possibly due to the nature of the poem, full of metaphors and mythological riddles. Describing the death of Achilles, Cassandra says he will be lamented by nymphs

αἵ φίλαντο Βηφύρου γάνος,
Λειβηθρίην θ' ὕπερθε Πιμπλείας σκοπήν

who love the waters of Bephyros
and the Leibethrian watchtower above Pimpleia. [tr. S. Hornblower]

All three toponyms here (Bephyros, Leibethra, Pimpleia) are associated with Pieria, but for this inquiry, the most interesting is the use of the phrase Λειβηθρίην... σκοπήν, as it is another instance of the word *skop(i)ē*, which must be rendered here as Leibethrian height, in reference to Leibethra and Pimpleia.[24] Here, once more, is how the passages from Apollonius and Lycophron were explained in the aforementioned scholia: 'Pimpleia, a place in Pieria; some say it is a mountain in Thrace, others that it is a spring and a village in Pieria' (schol. Ap. Rhod. 1,23–5); 'Pimpleia, meanwhile, is a polis, a mountain, and a spring in Macedonia' (schol. in Lycoph. 275). In both cases, the term *skopiē* is read as 'mountain' (ὄρος), and although the scholia attempt to present alternative explanations (city [πόλις]; land [χωρίον]; spring [κρήνη]), as both poets use the term *skopiē*, a reading pointing to 'a mountain' appears justified.

This general way of interpreting 'Pierian geography' also led to other explanations in the same vein: '[From Pieria]: Pieria, mountain in Thrace where Orpheus lived'.[25] Interestingly, this last information was not entirely false, but rather slightly altered. Pieria was, broadly speaking, a mountainous country where Orpheus and the Thracians lived, according to many ancient sources. However, such slightly misaligned geographic coordinates could lead to new phenomena, such as the 'Pierian mountains', which, at some point, developed from an acceptable periphrasis ('Pierian mountains', meaning mountains in Pieria, i.e. Olympus) into an independent entity. Hence, historians could point to 'Pierian Mountains' on their maps wherever they would place them, other than in the imagination of ancient commentators. A similar periphrasis – rather than a proper name – are Herodotus' 'Macedonian Mountains' (7,131) featured in the description of Xerxes' marching south with his army.

A reading which presumes the existence of a mountain in Leibethra and Pimpleia, or of a mountain of that name, ties into the matter of the cave where Orpheus was supposedly born and wherein he lived. The earliest account of a cave of Muses in Pieria is in one of Horace's odes (3,4,40), in which he encourages the goddesses to let Caesar (i.e. Augustus) rest in the 'Pierian cave' (*Pierio recreatis antro*).[26] Martial places it more precisely when he speaks explicitly of a Pi(m)pleian grotto (12,11): *cuius Pipleo lyra clarior exit ab antro?* – 'Whose lyre comes forth from the Piplean grotto with a clearer tone' [tr. D. R. Shackleton Bailey]. A complete proof for the existence of a metapoetic image of the cave of the Muses and Orpheus can be found in the aforementioned *Orphic Argonautica*

(1373–6). At the end of the piece, Orpheus returns from the journey of the Argonauts 'to snowy Thrace, in the region of Libethra, in my homeland, entering the famous cave where my mother gave birth to me on the bed of the brave Oeagrus' [tr. J. Colavito]. In this case the text mentions 'Thracian Libethra', but the mechanism for construing their image is similar to that employed in other accounts, as they link Muses and Orpheus to a 'Pierian' grotto appropriate to the poet or musician. The grotto may then be located in Pimpleia, Leibethra or Pieria in general, and all the toponyms loosely associated with Thrace. As a literary or metaliterary phenomenon this cavern is primarily a product of poetic imagination, not a real place. Of course, *Orphic Argonautica* is a product of Late Antiquity (fourth–fifth century CE), but its roots are in earlier traditions. Orpheus' grotto is encountered, although without details of its location, as early as Virgil's *Georgics* (4,508–10):

> He wept under a rock near the empty waters of Strymon,
> and in the ice-cold caves developed his song
> charming tigers and making the oak trees follow him. [tr. B. Graziosi]

In her commentary to this passage, B. Graziosi notes (2018: 193, n. 91) that this unclear phrasing may suggest a 'tradition of Orphic utterances emerging from caves'. She points out the depictions of Orpheus' prophesying head on fifth-century pottery (Figure 4), as well as Eurypides' (*Alc.* 969–71) mention of Thracian tablets.

Contexts and explanations

First, it bears repeating that Pimpleia was a village within Dion, and Leibethra was a town in southern Pieria (Strabo 7, fr. 10). Both were located on the slopes of Olympus, but not above. Neither Strabo nor Pausanias, nor Classical or Hellenistic authors suggest topographic features (mountains, springs, grottoes) seen in Roman writing, scholia, lexicons and commentaries. The general assessment of the material suggests a change in the meaning of the toponyms in the first century BC/AD, marking it as a tipping point. This is important for the evaluation of latter accounts of Orpheus and Greek myth in general.

How should the discrepancy between early sources and our knowledge of these historical toponyms on one side, and the geographic references in Roman literature and scholia on the other, be interpreted? The phenomenon has a number of causes. Firstly, the changes follow the spread of literacy, circulation of texts, and emergence of a literary culture replete with creative (and occasionally wrong, but erudite) readings and reinterpretations of texts from previous generations. This process is particularly noticeable in the multicultural and multilingual Roman world, which dealt in both reinterpretation and translation (*skopiē/mons*). Secondly, in a world of circulating texts and interweaving cultural phenomena, it was possible for literary and philosophical or religious notions, including Orphic or Neopythagorean, to cross-pollinate. Thirdly, the choice of geographic features for the images of toponyms (mountain, grotto, spring) related to Orpheus and the Muses may have been tied to the development of a metapoetic language in the culture of the period. Particularly influential here was the borrowing by the Romans of Greek patterns of interactions with the Muses, from the prototypical description of Hesiod's poetic initiation (*Dichterweihe*) to the geography of inspiration (with mountains, springs or grottoes as its sources).

Mountain

Mountains were highly pronounced in Orpheus' mythical geography from the beginning. Already in Aeschylus' *Bassarids* the Pangaion forms a backdrop to the hero's religious practices and his death. Mountains, alongside rivers, quickly became a fixture in the depictions of the hero's murder. Originally, that had little to do with Pimpleia and Leibethra, although Pieria was considered mountainous and both settlements were located on the slopes of Olympus. This justified referring to them as *skopiē* in Hellenistic literature. The Hellenistic phrase Πιμπληίς σκοπή[27] is reflected in Catullus' phrase '*Pipleius mons*' (105). However, the Greek noun *skopē* has a broader range of meanings (including 'height' or 'highland') rather than just 'a mountain'. Scholiasts follow the Roman poet's example by mentioning ὄρος ('mountain') where Hellenistic poetry only used *skopiē* (as 'height'). Of course, Catullus himself (or his source) is not mistaken here; instead, he reinterprets the Greek term based on his reading of a literary text. But this example demonstrates the evolution of the changes, with the phrase *Pipleius mons* giving rise to further transpositions and interpretations. As for the commentaries, such as the *scholia Bernensia ad Verg. ecl.* 7,21, the scholiasts did not aim to verify geographical data, but rather document any literary versions they knew of. Those, in turn, tended to be ambiguous, rich in association and bold metaphor, linking distant phenomena into evocative images. An example here might be the 'Bistonian Pieria' of Apollonius: a phrase originally clearly interpreted as an erudite reference to Orpheus' dual spatial traditions, but in a reading disconnected from Alexandrian scholarship it could be understood literally, as placing Pieria within Thracia. Similarly ambiguous were the passages from Lycophron (*Alex.* 274–5) and Virgil (*Ecl.* 7,21), linking the Muses to nymphs. The use of such ambiguous phrases in popular poetry caused cascades of reinterpretations of various metapoetic notions and descriptions of mythical scenery.

In ancient culture, mountains were considered a liminal space, well-suited for divine epiphanies and, by the same token, the right place for poetic initiations.[28] Particularly influential in Antiquity was the description of Hesiod's encounter with the Muses on the slopes of Helicon (*Th.* 1–105).[29] Poetic self-reflections adapted many features of that depiction of a poetic initiation, such as the liminal time of the encounter, conversational form, and especially the space where the epiphany happened: on a mountain, near a spring, later inside a grotto.[30] From a cognitive standpoint, the encounter with the Muses at Helicon became a kind of prototype and as such it modified other phenomena and imageries, even quite remote. Later metapoetic explanations, particularly spatial, could thus be interpreted according to the prototype and reinforced with its typical elements.[31] The prototypical *locus amoenus*, drawing especially on Hesiod's moment of poetic initiation, was also embodied in Roman villas, or even in the houses and libraries.[32] This phenomenon is also discernible when Catullus speaks of composition and a literary career as a process of climbing a mountain (of the Muses).[33] Thus, the close ties of both Pierian settlements to Orpheus and the Muses must be acknowledged as a key aspect in the geographic metamorphosis of Leibethra and Pimpleia, since both toponyms appear as epithets of these goddesses in Hellenistic and Roman literature.[34] One could logically infer that if other epithets clearly link the Muses to mountains (Olympus or Helicon), Pimpleides and Libethrides should be similar.

Caves

The image of a cave in Pieria, Leibethra or Pimpleia reinforces their interpretation as mountains, but also has its own, independent roots. This phenomenon may be tied to both the biographic tradition of poets and to Orphic or Neopythagorean writings. For example, the prophesying head of Orpheus is commonly depicted within a grotto (Figure 4); a Neopythagorean text from the late Hellenistic period depicts a transfer of mystical knowledge on Mount Pangaion; and the *Orphic Argonautica* evokes a mountain landscape in its description of Orpheus' cave.[35] There are also other potential sources of the imagery of Orpheus' grotto. 'Poets' grottos' were depicted since the Classical period, starting with Eurypides' grotto and ending with 'Homer's grotto' near Smyrna.[36] Both these instances indicate that a plot pattern tying poets or intellectuals to caves, be it as a place of isolation or a place of divine contact, existed as early as the fourth century.[37] Caverns were also a place of epiphany, revelation, or nympholepsy, as seen in texts from various periods.[38] Returning to Eurypides, it is worth mentioning that his supposed grotto was shown not only on Salamis, but also in Macedonia, where he reportedly lived in his final years.[39] The presence of caves in the images of Pieria and the Muses may also stem from the Hellenistic and Roman redefinition of the *mouseion*.[40] The change dates back to the Hellenistic period, since Pompey's Asian loot includes an artificial grotto with a horologium on top, listed in the source as a 'musaeum'.[41] It bears highlighting, however, that the cave of Orpheus appears relatively late in known literary traditions; it is not attested until Virgil and late Orphics. Of course, the cave of Orpheus in a mythical narrative does not mean a grotto was present in Leibethra or Pimpleia. To paraphrase Aristotle, mythical narratives deal not in what is true, but in what is likely, and there was no shortage of caves in the mountainous lands of Pieria or Thrace.

Spring

Another important element of the reimagination of Leibethra and Pimpleia as Orphean toponyms was tying them to springs or rivers. Based on late explanations by Servius and Hesychius, it was also not any fount, but one associated with the Muses, one whose waters brought poetic inspiration.[42] In this form, the idea, although again developed from the prototypical depiction of Hesiod's encounter with the Muses, is a Hellenistic and especially Roman phenomenon.[43] Thus, it is worth noting the reinterpretation of the goddesses of inspiration as nymphs. In particular, the phrase '*Nymphae Libethrides*' could have led to further associations with water, grottos and springs.[44] The phrase itself may originate from Lycophron (*Alex.* 273–5), where the nymphs of Bephyra, Leibethra and Pimpleia stand in for the Muses, keepers of Orpheus, or from phrases such as Euphorion's παρθενικαὶ Λ[ι]βηθρίδες ('Leibethrian girls' [fr. 416 SH]). Although Varro mentioned the ties between Leibethra and the Muses (*Ling.* 7,20, quoted earlier), the ambiguity of Hellenistic texts allowed for free reinterpretation. Camenae, river nymphs and Roman counterparts to the Muses, may also have influenced the change in the metapoetic language and the closer linking of the goddesses of inspiration to water and springs.[45] The typical Roman set of associations is best explained by Servius (ad Verg. *Ecl.* 7,21), drawing upon the authority of Varro:[46]

> that the poets invoke Nymphs (...), the reason is that, according to Varro, the Nymphs are also Muses; for they are said to exist in the water that flows from springs, as was the view of those who consecrated the spring to the Camenae; for it is the custom for sacrifices to be made to them not with wine but with water and milk; and not without reason, for the movement of water produces music.
>
> Translated by A. Hardie

The explanations of Varro, which have no parallels in any Greek text, coincide with the changes to the image of the Muses (and nymphs) after the Hellenistic period, as well as changes to the geographic meaning of Leibethra and Pimpleia (first century BC to first century AD) in the period of their great popularity in Latin literature.[47]

In summary, many arguments suggest that springs, mountains, and grottoes were late additions to the imagery of Leibethra and Pimpleia, and that the reasons for them were (meta)literary rather than topographic. In a world with no maps or encyclopaedias to provide fixed reference points, literature was often used to provide spatial orientation, with all the drawbacks of that solution. Erroneous or creative readings by Hellenistic and Roman authors then led to the creation of an entire range of new topographic meanings, absent from earlier ages or geographic works such as Strabo's and Pausanias'. Notably, the Romans did not passively accept Greek models, but rather reinterpreted them creatively, e.g. by implementing Camenae as Roman counterparts to the Muses.

Such reinterpretations usually draw on a collection of cultural prototypes, such as the scenery of the encounter with the Muses and poetic inspiration or the general imagery of the Muses and nymphs, associated as they were with mountains and springs. These general patterns had an immense influence on the creation of new texts and on linking toponyms important for the myth of Orpheus with new notions. The mechanism was therefore culturally conditioned and tied to prototypical visions of *mousikē*.

Another reason for identifying Leibethra with a mountain is made prominent in the aforementioned scholia ad Vergil *Ecl.* 7,21: its name is tied to Mount Libethrion in Boeotia. This phenomenon will be examined in the next chapter; for now, let us address the connections of Leibethra and Pimpleia to Thracians and Thrace.

Leibethra, Pimpleia and Thracia

The earliest known account defining Leibethra as a site in Thrace is probably the introduction to *Hieros Logos*, attributed to Pythagoras, its contents known to us from Iamblichus and Proclus (OF 507T). According to that work, Pythagoras went to 'Thracian Libethra' to be inducted into the mysteries and read (thanks to Aglaophamus) the *Hieros Logos*, a compendium of knowledge about the gods, authored by Orpheus, who had supposedly received it from his Muse mother on Pangaion. *Hieros Logos* is the most famous Neopythagorean pseudepigraph, one of many such texts written in the Roman context *c.* first century BC.[48] The tale clearly linked together two spatial traditions (Pangaion/Strymon and Leibethra/Thrace or 'Thracian Pieria') in a way very similar to Aeschylus/Eratosthenes (*Catast.* 24: death on Pangaion and tomb in Pieria) or Apollonius of Rhodes (1,34: 'Bistonian Pieria'). In *Hieros Logos*, the toponyms separate two stages of initiation: of Orpheus on Pangaion and of Pythagoras in 'Thracian Libethra'.

Within the Orphic circle, the ending of *Orphic Argonautica* presents Leibethra as a region of Thrace (v. 1373–4). It is unclear whether the adjective 'Thracian' expressed the idea of a 'Thracian Pieria' or pointed to Leibethra being situated in Thrace, particularly in context of the beginning of the text, where Orpheus sets out from Leibethra in Pieria (v. 50). It appears, however, that the author did not pay any attention to details of Thracian and Pierian topography, as they mix up toponyms and created links between e.g. Strymon and the Rhodopes or Leibethra and Haemus. It is, therefore, an 'imaginary geography', derived from literary reading, not geographical knowledge.

In the previously-cited *scholia Bernensia* for Virgil's 7th eclogue, the origin of the adjective Libethridae (nymphae) is explained as follows: 'Libethrus, a river in Thrace, where Orpheus was torn apart, where the Muses bathed'. This reminds us of Servius' explanation, which indicated that Oeagrus was a river god in Thrace (OF 894T), which in turn brings to mind the scene of Muses crossing the Strymon (leading to the birth of Rhesus from the Muse Clio and, again, a local river god).[49] Leibethra is also tied to Thracians according to Conon and appears in an entry on Orpheus in the *Suda* lexicon (*o* 654). The lexicographer places Leibethra in Thrace, but also indicates it is near Pieria (ὑπὸ τῇ Πιερίᾳ), combining both traditions. It may appear very erudite and bring to mind Apollonius' 'Bistonian Pieria', but at the same time is clearly an attempt to remove contradictions caused by ambiguous literary texts. In the world of imaginary geographies, many literary texts appear to confirm the existence of the presupposed 'Thracian Leibethra'.

Similar links to Thrace also exist for Pimpleia. In Apollonius' scholia for *Argonautica*, information about the place of birth of Orpheus is provided with an annotation claiming that 'according to some' it is a 'mountain in Thrace' (ὄρος Θράκης).[50] This is similar to the explanations of Leibethra and the word *skopiē* in his scholia for Lycophron (in *Alex.* 274). The same scholia for *Argonautica* later states (1,31–34a) that 'Pieria' itself is ὄρος Θράκης, ἐν ᾗ διέτριβεν Ὀρφεύς ('a mountain in Thrace where Orpheus lived'). This commentary explained the descriptor Πιερίηθεν from *Argonautica* 1,31, while Apollonius mentions that Orpheus used music to lead oaks 'out of Pieria'. The trees, once growing on the foot of Mount Olympus, were to follow the musician to Thracian Zone, where they remain 'today'.

The tale of the densely-growing oaks in the town of Zone on the coast of eastern Thrace was also known to Nicander of Colophon and Pomponius Mela (OF 952T). It likely originated in a literary explanation presenting unusually thick forests of the Thracian coast near Drys (*Oak*) and Zone (opposite the island of Samothrace) as an effect of Orpheus' actions. Considering the rise in the popularity of oaks in the story of Orpheus, this narrative must have been rather popular in the Hellenistic period.[51] Apollonius's literary play on the motif of travelling oaks involves another modification to the tale of Orpheus. Although the hero had been tied mostly to Mount Pangaion and the Strymon area, *Argonautica* suddenly places him in Bistonia, at the foot of the Rhodopes and west of the Hebros River, in eastern Thrace (1,34: 'Bistonian Pieria'). Book 4 of the epic thus refers to Orpheus' 'Bistonian lyre' (4,903–4). A digression to take a closer look at Thracian tribes linked to Orpheus in ancient sources becomes necessary.

Orpheus and Thracian tribes

In *The Mythical Poets of Greece*, Jeno Platthy notes (1985: 147): 'To make the relationships between the various Thracian tribes more difficult to follow regarding ancestry of Orpheus, Strabo says that he was from the Kikonian tribe.' His remark is correct: ancient sources provide divergent information on the hero's ties to various Thracian tribes and regions. Simultaneously, however, it is misguided in that the search is not for a real place of origin of a mythical figure. Thus, of interest are not complications introduced by Strabo or another author, but rather the reasons for choosing one tribe over others. Associating Orpheus with specific tribes is not neutral in meaning, but rather revealing of the context – frequently political – behind a given version.

This aspect was noted by Fritz Graf (1987, 87) when he indicated that choosing the Cicones was a 'purely poetical localisation, deriving from Homer's knowledge of this tribe'.[52] This commentary is something of a guidepost, as the specific presentation of the myth had to make reference to literary, historical, political and geographical contexts understood by the audiences. These usually took the form of allusions to commonly known texts and passages, to current politics (the Odrysian kingdom), and to a geographical framing close to the author and the audience (Odrysians, Bistonians, Bizaltians).[53]

One of the best-explored examples of transposing a myth into the political reality of the Greek world is the presence of the Odrysians in the narrative of Orpheus.[54] Their presence there should be linked to the territorial rise of the Odrysian kingdom *c.* 450–330 BC, its close ties to Athens, and in later years also the tribe's place in historical works, particularly by Thucydides and Xenophon. In later literary imagination, Thracians may have been generally associated with Odrysians or Homer's Cicones. The inclusion of tribes living in the Pangaion area and near Strymon, in turn, can be linked to two general phenomena. The first is the Athenian interest in this area starting in the mid-sixth century, but especially after the failed invasion of 465, and later the founding of Amphipolis by Hagnon (437/6). The area, rich in precious metals, became the most important area of Athenian activity in Thrace.[55] The other contributing factor was linked to the death of Orpheus being situated in this area in Aeschylus' *Bassarids*, a play dating to the 460s. The significance of the region, and Aeschylus' version of the myth, had a non-negligible impact on Greek imagination and always functioned as a reference point for geographical and ethnic choices of poets and mythographers. Local tribes of Edoni[56] and Bisaltians[57] appear in the narratives for similar reasons.[58] As for that last people, it is worth adding that Orpheus' association with Bisaltians may have already been mentioned by Asclepiades of Tragilos, who traced the origin of Thamyris, Orpheus' grandfather in one genealogy, to Bisaltia. This case is particularly interesting, as Asclepiades' own hometown of Tragilos was in Bisaltia.[59]

However, the most interesting and least researched case of a Thracian tribe tied to Orpheus in sources are the Bistones, living east of Strymon and Pangaion. The tribe was known from mythical stories of Diomedes and his flesh-eating mares (Strabo 7 fr. 44) and of Polymestor, ally to the Trojans and son-in-law to Priam (Tzetz. *Chil.* 3,14). However, in the third century, Bistonia was also linked to Oeagrus and Orpheus, with references to the area and the tribe of Bistones made in Phanocles, Apollonius, Nicander and in the *Lament for Bion*.[60] For some reason, all of these poets preferred the area, alongside Hebrus, Haemus and Rhodopes, over Strymon and Pangaion.[61] Later mentions are more probably a reflection of available reading.[62] It is exceedingly likely that linking Orpheus to Bistones (as well as Hebrus, Rhodopes and Haemus) was a Hellenistic innovation. We do not know what circumstances made this specific Thracian tribe appear in literature and where to look for the origins of this idea, but known accounts suggest two possible (and possibly complementary) interpretations.

A mythical story tying Orpheus to this area may be the result of the rise of the cult of the hero and his tomb on Lesbos sometime in the fourth or third century.[63] The link between the death in Bistonia and the burial of the head on Lesbos is first attested in Phanocles. The island tomb had to compete with the version known from Aeschylus' *Bassarids* and Eratosthenes' *Catasterismoi* (24), where the death takes place on Mount Pangaion, the body is thrown into the Strymon, and the hero's remains are buried by the Muses in Pierian Leibethra. We do not know if involving the Bistones, living at the feet of the Rhodopes and around the Hebrus River, was the idea of Phanocles himself or of another poet from the same period, especially since the Cicones, also pointed to by contemporaneous authors (Ps.-Arist. fr. 641,48), were a better geographic fit for a hypothetical 'Lesbian' reconstruction of the myth, and also had more literary fame. However, the Hebrus and the Rhodopes are closer to Lesbos, to which they were tied politically and economically since the Archaic period, and thus made perfect sense as an alternative scenery at the expense of Strymon and Pangaion, which were connected to Athens.

The geographical choices of Apollonius, a poet active in third-century Alexandria, provide another version. In his *Argonautica*, Orpheus moves from Pieria to Bistonia (1,34: 'Bistonian Pieria'), which may be read as a rejection of earlier (literary and metapoetical) connotations in favour of new possibilities and a typical Hellenistic journey to a 'new world'. In a sense, the travel of oaks and Orpheus to Bistonia may even be seen as transferring 'Pieria' (as the homeland of the Muses and thus literature) into a new place.

The phrase 'Bistonian Pieria' has posed a challenge for research into Orpheus for years and has been interpreted in various ways. Some scholars believe that it refers to a 'Pierian Thrace', or that it calls Macedonian Pieria a realm in Bistonia; others still point to the existence of two Leibethras/Pierias.[64] Faced with this geographical duality of Orpheus, Graf (1987: 90) unexpectedly declared: 'If the place where a hero has his grave is really his place of origin, Orpheus is not Thracian, but a Pierian.' Moreover, the spatial duality is also visible in the stories of Orpheus' death on Pangaion (Thrace) and burial in Leibethra (Pieria). Thus, the myth deals not only with Apollonius' opposition between the place of birth (Pimpleia) and the Thracian kingdom the adult Orpheus rules ('Bistonian Pieria'), but also with the return of the hero's body to Pieria (Leibethra) after his death and his burial there.

It appears that the simplest explanation of the ambiguity would be a reference to the specifics of Hellenistic literary practices, under the assumption that the poetic image of 'Bistonian Pieria' represents an attempt to merge two topographic traditions associated with Orpheus – Thracian and Pierian.[65]

Hellenistic writers, particularly those associated with the Ptolemaic court, had a clear propensity to a kind of 'seeing double', as Stephens (2003) puts it, and literary games involving broad geographic knowledge. As Thalmann (2011) shows, it was in part due to the rapid expansion of geographic horizons and the need to redefine changing group identities. The world was no longer just Athens and the environs of the Academia, and the Greeks were no longer its only inhabitants. Moreover, geographical knowledge had grown, and mythographic scholarship had accumulated. The emergence of libraries as an institution meant that poets could no longer ignore divergences in mythical narratives, and were able to express their attitudes towards earlier writers, for example by subtly mixing versions, finding rare solutions, or through intertextual allusions, proving not just their admiration for, but also knowledge and mastery of tradition. This manifested in many ways, including finding double toponyms and linking them, or connecting two separate locations into a single whole. This resulted in phrases like 'Pimpleian Thebes', 'Tritonian Thebes', or 'Paphian Cytherean'.[66] The passage from Apollonius may have therefore been the source of misunderstandings and a reason for 'Thracian Pieria' appearing in later literature, as well as for the placement of Pimpleia or Leibethra in Thrace.

But why did Apollonius choose Bistonia? The most likely reason is that in the third century, the region was under Ptolemaic control.[67] He may have indeed been proposing a rewrite of Orpheus' Thracian mythical topography, and the choice of that particular realm was possibly linked to contemporary Ptolemaic politics, understandable for an Alexandrian poet and his audience.[68] Of course, there were other tribes at the banks of Hebrus and the foot of the Rhodopes, but Bistones benefited from their prior presence in myths and perhaps from the local Lesbian tradition placing the death of the hero in that area. Thus, the two aspects of this interpretation converge. On one side is the reconstructed (but likely) interest in the death of Orpheus on the Hebrus or near the Rhodopes (it is worth noting that Lesbos also entered the Ptolemaic sphere of influence in the third century); on the otherside, the drive to remove Orpheus from Pieria, Strymon and Pangaion, as those areas were under Antigonid influence and belonged to the Athenian mythical tradition. In this context, Apollonius' moving of Orpheus to a '(new) Pieria' in Bistonia seems like a choice of the lesser-known tradition, as well as a proposal that could please Ptolemaic rulers.

Orpheus' ties to Thracian tribes take many forms in the sources and may be explained in various ways. Much like the spatial references in the stories of the hero, they were subject to modification and dependent on the cultural and sociopolitical context, preferences of the audience, and circumstances of presentation. This behoves us to search for reasons for each use of ethnic and spatial references in the sources. The analysis mainly concludes that mentions of Thracians in these narratives are not the expression of Orpheus' heritage, but rather stem from mythographic and literary premises.

Summary, Nysa and scholiasts

Late sources present three main types of explanations for the Thracian connections of Leibethra, Pimpleia or Pieria in general. The first ties the toponyms to Thrace in a very broad and ambiguous fashion: typically, the adjective 'Thracian' implies either the general placement of the location within Thrace, or the original Thracian nature of Pieria, which may thus also be called a part of Thrace. The other aspect came from Thucydides' and Strabo's information about the Pieres, which will be discussed in the next chapter.

The second type is the understanding of Leibethra/Pimpleia as 'Macedonian-Thracian' toponyms, which assumes an early presence of Thracians in Pieria and its later conquest by Macedon. This interpretation partly takes into account quasi-historical and geographic knowledge, but is based on literary texts, condenses temporal relationships, and creates imaginary political and geographic entities.

The third type places Leibethra/Pimpleia/Pieria in Thrace, likely outside of Macedon. This solution originates from the creative, but erroneous readings of earlier descriptions of Orpheus, in particular Apollonius' expression 'Bistonian Pieria'. Such ambiguous statements inspired readers and scholars to imbue Orpheus' portrayed Pierian-Thracian homeland with new notions. Changes to geographic coordinates can be seen in the consolidated image of a shared kingdom of Thracians and Macedonians in Conon's *Narratives* or in the increased density of Thracian and Macedonian territory (*AP* 7,9; *Suda* s.v. Ὀρφεύς). For the same reason, *Orphic Argonautica* and Nonnus have Pimpleia or Pieria for example in Bistonia or 'in Thracian land'. This version is the fullest realisation of the idea of imagined, literary space, with the authors drawing on a multiverse of earlier literary works for their interpretations.

This fluidity and ambiguity of space – somewhere between Pieria, Thrace and 'Thracian Pieria' – would thereafter become an important feature of Orpheus' mythical geography. It bears noting, however, that all known information on 'Thracian Pieria' comes from late sources, starting in the first century. The best expression of this change is the context for the phrase 'Bistonian Pieria' in Apollonius of Rhodes' *Argonautica* as contrasted with its later realisations by Roman poets and in scholia. In the third century, the depiction of the *spatium mythicum* in the narratives of Orpheus had had a vastly different quality from its late Hellenistic or Roman versions.[69]

Geographic evolutions similar to that of Pierian toponyms are encountered in the case of Nysa and Dionysus as well. The mountain is not fixed in space, but 'moves' alongside the god and the change of geographic realities in the story. When Dionysus becomes, in whatever way, tied to Libya, Nysa is already there. Our sources are not illogical here, they simply follow a different logic. From this perspective, scholia or lexicons discussing Leibethra or Pimpleia do not 'lie', they have a different truth to tell.[70]

In general, a scholiast or Imperial-era scholar did not aspire to geographic precision, but sought to document literary phenomena and only then tie them to ancient topographic knowledge. Thus, if literary texts (especially Roman poetry) present new interpretations and explanations for Leibethra and Pimpleia (spring/mountain, Thrace), the scholia had to account for them. This resulted in neutral and geographically relativistic entries, such as the one in *scholia Bernensia*. From a historical standpoint, all these explanations are valid, and to a degree true, if we assume they document versions present in literature and result from a process of reading and (re)interpretation. Nevertheless, if researching early images of Orpheus, such sources, particularly read literally and straightforwardly, can lead to misinterpretations.

4

Thracians, Pieria and Music

Reinterpretations of geographic values assigned to Leibethra and Pimpleia in late sources are not the end of our deliberations over the transmission and transformations of the myth of Orpheus, or over the role of Thracians in Pieria. We are roughly halfway to laying down a solid foundation for reconstructing the Pierian tradition of Orpheus from the Classical period. Our earlier analyses must be complemented by a reading of accounts indicating links between mythical musicians and Thrace, the presence of Thracians in Pieria and Boeotia, and their role in the cultural development of Greece. Such explanations were an ideological and quasi-historical basis for claims of Thracians roots of Pieria, and by extension Orpheus, in Antiquity, and remain so today. By emphasising the role of Thracians and Thrace in the stories of the hero, they make it difficult to spot the Macedonian element in the sources.

The capstone for nearly all modern interpretations that point to the Thracianness of Orpheus and a role of Thracians in the development of Greek culture are the explanations by Strabo and Pausanias. Let us therefore recall that Montanari (2015) explained s.v. 'Pimpleia' that it is a 'mountain in Pieria', and supported that interpretation by citing the author of *Geography* (Strabo 9,2,25). The account of Pausanias (9,29,2–3), meanwhile, is referenced by Larson (2001, 139 and n. 40), joining the Thracians to the cult of the Muses and the Leibethrian nymphs. The analysis will be complemented with accounts of Classical-era authors Ephorus and Thucydides, whose explanations played a major part in later descriptions of the roles of the Thracians in the early history of Macedon and Boeotia.

Strabo I: Leibethra and Boeotia

A critical reading of Strabo and Thucydides is crucial for understanding how Pieria was 'Thracianised' in Antiquity, as well as why these claims proved so resilient in the period and why they are still present in scholarship.[1] First, we shall approach the two complementary accounts of Strabo (C 471 [10,3,17]; C 410 9,2,25), afterwards, we will return to the Classical period and Thucydides' description of the origins of Macedon (2,99). Due to the significance the geographer's argument holds in both ancient and modern interpretations, the first passage is quoted here in full:

> From the melody, rhythm, and instruments, all Thracian music is considered to be Asiatic. This is clear from the places that the Muses have been honored: Pieria, Olympos, Pimpla, and Leibethron were Thracian places and mountains in antiquity (now they are held by the Makedonians), and Helikon was consecrated to the Muses by the Thracians who settled in Boiotia, those who also consecrated the cave of the Leibethriadian Nymphs. Those who paid attention to ancient music are called Thracians (Orpheus, Mousaios, and Thamyris).[2]

Strabo implies that Thracians had inhabited both Macedon and Boeotia. These two regions are linked by the cult of the Muses in 'Thracian' areas (Pieria and Helicon), the Thracian origins of the first musicians, and the similarity of proper names (Leibethron in Pieria and the cult of Leibethriadian Nymphs in Boeotia).[3] Geographer's arguments require a meticulous analysis.

First, let us examine the ties of Pierian Leibethra to Boeotia and Helicon. Such links have appeared in Strabo and the scholia and lexicons discussed above (e.g. schol. in Lycoph. *Alex.* 275). Crucial to the assessment of the relationship between Pieria and Boeotia is a passage from Pausanias (9,34,4), confirming the existence of the cult of Libethrian nymphs on the Helicon massif:[4] 'Some forty stades from Coroneia is Mount Libethrius, on which are images of the Muses and Nymphs surnamed Libethrian. There are springs too, one named Libethrias and the other Rock (Petra), which are shaped like a woman's breasts, and from them rises water like milk' [tr. W. H. S. Jones].

The Mount Libethrion (τὸ Λιβήθριον) named in the text is part of the Helicon massif, which, contrary to popular imagination, is not a solitary mountain, but rather stretches over some 800 km². The Greeks used the term 'Helicon' to refer both to the peak rising over the so-called Valley of the Muses near Thespia and to the massif itself, with Mount Libethrion as its eastern peak. Thus, Libethrian nymphs could be linked either with the massif as a whole, or solely with Mount Libethrion.

The passage in Pausanias indicates a presence of the statues of Muses and nymphs referred to as 'Libethriai' (Λιβηθρίαι) in the second century AD, as well as of a spring with a similar name – 'Libethrias' (Λιβηθριάς). Both names suggest a relationship with water (through the verb λείβω, meaning 'to pour, to shed'), common in such instances and tied here to the two springs on the mountain slope. The cult of nymphs as divine guardians of natural sites (mountains, grottoes, springs) at the fringes of the inhabited world is thus entirely reasonable in this location. Strabo and Pausanias discuss Libethrian nymphs in various ways however. Strabo points to the nymphs and their grotto (νυμφῶν ἄντρον), but does not mention Mount Libethrion by name. Pausanias names the mountain and mentions the statues, but not the grotto – perhaps finding it obvious in the case of the nymphs. More relevant here is that Pausanias is not clear on whether the name Libethriai refers only to nymphs or to the Muses as well. This is important insofar as Strabo – who wrote 150 years earlier – only mentioned 'Leibethrian nymphs' (τὸ τῶν Λειβηθριάδων νυμφῶν ἄντρον). Considering the significance of the connection between the Muses of Pieria and of Helicon in the geographer's argumentation, such a reference would be impossible to overlook.

We may thus suppose that only nymphs (called the Leibethriai) were worshipped on the mountain near Coroneia in Strabo's time, and the statues of the Muses appeared later. Such an intervention would be an instance of bridging the gap between socioreligious realities and popular stories, as well as of the creation of places, items, gestures or rituals considered a return to something forgotten, a restored memory, or a 'rediscovery' of an item, place or tomb. Similar examples include Hesiod's tripod, exhibited in the Valley of the Muses (Paus. 9,29–30), the scepter of Agamemnon in Chaeronea (Paus. 9,40–1), the monument to Corinna's victory over Pindar in Tanagra (Paus. 9,22,3), as well as the numerous graves of Homer, appearing throughout the Greek world as the poet's fame increased.[5] A similar case of adapting physical space in the polis to fit its literary image may have arisen with the altar and worship of the Muses at Ilissus.[6] It is thus possible that the cavern on Mount Libethrion in Boeotia was originally associated exclusively with nymphs, and the statues of the Muses were placed there once Pierian Leibethra grew in popularity and some readings began to connect both sites, while Libethrian nymphs (Libethriai) were identified with the Muses as Libethrides.[7]

Archaeological research on the Helicon massif has provided more information supporting the accuracy of this interpretation of Strabo and Pausanias. In 1985, a grotto dedicated to nymph worship was found on the northeastern slope of Megali Loutsa mountain (believed to be Pausanias' Libethrion) near Coroneia, at the altitude of ca. 820 m, west of the village of Agia Triada.[8] Its main room was around 8 by 10 metres in size. The eastern entrance was adorned with the inscription ΚΟΡΩΝΕΙΑ ΝΥΜΦΗ (*Coroneian Nymph* [see SEG 58,438]), clearly demonstrating the site's ties to the cult of nymphs and to the nearby polis. The excavation, started in 1989 under Vasilopoulou and still ongoing, has revealed a shrine functioning since Prehistory and well-furnished with artefacts. Nymphs were worshipped there from the Archaic period until Roman times, as evidenced by terracotta figurines and numerous votive offerings, and particularly by inscriptions on pottery shards. Objects discovered in the cave number in the thousands.[9] Many of the shards feature dedications: in some cases they only say [Λ]ειβεθριάδεσι ('for Leibethriades'), but others are clearly marked 'for the Nymphs Leibethriades' (SEG 49,517; 58,438).

The above findings do not contradict Strabo's and Pausanias' information and confirm the presence of a cult of Leibethrian nymphs throughout most of Antiquity. The grotto also has traces of worship of other deities related to the nymphs in various ways, but, very importantly, no proof of a cult of the Muses.[10] The huge amount of artefacts from various ages show no connection between local Leibethriades nymphs and the goddesses of inspiration.

Archaeological data combined with an analysis of written sources leads to the following conclusions: firstly, Strabo only knew of 'Libethrian nymphs', and the statues of the Muses described by Pausanias were a late, perhaps short-lived phenomenon. This would be unsurprising, considering the interest in the statues of these goddesses in the Roman period, as well as their popularity in baths, parks, libraries, theatres or gardens.[11] Secondly, the commentaries of Hesychius, Servius, or scholiasts of Lycophron and Apollonius suggest at some point the spring of Libethrias near Coroneia, associated with Mount Libethrion, and the Libethrian nymphs worshipped there, were identified with the Muses as Libethriades and with Pierian Leibethra. Such an identification may have resulted from the similarity of proper names, as well as from tales of the migrations of the Thracians and their ties to Boeotia. The spread of Hesiod's *Dichterweihe* as a topos, the ties between Helicon and Pieria/Olympus in metapoetic statements, and the general similarities between nymphs and the Muses in literature and worship may have also contributed to the process.

Strabo II: Ephorus, Leibethra and Thracians

Identifying Pierian Leibethra with Mount Libethrion was easier because the nymphs' cave was located in the Helicon massif. The perception of local nymphs as Helikoni(a)des, and therefore somewhat identical with the Muses known from Hesiod, may have been a side effect of literary interpretations and the expansion of the known world in Roman times. The latter aspect is confirmed in another passage from Strabo's *Geography* (C 410 [9,2,25]):

> Helikon, which is not far distant from Parnassos, is equal to it both in height and circumference. Both mountains are snow covered and rocky, and they do not circumscribe a large territory. Here are the sanctuary of the Muses and Hippoukrene, and the cave of the Leibethridian Nymphs, which would prove that those who consecrated Helikon to the Muses were certain Thracians, the ones who dedicated Pieris, Leibethron, and Pimpleia to the same goddesses. They were called the Pieres, but they have disappeared and the Makedonians now hold those places. It has been said that the Thracians were settled in this territory, having used force against the Boiotians, as did the Pelasgians and other barbarians.
>
> Translated by D. W. Roller

The overlap in the depictions of Pierian and Boeotian locations, seen in the text above, results from the similarity of proper names, although both were typical of Antiquity (Libethrion–Leibethra); the near-identical epicleses of the nymphs and Muses from either location; and the general links between nymphs and Muses. However, the connections between the toponyms have no historical basis, they are entirely literary or metapoetic in origin.[12] Based on earlier conclusions, our reconstruction presumed that at some point in the first century BC or first century AD, the portrayal of Pierian Leibethra was expanded with new components – a mountain and a spring. We should note that similar natural features are present on Boeotian Mount Libethrion and in the worship of Libethrian nymphs. This transformation was reinforced by the *Dichterweihe* model, where a mountain (originally Helicon) and springs (Permessus and Hippocrene: Hes. *Th.* 1–8) played a crucial role. Metapoetic phrases like Virgil's 'Nymphae Libethrides' (*Ecl.* 7,21) probably contributed to it, as well as Pierian Muses being called 'nymphs' from Leibethra, Pimpleia and Bephyra in Lycophron's *Alexandra* (274–5). The latter piece did so only as part of a literary riddle, but the phrase, much like 'Nymphae Libethrides', allowed for a literal reading.

The lynchpin of Strabo's argument was not the similarity of proper names, but rather the role of the Thracians. He assumed they had been originally present in Pieria and Boeotia, allowing him to link both regions, their toponyms, and associated phenomena into a quasi-historical explanation. What led the geographer to this conclusion, particularly regarding Boeotia?

The answer to the latter part of the question (regarding Thracians in Boeotia) is usually linked to Ephorus of Cyme.[13] Indeed, the geographer admits earlier in Book 9 (C 400 [9,2,3–4]) that his source for the history of Boeotia was the work of Ephorus (BNJ 70 F119):[14] 'Ephoros says that the Thracians, having made a treaty with the Boiotians, attacked them at night'.

A more in-depth reading of the passage suggests, however, that the historian was mostly concerned with military and political events related to the expulsion of Thracians from Boeotia.[15] It therefore appears that Strabo only used Ephorus' information about the Thracian presence in the region and tied Boeotian Thracians to Pierian Thracians by his own reckoning later in the narrative (C 410 [9,2,25]; C 471 [10,3,17]).[16] Apparently, the two stories (about Thracians in Pieria and about Thracians in Boeotia) could be connected by the Muses (Pierides and Helikoniades), the similarity of proper names, and Orpheus' Thracian lineage. If the son of a Muse was himself a Thracian, then the goddesses had to be Thracian 'invention' as well, and if Thracians had also lived in Boeotia, as Ephorus seemed to imply, then their journey south would connect two of the most important sites of the cult of the Muses – Pieria/Olympus and Helicon – and complete the argument. This hypothesis seems to be confirmed by how the geographer presents his proof in C 410 [9,2,25] (ἐξ οὗ τεκμαίροιτ' ἄν τις): Strabo makes no reference to any authority, but rather draws conclusions from the information he presented.

It still remains to be determined if Ephorus' story of a prehistoric Thracian presence in Boeotia is believable and what are its origins. Few believe today that Ephorus and other Classical historians had real knowledge of events before the Archaic period beyond myths and later attempts at explaining them.[17] For this reason, Ephorus and Strabo are now typically commented on as part of research into mythical traditions. In his introduction to Greek mythology, Ken Dowden cites passages from those authors and the Thracian night raid on Boeotia as examples of the complicated relationship between myth and history.[18] In his conclusions, he explains (1992, 60): 'This is not an historical record or an allegory of tribal movements. There has got to be a ritual behind this story: here is a nocturnal event with typical inversion of normal rules of behaviour, prominence of pre-people (reversion to Stone Age), crisis over the division of duties between the sexes and resolution through trial.' The scholar observes that the story of Boeotian Thracians is not about real Thracians, but rather it expresses ideas vital to society by using Thracians (and other 'Others'), as myths are wont to. He also remarks that since mythical narratives are malleable in later periods, Thracians should be seen here as mere stand-ins, exchangeable for Leleges, Pelasgians or other 'aboriginal' peoples. They are an ethnically irrelevant detail, a role to be cast.

We should remember here that the ethnogenetic myth focusing not on 'whence' and 'who' is being expelled, but rather on 'where to' and 'by whom', operates on two basic categories of space and identity: locality and externality.[19] In other words, they portray the ancestors of a people as either autochthonous (e.g. Lelex in Sparta, Pelasgus in Argos) or allochthonous (Cadmus, Danaus, Pelops).[20] In most cases, both of these presentations are used, either in conjunction or interchangeably, depending on sociopolitical needs and circumstances. The territorial and political formation of Boeotia is one of the best examples for such a process.[21] Ephorus and Strabo depict Thracians as just one of the groups supposedly living in Boeotia in the mythical age. Stories also include peoples like Pelasgians or Leleges, whose names served as collective terms for many ethnic groups encountered by the Greeks, typically in the sense of 'the aboriginal men'.[22] Their basic function in the foundational narratives of cities or peoples was to form a backdrop for the (arrival of) the Greeks, who replaced them, expelled them, or fought them. In the case of Boeotia, these groups may have been an alternative or a complement to the autochthony of Boeotians/Thebans as the descendants of Cadmus. Pelasgians, for example, were situated in various places from Italy to the Aegean, with sources listing around 150 locations they supposedly inhabited before the Greeks. Even more interesting are the Aones, fictitious aborigines whose name was back-formed from Aonia, an unclear descriptor for Boeotia or parts of it.[23] The oldest versions of the Boeotian foundational myth usually only mention the Ektenes or Hyantes; it was only later that it was expanded with stories tied to other groups, like Aones, Pelasgians or Thracians.

How did the Thracians appear in a fourth-century story about the origins of Boeotia? Why was it they who were tied to the story of a treacherous night-time attack? One explanation assumes that it may be a historical memory of a Thracian attack on Mycalessus during the Peloponnesian War (Thuc. 7,27), a notorious example of Thracian barbarity and cruelty. As Classical Greeks viewed Thracians as uncivilised, they imagined them as existing 'before' civilisation: in time protohistorical.[24] Moreover, Thracians were associated with Daulia in Phocis even before that, and through that with the invasion of Eumolpus on Attica.[25] Mythographically, the various narratives placed them so close to Boeotia that adding them to a story of its origins was unsurprising for a contemporary audience.[26]

The above can be summarised with a remark by Ganter (née Kühr), a specialist in ancient traditions of the founding of Boeotia (2014, 230): 'From a modern point of view, such an account reflects less what really happened in the Bronze Age or during the Dark Ages than what people telling these foundation stories believed had happened at the dawn of local history.' The probability of a 'memory' of such events surviving in the consciousness of Pierians or Boeotians is remarkably small. Meanwhile, much suggests the image being tied to the construction of Boeotian identity through references to allo- and autochthony. Mythographers merging contradictory stories about expulsions from Boeotia also played an important part in the creation of Ephorus' account by creating 'coherent' narratives with multi-layered, chronological systems of invasions, escapes and 'returns'.

What does this imply? Placing Ephorus and Strabo in a broader context of mythical tradition, as well as examining the circumstances surrounding the appearance of specific plot elements, suggests that we are dealing with an aetiological tale where Thracians appear in the backdrop, purely by accident. In such narratives, it is not important that they happen to be the enemies of the Boeotians. Their role in the tale can be explained in other ways and is irrelevant for the historicity of their presence in the area.

Once we cast doubt on the credibility of Ephorus as a historical source and consider the patterns in the narratives about peoples encountered by the Greeks in the mythical era, Strabo's thesis, derived from that information, completely loses its historical basis. In light of the above remarks, Strabo's key argument for ties between Helicon and Pieria has to be considered an artefact of mythography, not proof of a sound geographic and historical analysis. Stories describing the culture-creating role of the Thracians could not have their sources in Prehistory or in the Classical period. We know nothing of the early ages, and the depictions of Thracians in the fifth and fourth centuries present an underdeveloped civilisation, culturally dependent on the Greeks.[27] This question will be returned to later in this chapter.

Thucydides 2,99: Pieres are not Pierians

Strabo's chief and final claim is the supposed aboriginality of Thracians in Pieria and their influence on local culture.[28] The argument in this form is relevant for two reasons. Firstly, it is the ultimate 'historical' basis for the 'Thracian' connotations of Pierian Leibethra in the sources and in modern scholarship (e.g. LSJ, Montanari). Secondly, it is backed by the authority of Thucydides, as it was he who first wrote about Thracians (of the 'Pieres' tribe) in Pieria.

Most researchers still maintain that Strabo's and Thucydides' information has historical value. This acceptance has formed largely thanks to Hammond's interpretations and explanations from the first volume of his *History of Macedonia*.[29] And so, the well-known commentaries to Thuc. 2,99 by Hornblower or Rhodes contain no analysis of the problem, merely a reference to Hammond.[30] The discussion was finally reopened by Sprawski (2010), who critically assessed both the information of Thucydides and the simplified model of the development of the Macedonian state derived from the work of the Athenian historian. The following attempts to elaborate on his proposed interpretations and supplement them with further argumentation.

Thucydides begins his account of the origins of Macedon with the story of Sitalces (2,95–101), which, as observed already by Hammond (1972, 435), brackets a digression about the Thracian invasion of 429/428. The relevant passage is 2,99,3:

> The country on the sea coast, now called Macedonia, was first acquired by Alexander, the father of Perdiccas, and his ancestors, originally Temenids from Argos. This was effected by the expulsion from Pieria of the Pierians, who afterwards inhabited Phagres and other places under Mount Pangaeus, beyond the Strymon (indeed the country between Pangaeus and the sea is still called the Pierian gulf) of the Bottiaeans, at present neighbors of the Chalcidians, from Bottia.
>
> Translated by R. Crawley

The historian's narrative claims that Macedon emerged through contact with the Thracians, specifically the conquest and expulsion of the original inhabitants. This is evidenced by the names of Macedonian regions (Pieria, Bottia, Almopia), derived from Thracian tribes that originally inhabited them.[31] Conquests and migrations are always a possible scenario of demographic change, but could such a narrative be supported entirely by the similarity of proper names? Leaving the other toponyms aside, we shall focus only on Pieres and Pieria. Thucydides' story in its surviving version is questionable for a number of reasons.

First, we should remember that Pieria is a Greek name (from πῖαρ – 'fat'), and much like many other toponyms in the area (Leibethra, Pimpleia, Petra), it was inspired by local geography.[32] Early ties of the name to the fertility of the soil are also visible in Epicharmus' account from the turn of the fifth century (fr. 39 PCG). Rather than the presupposed original Thracian or even Macedonian toponyms, we are dealing with somewhat typical Greek local names linked to the natural characteristics of the area. Moreover, the name Pieria/Pieris is quite usual in Greek culture and already appears as a first name in Homer (*Il.* 14,226).[33] Can, therefore, the name Pieria come from the tribe of Pieres? A similar case of quasi-historical explanations being created based on phonetic similarities has already been discussed above: Strabo's linking of Leibethra in Pieria and Mount Libethrion in Boeotia. A parallel use of the similarity of names is known from Thucydides (2,29), who notes that the mythical Tereus was conflated with Thracian king Teres, father of Sitalces. In that case, however, the historian states that the likeness is accidental and imprecise. This does not change the fact that in his time Athenians apparently used that argument in their relations with the Thracians, as the phonetic similarity of proper names was one of the more popular ways of creating connections – including between the past and the present.

All this suggests that the name (Pieria) is obviously Greek and cannot be a relic of earlier Thracian inhabitants. This problem with Thucydides' information was noted even by Hammond, who concluded that the Pieres must have taken their name from Pieria, rather than the other way around.[34] This solution seems risky, contradictory to Thucydides' intended argument, and difficult to accept in this form. Taken together, this line of thought lays bare the frailty of the Athenian historian's argumentation and Hammond's mythmaking explanations, which create untenable ties between sources to sustain Thucydides' credibility.

Of course, it is difficult to deny that Pieria may have been integrated into Macedon through conquest, resettlement and other ethnic movements as well. A lack of tribal organisation of the kind seen in Upper Macedonia could be evidence of that (Hammond 1972, 417). However, this does not mean that Thucydides correctly recounted the historical process which created the Macedonian state.[35] From his point of view, the similarity of names – a frequent reason for convoluted explanations and creating associations between distant phenomena – is enough to assume a direct link to an insignificant group of Thracians, whose expulsion beyond the Strymon supposedly turned Pieria into a part of Macedon.

The adjective 'insignificant' is used here because the Pieres are only originally mentioned twice: by Herodotus (7,112; 185) and Thucydides (2,99); any further references to them follow the works of those historians. They are also never linked to Orpheus as some sort of 'Piero-Thracian', even though the passage from Thucydides and the Pieres' settlement around the Strymon River and Mount Pangaion could have suggested such an interpretation.

After the fifth century, we only encounter Pieres in Strabo (7, fr. 7 and C 471 [10,3,17]) and Pliny (*HN* 4,35). In particular, Strabo, based on Thucydides and Ephorus, developed the theory of a Thracian presence in Pieria by adding 'Thracian origins' of Orpheus and other mythical musicians. In his framing, claims of the Athenian historian became proof positive of the Thracian lineage of the Muses, *mousikē*, mythical musicians, and even of Thracian settlement on the distant Helicon.

In discussing the Pieres, it is worth remembering Hammond's cautious remarks on their ethnicity. He noted that (1972, 417) 'the description of them as Thracians has geographical and linguistic meaning rather than an ethnographic association'.[36] Hammond also brings up examples of other peoples taken under the 'Thracian' umbrella because of the areas they inhabited: Greeks used 'ethnicity' as a far more flexible category than it has been since the nineteenth century (Gruen 2013; 2020). Thus, similarly as in Barth's analyses (2002) of Iranian highlanders and farmers, it was possible to 'become' Thracian by living in a specific area and following a specific lifestyle. The general similarity of language and customs, unsurprising in largely pastoral peoples inhabiting lands north of the Aegean Sea and further up to the Danube, was sufficient for this purpose. Greeks clearly saw a continuity between Thracians and Macedonians and it appears that for a long time the latter were closer in material culture and modes of living to the 'Thracians' than to Greeks. The so-called Hellenisation of Macedonians (in the fifth century) progressed much faster than in the case of the Thracians and became an important step on the way to a coherent political and cultural identity.

According to Sprawski, the most convincing theory of the territorial and political development of Macedon assumes that during the Persian wars and shortly afterwards, some inhabitants of the area between Strymon and Peneus found it advantageous to become 'Macedonian', as the leadership of Alexander I offered them security.[37] The cultural cost of the changeover was likely negligible, as the 'Macedonisation' was mostly restricted to politics and religion. Thus, the crucial stage was the so called Hellenisation of the country in the fifth century, particularly at the end of the transformation, under Archelaus. This change should be regarded as an extended process, not simple the conquest and expulsion of Thracians by Macedonians. The political aspect was certainly the most important element of the changes, with the royal family providing a continuity of rulership, which is visible in local ethnogenetic narratives, focusing on the founder of the dynasty instead of Macedonians in general.

Thus, when Hammond (1972, 417) claimed that the archaeological material in Pieria includes typically Thracian tombs, he actually referred to tumuluses characteristic of a culture spanning from Macedonia to the Black Sea or even beyond. Before the sixth/fifth century, Macedonian material culture did not differ greatly from that of their northern and northeastern neighbours. Pre-550 archaeological data, of which we do not have enough for far-reaching conclusions in any event, cannot yet aid in an analysis of the 'ethnicity' of Pierians before the rise of Macedon.[38] In summary, too little is known of Macedonia before the mid-sixth century for clear conclusions on the formation of statehood in the region; later, in the fifth and fourth-centuries, Macedonians remain a loose conglomeration of peoples ruled by Argeads or Temenids, rather than a group with a clear identity distinct from the Thracians.

In light of this, is it possible to suspect a Macedonian invasion displacing Thracians from Pieria sometime in the eighth or seventh-centuries? Everything appears to suggest that the interpretation of events between 1300 and 650 proposed by Hammond (1972, 414–18), based on Thucydides, is as anachronistic as that of the Athenian historian.[39] Notably, the original expulsion of Thracians by Macedonians could not take place inasmuch as one can hardly talk of Macedonians before the sixth century, and as Hammond himself points out, Thracians were a flexible, mostly geographic concept.[40] If the point of view presented by Thucydides reflects anything, it is the political situation in his time and the contemporary thinking on how such events could proceed.

To recapitulate: the consolidation of the Macedonian state is better described through a gradual invention of a 'Macedonian identity' by the rulers and its negotiation between various ethnic groups of Lower and Upper Macedonia (leading to the creation of a hybrid identity).[41] This process was clearly linked to demographic movements, while groups resistant to the Argeads could be otherised and pushed out. It is perhaps they who were labelled the 'Thracians' based on their eventual area of settlement – e.g. beyond the Strymon, as with the Pieres.

This vision is supported by Archaic sources depicting Pieria as a 'no man's land', as Mari puts it.[42] In the hymn to Hermes (*h. hom.* 4,71), dated to the second half of the sixth century, this land is where Apollo grazes his herds. The first trace of Macedonia in the sources is, in general consensus, Makedons's lineage in Pseudo-Hesiod's *Catalogue of Women* (fr. 7). The account dates to approximately the mid-sixth century.

Meanwhile, the first inscription confirming the currency of a Pierian collective identity within the Macedonian state dates from the late sixth or early fifth century.⁴³ This proves that Pierians were a group aware of their distinctiveness since the rise of Macedon, which must also connect to the first mention of Pierus, likely as the eponym of the area, in an early fifth-century play by Epicharmus. Aside from Thucydides, the next account – in Euripides' *Bacchae*, i.e. from the late fifth century – already links Pieria to the Muses and Orpheus.⁴⁴

Thucydides' account should be treated judiciously for mythographical reasons as well. As indicated before, the ethnogenetic myth focuses not on who is expelled and from where, but where to and by whom. Therefore, the crucial element is the arrival of the Macedonians and the absorption of Pieria, while other elements of the story result from various narrative devices. These may come from an assumption that ethnicity is defined primarily by highlighting differences from out-groups. As the Macedonian identity was taking shape at the time, and additionally gravitated towards Hellenicity, it was desirable for its architects to differentiate it from that of the Thracians, its nearest cultural neighbours. In this context, a narrative of the creation or consolidation of state territory through expulsion of 'barbarian Thracians' may be understood as highlighting the differences. Presented thus, the story appears to have some historicity (invasion, conquest, migrations), but it actually focuses on setting Macedonians apart from their expelled predecessors the Thracians; a cultural border becomes a physical border. Such narratives may have been in circulation in the sixth and fifth centuries, creating the grounds for Thucydides' selective interpretation, which focused entirely on the one aspect he considered historically credible.

Macedon's strong ties to Greek culture are particularly visible in genealogies, which also offer alternative interpretations of the origins of Macedonian statehood and identity. In Pseudo-Hesiod's *Catalogue of Women* (fr. 7), Makedon, the country's eponym, is the son of Zeus and Thyia, daughter of Deucalion, and so a brother-in-law to Hellen, but Hellanicus makes him the son of Aeolus.⁴⁵ Moreover, since at least the fifth century we also have references to Pierus as the eponym of Pieria and son of Makedon.⁴⁶ These genealogies preclude a Thracian lineage, proving that Makedon was originally linked to the land and Pieria/Pierus had natural, familial ties to Macedonia/Makedon. This local nature is highlighted by Pierus' links to Methone (wife or sister), most likely dating from the fifth century.⁴⁷ Meanwhile, Pseudo-Scymnus describes Makedon as an autochthon, born of the earth,[48] showing how the mythical narratives of the founding of Macedon had a full range of possible interpretations.

The Macedonian, autochthonous visions are older and better attested than Thucydides' allochthonous version; moreover, they are Macedonian rather than foreign. This obviously does not make them more factual, but both variants must be analysed within a historical context as a useful construct for expressing and supporting the Macedonian identity or describing it from without. We may presume that in the Classical period there were at least two groups of stories about the founding of Macedonia; such pluralism is typical of the era.[49]

The placement of the 'Macedonian digression' in Thucydides' narrative of Sitalces' invasion demands a comment. The passage is evidently a deliberate design, as seen in its use of ring composition in 2,95–9: Thucydides pauses the description of Sitalces' advance to explain the beginnings of the Macedonian state, which, as the narrative reveals, had been previously inhabited by Thracians. Thus, the digression ends by resuming the description of the Odrysian army. This prompts the question of whether the information being provided in this form and at this moment in the narrative was not an expression of Athenian or Thracian propaganda justifying the attack on Macedon. In such a context, it would in fact constitute a return to ancient Thracian lands, rather than a barbarian raid inspired by Athenian hostility towards Perdiccas' Macedonia.[50]

In summary, Pieria is a well attested Greek name, not tied to the Pieres tribe; the Pieres' name being taken from the region, as Hammond claimed, is unlikely. As more critical researchers have already noted, this proves that Thucydides suggested the ties between that people and a region at the foot of Olympus on the basis of the similarity of proper names and a general concept of conquest of the lands later included in the Macedonian state. The choice of Thracians as the 'expelled' seems natural due to Macedonia's surroundings and the ongoing (in the fifth century) fights with neighbouring nations, while the choice of Pieres specifically may be conditioned by their settlement near Mount Pangaion, where Thucydides' family also held possessions (Thuc. 4,1–4,105).

The analysis also makes it uncertain if the Pieres can even be considered Thracian for any non-geographic reason. The group in question is completely unknown, appearing only in Herodotus and Thucydides, and later only mentioned based on the popularity of the great writers' works. Drawing far-reaching conclusions on the Thracian lineage of the Muses, Orpheus and Greek music in general from the above, as Strabo did, is thus highly problematic. A Thracian presence in Pieria is so far unproven even in archaeological research, partly because material remains are difficult to translate into ethnologic conclusions. The analysis is further complicated by the general cultural similarity of the peoples living north of Thessaly and the probable ethnic hybridity of Macedon.

Ultimately, even under the assumption that Thracians did inhabit Pieria before, it is impossible to support an argument justifying Thracian origins of the Muses, Orpheus and *mousikē*. It is so firstly because even Thucydides (in 2,99) himself says nothing of Pierian/Thracian cultural influence on the Macedonians; he only talks of their expulsion. Later concepts result from a far-reaching expansion of the Athenian's narrative, either by Strabo or by one of his sources.[51] Secondly, the level of development the Thracians had achieved in the fifth century (see below) renders it inadvisable to suppose they inspired Greek cultural progress. This reinforces an already strong notion, based on a reading of the sources, that primeval Macedon was tied to the Thracians through (Thracian-Pierian) Orpheus, not some knowledge of ancient Thracian musicality. Thirdly, the cult of the Muses likely does not appear in the Greek world until the late sixth century, with earliest evidence dating back to the fifth century. Thus, stories of a prehistoric Thracian influence on its introduction could, at best, serve to justify the originality of this phenomenon in a given location and were entirely ideological in nature.

Thus, due to the lack of convincing arguments for the credibility of Thucydides' account, from which we learn more of the fifth-century state of knowledge and alliances than about pre-eighth-century Macedonia lands, his passage should not serve as a point in favour of Thracian origins of Orpheus, the Muses or *mousikē*. His information fed into theories we already know from Strabo and Pausanias, both of which are quasi-historical constructs.

Once Thucydides' account is questioned or sidelined as unverifiable, Strabo's loses all credibility. The ties of Leibethra to Mount Leibethrion, and more generally of Pieria to Boeotia, have been challenged earlier in this text. Of the geographer's minor arguments, we are yet to consider Thracian origins of the mythical musicians and *philomousia* (proclivity towards music) and the culture-creating activity of the Thracians.

Thracians and *mousikē*

First, a brief recollection of the remarks made in Chapter 2 about the Thracian origins of mythical musicians, since the argument appears in Strabo and many works by modern scholars.[52] An analysis of mythographical data indicates that Thracian ties represent only a small fraction of the portrayals of mythical musicians and are not an inherent element of their depictions. It appears Thrace was not crucial to their presentation, although choosing it may have been important in some instances, for example for political or ideological reasons. In Imperial-era accounts, it is also possible that a writer could decide to link other musicians to Thrace under the influence of the (late) depiction of Orpheus as a Thracian. Assimilation and uniformisation are mechanisms typical of mythography.

In this context, it is worth noting that F. Graf's (1987, esp. 99–100) commonly accepted explanation for the Thracianness of the mythical musician is not as self-evident as it may appear. He assumed, for example (100), that Orpheus or another mythical musician, as a Thracian, 'was felt as foreign, strange to this system, at least in archaic and classical times, when most myths gained their definite forms. (...) [T]heir foreignness must point to an otherness not quite congruent with the daily life of the polis which archaic Greeks felt in relation to poetry and music, and to poets as well.'

While not rejecting these explanations entirely, we must note that the matter is more complicated. The examples of Olen, Thamyris and possibly Olympus, appear to match the pattern of an outsider, unadjusted to the structures of Greek polis. This may express a general awareness of borrowings, particularly Eastern, within music. But the cases of Ardalos (Troezen), Amphion (Thebes), Musaeus (Athens) or Linus (Thebes, Epidauros, Thespiae) demonstrate that at times the situation is clearly the opposite, with strong local ties between a mythical musician and the given area. Orpheus' links to Pieria are likely similar. The hero is an important part of Pierus' genealogy and of the equally-local Pierides, not a foreign attachment (see Chapter 5). The ethnicity or spatial references of a hero in a myth are thus not a result of the otherness of musicians and music in a polis, or of a primal musicality of Thracians, but rather a confluence of diverse factors, including the political context, mythographic or poetic decisions, and *ad hoc* choices for a given circumstance.

Finally, we shall consider if early sources confirm the hypothesis of an extraordinary link between Thracians and *mousikē*, music or the Muses. It is an important question, as modern experts either believe in the role of the Thracians, or question accounts discussing it without presenting arguments. Some researchers would apparently prefer, such as Alcidamas (*Ulix.* 24), if Thrace (and Orpheus) were the source of the invention of writing and wisdom, even if that is contrary to our knowledge of historical Thracians. Others, meanwhile, such as Androtion (BNJ 324 F54a), consider Thracians barbarians and the matter irrelevant. Thus, the 'Thracian kithara', Thracian roots of the Muses, or the original and near historical Thracian identity of Orpheus, are still given scientific currency, and, taken together, seen as proof of some sort of primeval *philomousia* of these peoples.[53] The present book lacks space to consider all accounts, and so only select examples, widely cited by scholars, will be analysed.

Aside from Strabo, our primary information on the role of Thracians in Greek cultural (and religious) development is a passage from Pausanias (9,29). While describing the Valley of the Muses, the writer recounts the origins of their worship on Helicon (introduced by Aloadae), provides the original number of the goddesses there (three), and how it grew to nine (9,29,2-3):

> The sons of Aloeus held that the Muses were three in number, and gave them the names of Melete, Mneme and Aoede. (...) But they say that afterwards Pierus, a Macedonian, after whom the mountain in Macedonia was named, came to Thespiae and established nine Muses, changing their names to the present ones. Pierus was of this opinion either because it seemed to him wiser, or because an oracle so ordered, or having so learned from one of the Thracians. For the Thracians had the reputation of old of being more clever than the Macedonians, and in particular of being not so careless in religious matters.
>
> Translated by W. H. S. Jones

Analysing this passage, Alex Hardie (2006) concluded that Pausanias' story serves purposes other than a straightforward transfer of knowledge about the past. He found the names of the three Heliconian Muses particularly doubtful, as they originate from the fourth century rather than the Prehistoric period. In this form, the narrative 'is most likely a fiction', part of a 'Heliconian ideology that retrojected three Muse names back to the mythical origins of worship on the mountain' (p. 47).

Elaborating on Hardie's remarks, it is possible to assign ideological functions to information about Pierus and the Thracians. In this form, the story served to explain the relation between the nine Olympiades/Pierides and the three Heliconiades, justifying the precedence of Boeotian Muses.[54] The most likely context for their appearance was the introduction of Muse worship in Dion in Macedonia and in the Valley of the Muses (late fifth century to early fourth century), leading to a struggle for primacy among these centres. Of note is that the chronology of their rise correlates to Hardie's proposed dating of the three Boeotian Muse names. Ovid's story of Thespiades (i.e. Heliconiades) as the real Muses, and Pierides, daughters of mortal Pierus, as false, may also have arisen from this debate over cultural primacy (since it would indeed decide the origins of *mousikē*).[55]

If the accounts of Strabo and Pausanias are not credible and thus discounted, what else could prove the musicality of Thracians? Could the image of Thracian musicality be, for instance, an effect of Athenian or Greek experiences with Thracian tribes in the sixth or fifth century? Classical accounts include some description of feasts organised by Thracian elites, especially kings, but none of them suggest Greeks would estimate Thracians as cultivated and educated people. They were a rare fit for the term proverbially applied to Leibethrians: *amousotatoi* (deprived of the gifts of the Muses, uncivilized). The sources depict barbarous habits and instruments associated with warmaking (e.g. trumpets, horns), not the aulos or string instruments typical for a Greek symposion.[56] If a Greek element appeared in such a description, it involved Greek musicians, invited to the feast to accompany songs involving Greek mythical motifs. The part the Greeks would rate as civilised was therefore composed entirely of borrowings and Hellenisation. A Classical Greek perception demonstrates no sign of the Thracian's *philomousia*.

Hence, the presence of a string instrument scholars call a 'Thracian kithara' in vase iconography has to be seen as a period creation and fantasy, founded in myth, not in historical realities.[57] Notably, Euripides in *Hypsipyle* (fr. 759 Kn.) gives Orpheus an 'Asian kithara', likely because the Greeks associated that instrument with Asia more than the barbarous custom of the Thracians. In the myth, Orpheus' kithara was a gift from Apollo, not linked to Thracian 'musicality' in any way. Oeagrus, as Orpheus' father, was not generally linked to music either.[58] This obviously does not mean that historical Thracians would not engage in music or had no string instruments, but rather that contrary to late accounts they were not salient in that area of life.

Conclusions

The portrayal of Thracian roots of Orpheus and his music was certainly not a reflection of Greek experience or ethnographic knowledge of Thracians as admirers of *mousikē*. Rather, it arose from the transposition of traits attributed to Orpheus onto Thracians, i.e. his audience in early iconography. In this form, the image of the hero as a Thracian appeared not out of any knowledge of prehistoric phenomena, but entirely as a mythographic, quasi-historical construct. Although the sources of the imagined Thracians in Pieria have roots in the Classical period (Thucydides, Ephorus), these interpretations are not linked to narratives of Orpheus until Strabo. Much as with 'Thracian' Leibethra and Pimpleia, key changes to the image of the hero are again a late first-century product.

Of course, explanations featured in the works of Strabo or Pausanias are an extremely interesting sign of explorations into the origins of, in this case, music or literature and, more broadly, Greek culture. In the form we know them, however, they are not a credible proof of Thracian roots of mythical musicians and music as a whole. They also fail to prove a Thracian origin of Orpheus and his myth. A reconstruction of the circumstances in which the explanations of both authors were formed leads to the conclusion that in this version they say more about the authors, their environments and audiences, or literary culture of the period, than about historical Thracians or the early days of Macedonia. If we were to look for information about Orpheus in those accounts, they would only be useful for an analysis of the myth's transmission and for tracking the changes to the story.

And so, if Orpheus was only *sometimes* a Thracian, due to cultural circumstance and poets' choices, then how should accounts linking the hero to Macedonian Pieria be evaluated? What role did the region play in the stories of the first musician? Moreover, if the myth can be considered historical due to its immersion in reality of the period when it forms, why did Pieria appear in Classical accounts of Orpheus? This leads us to consider the 'Pierian tradition' of Orpheus, and we return the hero from Bistonia to Macedonia.

5

Orpheus in Pieria

Plutarch's *Life of Theseus* reads (10):

> He also slew Sciron on the borders of Megara, by hurling him down the cliffs. Sciron robbed the passers by, according to the prevalent tradition; but as some say, he would insolently and wantonly thrust out his feet to strangers and bid them wash them, and then, while they were washing them, kick them off into the sea. Megarian writers, however, taking issue with current report, and, as Simonides expresses it, 'waging war with antiquity,' say that Sciron was neither a violent man nor a robber, but a chastiser of robbers, and a kinsman and friend of good and just men. For Aeacus, they say, is regarded as the most righteous of Hellenes, and Cychreus the Salaminian has divine honours at Athens, and the virtues of Peleus and Telamon are known to all men. Well, then, Sciron was a son-in-law of Cychreus, father-in-law of Aeacus, and grandfather of Peleus and Telamon, who were the sons of Endeïs, daughter of Sciron and Chariclo. It is not likely, then, they say, that the best of men made family alliances with the basest, receiving and giving the greatest and most valuable pledges. It was not, they say, when Theseus first journeyed to Athens, but afterwards, that he captured Eleusis from the Megarians, having circumvented Diocles its ruler, and slew Sciron. Such, then, are the contradictions in which these matters are involved.
>
> Translated by B. Perrin[1]

Plutarch's account is a good demonstration of how Greek culture would occasionally be a battleground between two local versions of a narrative (Athenian and Megaran in this case), one of which would become Panhellenic and universal.[2] Naturally, the latter, more widespread story, always had a better chance to survive in writing. What remains of the Greeks in nearly all cases are the results of a story gaining widespread popularity, transcending into literature, and rising to the rank of a more-than-local tale. The process was long and circuitous, however, and so regional versions, and entirely local myths are rarely seen in sources. Any such case is therefore all the more valuable to a historian. The Pierian tradition of Orpheus, postulated here, is one of those local stories of Panhellenic heroes.

What justifies the term 'Pierian tradition'? Is it the interest of poets in Pieria and its presence in literary works about Orpheus? That would clearly be an insufficient argument. After all, locating Mount Nysa in Arabia does not make for an 'Arabian version'. What is required is an entire collection of diverse accounts, including, for example, genealogies, produced by a mythographic and religious activity and tying a physical area to mythical figures and events. Such local practices extend beyond literary phenomena and usually bind a hero or deity to the polis or region, integrating them into the lives of a local community. Is there trace of such phenomena in the case of Orpheus and Macedonia? The author believes so, and is not the first to hold that opinion. An awareness of a certain role of Pieria in the myth of Orpheus has been pronounced in earlier research as well.[3] However, the matter of how that tradition was expressed and how it ought to be interpreted has remained contentious. Until now, published texts focused on other elements of the portrayal of Orpheus and were distrustful of the presence of Pieria/Macedonia in the accounts about the hero. This was made more problematic by late *testimonia* tying Pierian toponyms to Thrace and attributing to them various elements that generated confusion. The key part of the change in the approach to this issue is the inclusion of information about Orpheus' grave and statues, as well as indicating the proper context for such religious innovation in Macedonian history.

Birth, life and music in Pieria

Free of the baggage of the 'Thracian tradition', which has been discussed in the previous chapters, we may now re-examine Orpheus' connections to Pieria. The sources indicate a tradition which held that Orpheus was born in Pieria. According to Apollonius' account (1,23–4), cited above several times, Orpheus was born near Pimpleia. His birth in the Leibethrian grotto is described similarly by the *Orphic Argonautica* (1373–6). In both poems, Orpheus' connection to Pieria is undoubtedly his mother, a Muse. This connection between the goddesses and Pieria and Olympus is known from the earliest literary texts, with Hesiod expressly stating that the goddesses were born in Pieria.[4] For heroes, such a birthplace, aside from exceptional cases, nearly always links to local mythical traditions.

In some texts, Orpheus was linked to Pieria without any additional detail; he simply lived there and spent his days playing music. The earliest sources here include passages from Euripides' *Bacchae* and Timotheus' *Persians*. Both works were written in the late fifth century. In the second stasimon of *The Bacchae*, the chorus calls on Dionysus and asks him where he would lead the 'sacred bands' (550–9). Afterwards, they enumerate the sites connected with the god: Nysa, Corycia's peaks, and the leafy coverts of Olympus (556–61). The first two locations are mentioned very briefly, but the third is unexpectedly expanded with an image of Orpheus' Olympus (560–5):

τάχα δ' ἐν ταῖς πολυδένδροισιν Ὀλύμπου
θαλάμαις, ἔνθα ποτ' Ὀρφεὺς κιθαρίζων
σύναγεν δένδρεα μούσαις,
σύναγεν θῆρας ἀγρώστας.
μάκαρ ὦ Πιερία

Perhaps in the leafy coverts
of Olympus where Orpheus, playing his lyre,
once assembled the trees by his song,
assembled the beasts of the wild.
Happy Pieria [tr. D. Kovacs]

The vision of the musician leading trees ties in with Apollonius' (1,23–34) description of oaks led out of Pieria to the Bistonian coast and probably reflects the general knowledge of Macedonia's abundant woods. However, it focuses on the hero's exceptional musical skills, linking them closely to the scenery of Pieria, a land at the foot of Olympus.

What could have been the reasons to place the portrayal of the mythical musician at this point in the play? Olympus and Pieria must have been associated by the poet and his audience with the Muses, one of whom was Orpheus' mother. This much is known for certain. Another possibility would be the similarity between the fate of the hero – specifically his death – to the rending of Pentheus by the bacchantes later in the play. Aeschylus'

Bassarids featured a similar narrative, certainly known to Euripides and his contemporaries, but it placed the death of Orpheus on Pangaion. Why, then, is it actually Orpheus that Euripides' chorus mentions when discussing Mount Olympus? It appears that the most probable explanation is that at the time the hero was linked to that area, for example because it was viewed as the site of his birth and the home of his mother. But why did Euripides select this myth, and what could have been his relation to a local Macedonian tradition? It is worth remarking here that according to biographic tradition, Euripides was, near the end of his life, invited to the court of the Macedonian king Archelaus, for whom he wrote the tragedies *Archelaus*, *Temenus* and *Temenidai*, and was believed to have also written (or perhaps merely performed) *The Bacchae* while there.[5] It appears, therefore, that the mention of Orpheus in that play was no accident or poetic fantasy, but possibly a reflection of a local mythical tradition. In this form it is parallel to Euripides' decision to place Orpheus in Thrace in *Hypsipyle*, where he looked after Euneus and Thoas, the sons of Jason. This Athenian tradition tied into the Athenian Euneid family, which demonstrates how different versions were chosen depending on the context and the needs of audiences.

Orpheus' connections to Pieria are confirmed in *The Persians* by Timotheus, one of the chief proponents of the 'New Music'.[6] Verses 221–4 of this poem (fr. 791 [OF 883+902T]) inform us that Orpheus, born in Pieria, was the first musician, or the first to create 'dappled music':[7]

πρῶτος ποικιλόμουσον Ὀρ-
φεὺς >χέλ<υν[8] ἐτέκνωσεν
υἱὸς Καλλιόπα<ς ⏑–
–˟> Πιερίαθεν[9]
Orpheus, son of Calliope daughter of Zeus and native of Pieria, was the first
to beget the tortoise shell lyre of dappled music. [tr. P. LeVen]

Whether or not we accept the papyrus version or Page's conjecture for the last verse, Orpheus is only connected to Pieria. The choice of this toponym becomes more difficult to explain if 'Orpheus is always a Thracian'. Firstly, Timotheus presents here the history of innovation in music, beginning with Orpheus, and making himself and Terpander the heirs and continuators of that tradition. Such a choice should be linked to the portrayal of Orpheus as the ancestor of

Homer and Hesiod (OF 871T) and his general placement at the beginning of the Greek musical tradition, well attested for the fifth century[10] However, did Greeks understand that to mean that their musical tradition began with a Thracian? That seems unlikely in the fifth century. Consequently, Orpheus' links to Thrace must have been perceived as episodic and not an 'ethnic' reference: the hero sang to Thracians, and died in an area considered 'Thracian'. However, when presented as the originator of Greek musical tradition, he was probably not viewed as a foreign Thracian, but rather a Pierian son of a Muse. Not without relevance here are the genealogies tracing Orpheus' ancestry from Apollo, not Oeagrus. As the son of Apollo and Calliope, the hero would be tightly linked to Pieria as the Muses' homeland.

What else could have influenced the choice of Orpheus' location in Timotheus' poem? The poet, much like Euripides, was invited to the Macedonian court by king Archelaus.[11] What may have been a coincidence for one author could hardly be so when it happens to two: both of them present accounts proving that Orpheus must have been tied to Pieria/Macedonia in the fifth century. Their links to Archelaus' court make it very likely that it was a Macedonian tradition, rather than pure poetic invention, especially if we were to assume that the tomb of Orpheus in Leibethra had already existed in that ruler's lifetime (see Chapter 6). Many minor accounts, including the genealogy featuring Pierus and Methone (see 'Genealogies of Orpheus' below), suggest that Orpheus was already connected to Pieria in mythical tradition and worship by the time the accounts of Euripides and Timotheus were written.

Examples of the general link between Orpheus and Pieria as his homeland appear in the works of other authors as well. For example, when Hyginus (*Fab.* 14,44), who was likely informed by Classical and Hellenistic mythography, enumerates the Argonauts in his *Stories*, he includes information about Orpheus' origins near Olympus: 'Orpheus, son of Oeagrus and the Muse Calliope, Thracian, from the city Flevia, which is on Mount Olympus, near the river Enipeus'. It appears near certain that the word 'Flevia' in the manuscripts is meant to be Pimpleia, a name known from so many accounts. This is suggested by the city's unequivocal placement 'in Olympo monte'. *Orphic Argonautica* also has Orpheus live in Pierian Leibethra (50–5), where Jason finds him to invite him for the journey. Similar information is presented by Strabo, Conon, Pausanias, and many other later scholars or commentators.[12]

Orpheus' death in Pieria

According to many ancient sources, Orpheus' death also took place in Pieria, or he was buried there.[13] This aspect of the tradition has been highlighted relatively poorly in Bernabé's collection, probably as a consequence of the scholar's focus on how Orpheus died (women, maenads, dismemberment) over where he died. The choice of the location in a mythical narrative is obviously not accidental, although it says little in itself (as in the case of Nysa in Arabia). Assessing choices made by a poet or mythographer usually requires a broader context.

The earliest of these accounts is a statement by Menaechmus (BNJ 12F2) cited in the scholia to Pindar's fourth Pythian ode, inbetween remarks on Orpheus' origins as an Argonaut. The text of the scholion cites, after third-century BC grammarian Chaeris, an oracle 'which [Menaechmus] records in his *Pythikos*': 'Pierians who dreadfully suffer, you will expiate your hateful offence, because you have killed Orpheus, Apollo's beloved son' [tr. P. A. Tucci].

This Menaechmus is identified with a historian from Sicyon, the author of a local history of the city and a lost work about Alexander the Great. It is believed he started writing no later than the 330s, as his work about the Pythian games (*Pythikós* or *Pythionikos biblios*) was superseded by a list of victors composed by Aristotle. The oracle he quotes is relevant for two reasons: firstly, it points to Apollo as Orpheus' father; secondly, it connects his death to the 'Pieres'. The term could be understood as a reference to the Thracian tribe of Pieres, but considering the role of Apollo and the context of the work (a kitharode competition in Delphi), it is more likely that it talks of the inhabitants of Pieria. Moreover, the context of the curse is very reminiscent of the proverb about Leibethrians, residents of a Pierian town who lost their musical skills and aesthetic sense as a result of Orpheus' death.

Another notable account comes from Eratosthenes' *Catasterismoi* (24), in which the Alexandrian scholar cites Aeschylus' *Bassarids* in his description of the catasterism of the lyre. His narrative presents the history of the first instrument from its invention by Hermes, through its passing to Orpheus by Apollo, to the hero's death and the lyre's catasterism by Zeus. This story was very popular in Antiquity and was retold many times with minor modifications (OF 975T). For the current argument, the most interesting part is a mention of the fate of the lyre before it was placed in the sky: 'Hence Dionysus, being angry with him [sc. Orpheus], sent the Bassarids, as the tragedian Aeschylus says, who tore him to pieces and threw his limbs in different directions. But the Muses gathered them up and buried them in the place called Leibethra' [tr. S. Burges Watson].

First, let us note that the story of Orpheus' death on Pangaion and burial in Leibethra implies a connection between his activity and Thrace while underlining his familial relationship with Pieria. In this form, this version is identical with Apollonius' (1,23–34: birth in Pimpleia and journey to Bistonia with the oaks). This version of Orpheus' burial in Pieria was clearly very widespread and within the mythographic mainstream, as it is also mentioned by Apollodorus' *Library* (1,14): 'he was buried near Pieria after he was torn apart by maenads'. Such a narrative of Orpheus' death does not consider the possibility of separate treatment for the head or especially the catasterised lyre and their burial on Lesbos. It appears we are encountering two contradictory (local) traditions, one of which (the Pierian) seemingly became the Panhellenic version (see Apollodorus).

Returning to Eratosthenes' description, there is a debate in academia today over whether his information and his final citation of Aeschylus mean that a description of Orpheus' burial was also part of the tragedian's play. In that case, *testimonia* of the grave being at Pierian Leibethra would precede Menaechmus by over a century. However, Linforth (1941) already had some doubt in that regard, recently reinforced by Trzcionkowski (2015, 166), who pointed out the compilatory character of the description of the catasterism of the lyre. He states that it is difficult to prove that at this specific point Eratosthenes or the compiler follows a single source.

There are, therefore, two options: either the second part of the information comes from Eratosthenes and expresses views from the mid-third century, or it comes from *The Bassarids*, which would require a more substantial support. First, let us consider the splitting of the place of death (Pangaion) and burial (Leibethra) in Eratosthenes' story. This phenomenon resembles other Hellenistic instances of dividing the myth of Orpheus into two topographic parts, especially between his birth in Pieria and life in Thrace, as Apollonius does. Would such a split be justified already in the 460s, when Aeschylus' play was performed in Athens? Pangaion and Strymon were within Athenian spheres of interest and influence at the time, and so placing the death of Orpheus there would be understandable to Athenian audiences.

That is not the case with Leibethra, as this burial site would be in Macedon, a state that Athenians had poor relations with during the 460s.[14] Placing the tomb of the hero in Macedonian Leibethra would clearly require a particular reason from Aeschylus. It would be possible if a tomb of Orpheus was already displayed in Pieria and if it enjoyed more-than-local fame. However, in this form it would be a testimony a half century or more older than other instances of poet worship (Kimmel-Clauzet 2013; see Chapter 6), and originating from a periphery of Greek culture. Of course, Aeschylus could freely select the backdrop for mythic events, but in reality poets were always more or less restricted by tradition, expectations of audiences, the political situation, and the geographical knowledge both his own and of the audiences. This would make it very difficult to cite for no clear reason a toponym absent from pre-fourth-century accounts and thus probably unknown to the Athenians. This suggests, particularly in light of the tensions between Athens and Macedon in the period, the physical distance, and a lack of knowledge or interest in Macedonian topography or religiousness from Athenians, that it was unlikely Aeschylus would just invent this location for the tomb. Meanwhile, any detailed information about the tomb, statues and hero worship of Orpheus in Leibethra appears only in later sources, thus constituting no evidence for the existence of those phenomena in the mid-fifth century. All of the above arguments advocate for the separation of the two facts in Eratosthenes' description and attributing only the story of Orpheus' death on Pangaion to Aeschylus. The passage from *Catasterismoi* would therefore link two traditions from different time periods: one of the hero's death in Thrace, from *The Bassarids*; the other of his grave in Leibethra, created after the spread of the depiction of Orpheus' 'Pierian tomb' in the fourth to third century. The conclusions drawn here match the remarks of Linforth and Trzcionkowski.

Another Hellenistic account tying Orpheus' death to Pieria is Lycophron's *Alexandra* (regardless of how the author be dated).[15] It features a description of nymphs lamenting the death of Achilles (272–4): 'wept by the nymphs who love the clear water of Bephyras and the high seat of Leibethron above Pimpleia' [tr. A. W. Mair]. As usual in the case of *Alexandra*, it is not a clear, straightforward piece of information, but a geographic and mythographic riddle. We can quickly surmise that the 'nymphs' of Bephyras are Muses, who grieved Achilles in the *Odyssey* (24,58–64) or in Pindar (*I.* 8,57–8), as well as many other literary texts.[16] This identification of nymphs with Muses is also clearly suggested by Pierian toponyms, in particular Leibethra and Pimpleia, which are known for their ties to the Muses from other works as well.[17] The question here is, at most, what is the function of the Bephyra River? Thanks to Pausanias (9,30,8), however, we know that it flowed near the Pierian city of Dion, and so this reference alludes to the Muses as Pierides.

The riddle, however, also has a second level, which has not been sufficiently examined until now.[18] The role of all these toponyms, but especially Bephyra, is to point to Orpheus and his death in Pieria. He is the third link connecting the Muses (as a son of one) to Pieria and Achilles. As seen with Eratosthenes, the musician's violent death would be grieved by the Muses, exactly like Achilles'. The choice of toponyms in the scene evokes the vision of the death of 'Pierian' Orpheus, making it parallel to the portrayal of the death of Achilles, with 'Pierian nymphs', i.e. the Muses, connecting the two figures in an adept mythological riddle.

But why is the Bephyra River the best argument for this reading? It plays no part in the stories of Achilles' death, but is relevant to the portrayals of the death of Orpheus. The pieces of the hero's torn body are thrown into water, usually of rivers Strymon or Hebrus, but in one version into Baphyra River in Macedonian Pieria. This is relayed by Pausanias (9,30,8):

> There is also a river called Helicon. After a course of seventy-five stades the stream hereupon disappears under the earth. After a gap of about twenty-two stades the water rises again, and under the name of Baphyra instead of Helicon flows into the sea as a navigable river. The people of Dium say that at first this river flowed on land throughout its course. But, they go on to say, the women who killed Orpheus wished to wash off in it the blood-stains, and thereat the river sank underground, so as not to lend its waters to cleanse manslaughter.
> Translated by W. H. S. Jones

Inasmuch as the name Helicon, not attested for Pieria in any source, can be considered a local or literary fantasy, Baphyra River is a real place in that region of Macedonia.[19] Pausanias' phrasing, 'The people of Dium say', also indicates that the river must have been part of a local legend associated with Orpheus. Moreover, two of the four versions of the hero's death presented by Pausanias (9,30,5–11) place the events in Pieria. The first of these is linked to Dion; the second describes the tomb in Pierian Leibethra (9,30,9–11). In both cases, Pausanias confirms the existence of a local legend connecting Orpheus to the area. Lycophron's riddle, addressed to the erudite readers of *Alexandra*, therefore suggests the name of the river also appeared in other texts regarding Orpheus' death in Pieria, and the extensive topography of the hero's life and death (Pimpleia, Bephyra, Leibethra) was widely known at least since the Hellenistic period.

The presence and importance of the river in the description of Orpheus' death is also seen in Conon (45), where Orpheus dies in Leibethra (ἐν Λιβήθροις) at the hands of Macedonian and Thracian women. After the violent death of the hero, 'the country suffered from a plague because the women had not paid the penalty for their crime, those who sought relief from their ills received an oracle that if they found the head of Orpheus and buried it, they would receive relief. They found it, after much difficulty, near the mouth of the river Meletos thanks to a fisherman' [tr. S. Blakely]. The entire story contains so much detail, including the aition (cause, beginning) of a religious custom related to the tomb and temple of Orpheus, that it is hard to perceive it solely as a literary invention. Rather, one may conclude it describes more or less exactly the details of the worship of Orpheus in Pierian Leibethra, and thus also some local version of the myth.

Strabo (7, fr. 10) also placed the death of Orpheus in Pieria. In his description of Macedonia, upon explaining the location of Pimpleia, the geographer presents the hero as a sorcerer, a soothsayer and a trickster. According to this story, Orpheus lived in Pimpleia and was killed for political reasons. At the end of the narrative, immediately after discussing the death of the musician, Strabo adds: 'Nearby is also Leibethra'. The entire account is a clear rationalisation of the myth, owing much to the Neopythagorean tradition, but at the core it repeats information known from other literary works and once again proves the knowledge of a narrative of Orpheus' death in Pieria.

The proverb about Leibethrians

Lastly, a lesser known testimony: the proverb about the Leibethrians' *amousia* ('lack of culture').[20] The saying survives in many versions within a convoluted paremiographic tradition; however, in spite of their many differences, all of them include information about Orpheus' death in Leibethra.[21] The most important mentions appear in texts by Zenobius and Diogenianus of Heraclea Pontica, second century AD authors whose works were compiled from a lost first-century collection by Didymus Chalcenterus and Lucillus of Tarrha.[22] The following references cite Zenobius' version, which is the earliest still extant. The proverb comes from the oldest Mount Athos manuscript (fifth century AD) and as such the tradition is referred to as 'Zenobius Athous' (3,1)[23] [OF 1069T]:

> Zenobius Athous prov. (coll. Miller 3,1: Mel. p. 369) ἀμουσότερος Λειβηθρίων: Λειβήθριοι ἔθνος ἐστὶ Πιερικόν, οὗ καὶ <Ἀριστοτέλης> μέμνηται ἐν τῇ Μεθωναίων πολιτείᾳ. λέγονται δὲ ἀμουσότατοι εἶναι οἱ Λειβήθριοι, ἐπειδὴ παρ' αὐτοῖς ἐγένετο ὁ τοῦ Ὀρφέως θάνατος.

> less civilized[24] than Leibethrians: Leibethrians are Pierian ethnos, mentioned [by Aristotle] in the *Constitution of Methone*; it is said that Leibethrians are very uncivilized, as it was among them that Orpheus' death happened.

Some researchers believe the Leibethrians in the proverb are a Thracian tribe, but the reference is clearly to the citizens of the polis of Leibethra.[25] After all, the passage does not mention Thracians, but Leibethrians, whom it describes as 'Pierian *ethnos*'.[26] The account is therefore another confirmation of a link between Orpheus' death, Pieria and Leibethra. The key question is its dating.

The only researcher to investigate this text was Romero (2011), who concluded that the proverb originated from a comedy by the poet Thugenides (fifth century BC). Such an attribution and dating is, however, unlikely to be correct, as it is based entirely on Tittmann's fanciful correction (1808, CXLVI: Θουγενίδης for Θουκιδίδης) in a version of the proverb only known from the thirteenth-century lexicon of Zonaras.[27] Interestingly, that emendation is also accepted by Kassel and Austin (editors of PCG), who also add the *testimonium* of Thugenides in *Poetae Comici Graeci* (fr. 5).

However, there is another possible dating for the proverb, as the Mount Athos manuscript provides additional information missing from later codices.[28] The editor of the proverb cites the *Constitution of Methone*, a work from the school of Aristotle, conventionally presented alongside his fragments (fr. 552 Rose). It is worth noting here that the 'Zenobius Athous' manuscript includes more such citations. For instance, 2,107 mentions the proverb *Aisopeion haîma*

('The blood of Aesop'), after which the author refers to the *Constitution of Delphi* (Arist. fr. 487 Rose). These and other examples show that the early tradition of the collection of proverbs included information about their sources, now gone from some manuscripts. We also know that the works from the school of Aristotle, particularly the series about the constitutions of Greek poleis, included mythical material, proverbs and anecdotes.[29] This is unsurprising, as the Lyceum generally started the later Greek interest in proverbs, with both Aristotle and Theophrastus using myth and proverbs in their writings.[30]

If the source of the remark on Leibethrians was the *Constitution of Methone*, the proverb can be dated to the fourth century. Notably, Aristotle, as a person otherwise acquainted with the history and topography of Macedon, may have had first-hand knowledge of Methone, since its citizens were invited to Athens after the city was razed by Philip. The question would be: how could Leibethra, a city on the other side of Pieria, be connected to Methone, and why would the proverb about Orpheus' death end up in Aristotle's work about the city?

Genealogies of Orpheus: Pierus and Methone

These questions can be answered with the help of a genealogy that links Orpheus to Pieria. It is present in an extended form in two second-century AD sources: a work by the sophist Charax of Pergamum[31] and in *Certamen Homeri et Hesiodi* (4). The following is the latter and more extensive version:

> Now some say that he was older than Hesiod, others that he was younger, and related to him. This is the genealogy they give: from Apollo and Thoösa, daughter of Poseidon, they say Linus was born, from Linus Pierus, from Pierus and the nymph Methone Oeagrus, from Oeagrus and Calliope Orpheus, from Orpheus Ortes, [from him Eucles,] from him Harmonides, from him Philoterpes, from him Euphemus, from him Epiphrades, from him Melanopus, and from him Dios and Apellaios; from Dios and Apollo's daughter Pykimede, Hesiod and Perses; from Apellaios Maion, and from a daughter of Maion and the river Meles, Homer.
>
> Translated by M. L. West

Certamen contains elements of Homer's (and Hesiod's) biographic tradition dating at least to the Classical period.[32] The lower part of this genealogy, between Orpheus and Homer and Hesiod, also originated in that era, as unrelated accounts show several fifth-century mythographers proposed a similar lineage. The most important one of these is the *Life of Homer* by Proclus (5,4):

> Hellanicus, Damastes, and Pherecydes trace his lineage back to Orpheus. They say that Homer's father Maion and Hesiod's father Dios were the sons of Apellis, son of Melanopus, son of Epiphrades, son of Chariphemus, son of Philoterpes, son of Idmonides, son of Eucles, son of Dorion, son of Orpheus. And Gorgias of Leontini takes him back to Musaeus.
>
> Translated by M. L. West

Proclus' information is confirmed in the commentary and scholia to Hesiod, reinforcing the view that Hellanicus played an important role in the appearance of this genealogy.[33] This is also supported by the insertion of characters connected with Cyme, a city opposite the mythographer's home island of Lesbos, into the generations between Orpheus and Homer and Hesiod.[34] While Homer's own link to Cyme is an element of an older tradition,[35] the insertions into the genealogy suggest a mythographic exercise of calculating the number of generations between the mythic age (a generation before the Trojan War) and the eighth century and then filling the gap in with inventions. Moreover, most of the names are meaningful, pointing to personal ties to *mousikē*.[36]

In its surviving form, the genealogy linking Orpheus to Homer and Hesiod is a product of the fifth-century debate over the origins of Greek literature and culture. This is further indicated by the presence of alternative options, particularly the (probably Athenian) lineage of the first 'historical' poets from Musaeus (Gorgias 82 B25 DK). The dispute is also rooted in the debate over the origin and dating of Orphic texts.[37] Some role was also played by the burgeoning fifth-century interest in the biographical details on Homer and Hesiod and the relation between them; some sources are clearly focused on attempting to answer the question of which one came first.[38] All of the above indicates that the so-called 'lower' part of the genealogy (from Orpheus to Homer and Hesiod) was sourced from the second half of the fifth century and was likely related to Hellanicus activity as mythographer and historian.

From our perspective, the 'upper' part of it (Apollo/Thoosa–Linus–Pierus/Methone–Oeagrus/Calliope – Orpheus) is more interesting, as is the question of whether it was also invented by Hellanicus or at least during his lifetime. There are some arguments in favour of this hypothesis. First, the genealogy tries to unite two divergent traditions: one linking Orpheus to Apollo, one to Oeagrus. The former lineage is well-attested already in the Classical period.[39] Notably, the way the two genealogies are merged – by replacing two parallel, contradictory versions (Apollo or Oeagrus) with a vertical chronological arrangement (Apollo → […] → Oeagrus) – is characteristic of mythography, and especially of Hellanicus' practice of it. We know examples of similar procedures, e.g. the genealogy of Pelasgus (F36), and of other methods of removing conflicts, e.g. the reduplication of characters (F4; 91; 114). This is what Robert Fowler means when writing about the specifics of Hellanicus' mythographical activity (2013, 684): 'More than his predecessors Hellanikos sought to resolve the contradictions between different genealogies, and to convert these into a chronological framework, thus laying the foundation for later chronography'.

Naturally, an adroit arrangement of divergent elements does not prove the early origins of Orpheus' upper genealogy. However, such early provenance could be indicated by the presence of Methone in the genealogy, as she was linked from a very early period to Pierus, the eponym of Pieria. Tzetzes' commentary to Hesiod's *Works and Days* mentions, citing Melisseus (BNJ 402 F1), that: 'Pieria originally founded by Pieros, the brother of Methone and the father of Linos, had been called Pieria'.[40] A similar version is found in the *Chiliades* (6,53), where Tzetzes claims Pieria was 'a town that was built by Pierus, / Who was brother to Methone and father of Linus', as well as in the *Etymologicum Magnum* (671,37). In all these *testimonia*, Methone is Pierus' sister, not his wife. Moreover, all instances also mention another mythical musician, Linus. A slightly different version of Methone's relation to Orpheus is featured in Plutarch's *Questiones convivales* (11 = Mor. 293a–b). It answers the question 'Who are the Ἀποσφενδόνητοι?' by stating they were Eretrians driven away from Korkyra who then sailed to Thrace, took control of the region and settled in the place that was originally home to Metho, the ancestor of Orpheus, and named their city Methone.

In all of these versions, regardless of the minor divergences between them, Metho/Methone and Pierus are ancestors of Orpheus. In the genealogy cited earlier this would make Oeagrus and Orpheus Pierians by blood, native-born sons of Pieria. This also explains the remark from Zenobius, who, in his description of the proverb about people 'less civilised than Leibethrians', cited Aristotle's *Constitution of Methone*. Apparently the genealogy including Methone and Pierus made it into the mythographic part of the description of Methone's political system and history, since probably all of Aristotle's *Constitutions* began in the mythical age. From there it would be only a step to mentioning the death of Orpheus in Pieria and citing the proverb.

But is it certain that the Methone genealogy is an early tradition? Indirectly this could be indicated by the proverb itself, but it also appears that there are other arguments for its early origins and ties to Hellanicus. According to historical sources, the city of Methone was conquered and razed to the ground by Philip II in 354, with the survivors going into exile, never to return to Pieria. The polis was not rebuilt, although a Macedonian settlement may have arisen in its place two or three generations later.[41] This removed the reasons for new versions of the myth to arise after that year, whether to present the city in a positive light or to include its eponym (Metho/Methone) into a new genealogical system. Everything points to mythical information about Methone and its eponym being older than that caesura, that is, originating between 450 and 350.

The appearance of Pierus as the eponymous hero of Pieria on the list should be dated similarly.[42] He does not appear in surviving Archaic sources and only appears (alongside Pimpleia) in Epicharmus in the first half of the fifth century (fr. 39 PCG). After the dissolution of Alexander's empire in the late fourth century, the geopolitical situation changed so radically that Pierus apparently lost any propaganda value as an eponym.[43] Thus, it appears the time frame for mythographic activity making reference to the character of Pierus was particularly the period *c.* 450–300.

In broader terms, the genealogy of Orpheus in the form seen in *Certamen* and Charax should reflect some political changes and an intensified 'propaganda' activity of Macedon, as indicated by the crucial role of Pierus and Methone. Such actions are particularly likely between the rule of Alexander I and Alexander the Great, but they fit best in the era of Archelaus, who attempted to portray Macedon as a civilised country. Pierus as the son of Linus,[44] grandson of Apollo and grandfather of Orpheus, the son of the Muse Calliope who stands at the beginning of the lineage of Homer and Hesiod, is a chronological arrangement that was possibly aimed (aside from resolving contradictions in the narratives of Apollo and Oeagrus) at highlighting the significance of Pieria

(Macedon) in the history of Hellenic culture. In this form, the upper part of the genealogy (Apollo/Thoosa–Linus–Pierus/Methone–Oeagrus/Calliope–Orpheus) would tie Orpheus to Pieria (and Methone) as proof of the original Hellenicity of Macedonia. Considering our knowledge of the Classical period, such a daring propagandistic manoeuvre would make particular sense during the reign of Archelaus, which, notably, would concur with the conclusions drawn from the analysis of Euripides and Timotheus.

The connection between this part of the genealogy and Hellanicus is supported by another detail. Firstly, one of the surviving fragments from that author (F74) indicates his interest in Macedon, as it contains a version of the genealogy of the country's eponym, Makedon. It is different from the one known from Ps.-Hesiod's *Catalogue of Women*, as Hellanicus presents Makedon as the son of Aeolus, and so a paternal grandson of Hellen and the great-grandson of Deucalion.[45] This version would add prestige to Makedon's origins, making him more 'Hellenic'. Secondly, the Suda lexicon claims Hellanicus resided in Amyntas' court in Macedon for some time.[46] These two claims would make Hellanicus' links to not only the lower part of the genealogy (from Orpheus to Homer/Hesiod) but also to its upper part, known from Charax and *Certamen*, far more likely.[47]

However, Hellanicus' authorship is not the key element of the present argumentation. It is only considered here as a hypothesis; the early origins of the genealogy (fifth to fourth centuries) and its Macedonian background are the crucial parts for Orpheus' ties to Pieria. These, in turn, are seen in the inclusion of Methone and Pierus, and in the proverb about Leibethrans quoted in the *Constitution of Methone*, which dates from roughly the same period. All of the above accounts thus indicate an early origin for the story of Orpheus' birth, life and death in Pieria, local roots of the myth (topography and genealogy), and the spread of that version of the narrative on the Panhellenic level (Apollonius, Lycophron, Apollodorus).

Pierian toponyms and the Muses

The popularity of the Pierian toponyms (Leibethra and Pimpleia) and their ties to the Muses as Pierides is another proof of the more-than-local significance of the Pierian tradition of Orpheus.[48] Incidentally, not all notable accounts are clearly tied to Orpheus' name and not all can be found in collections of *testimonia*. It has been the case, for example, with Lycophron's account (*Alex.* 272–4), which conceals the hero behind toponyms and distant associations with Achilles. The following will examine other such lesser known *testimonia* indicating the Muses' ties to Leibethra and Pimpleia, as the presence of those toponyms quite frequently suggests a widespread Pierian tradition of Orpheus. The first text of interest is an epigram by the poet Leonidas of Tarentum. Book 5 of the *Anthologia Palatina* includes a piece describing a dedication of instruments by two musicians at the end of their careers:

> Melo and Satyre, the daughters of Antigenides, now advanced in age, the Muses' pliant workwomen, made dedications to the Pimpleian Muses. Melo dedicated her swift-lipped flute and this boxwood flute case, and amorous Satyre dedicated the reed that she daubed with wax, with which she accompanied wine drinkers in their evening revels—a sweet whistler, with which all through the night's darkness she limned the dawn, without an ill thought for the courtyard doors closed against her.
>
> Translated by W. R. Paton

It is believed the women in the passage may have been relatives of Antigenides, a famous Theban auletist of the first half of the fourth century BC and teacher of Alcibiades.[49] Setting that interpretative possibility aside, we can see the instruments were dedicated 'to the Pimpleian Muses'. Instead of the expected traditional appeal to Helikoniades or Pierides, there is a call to the relatively obscure Muses from Macedonian Pimpleia. Notably, the poet comes from Tarentum in Italy, while the musicians were most likely from Boeotia. Selecting the 'Pimpleian Muses' thus has literary connotations and indicates the spread of a tradition connecting the Muses to Pimpleia, demonstrating that toponym's exceptional career in Hellenistic literature.

Other examples include the *testimonium* of the poet Euphorion (SH 416), which alludes to the Muses as παρθενικαὶ Λ[ι]βηθρίδες ('girls from Leibethra').[50] Some fragmentary Hellenistic texts contain similar phrases.[51] The popularisation of the terms 'Libethrides' and 'Pipleides' as epithets of the Muses in the Hellenistic period is attested especially well by Varro (*Lat.* 7,20). This, in turn, explains how Virgil can eruditely and intertextually summon the (Macedonian) Muses as *Nymphae Libethrides* (*Ecl.* 7,21). It is no surprise that the two Pierian toponyms became very popular in Roman poetry, where they turned into a permanent feature of the metapoetic language and part of a 'geography of inspiration'. Literature of the Roman Empire mentions Leibethra and Pimpleia as often as Helicon, Parnassus or Pieria.[52] Orpheus' Pierian tradition was innovative in the Hellenistic period, but did not forgo the traditional metapoetic vocabulary (Muses and mountains).

This broader context also explains the words of Callimachus (*h*. 4,7–8): 'the Muses hate the singer who does not sing of Pimpleia'. The choice of this toponym may have been a product of a typical Hellenistic tendency to look for rare and local versions. Without surrendering that proposition, it also undoubtedly resulted from the spread of the idea of Pimpleia and Leibethra as Orpheus' *spatium mythicum*.

One more group of texts worth examining are the so-called Orphic writings. Some Orphic poems would begin with an apostrophe to the Muses of Pimpleia or Leibethra.[53] This role is confirmed by the much later *Orphic Argonautica*, which also ties Orpheus to Leibethra and has the hero himself returning from a journey to 'the famous cave where my mother gave birth to me on the bed of the brave Oeagrus' (1375–6). Such accounts prove the weight of the Pierian toponyms in Orphic texts and their linking of Muses and Orpheus to the Pieria area.

Meanwhile, Iamblichus' *Vita Pythagorei* and Proclus (OF 507T) mention that the first-century Orphic text *Hieros Logos* described Orpheus receiving knowledge about the gods and the world from Calliope and then passing it on to Aglaophamus (his apprentice), who then taught it to Pythagoras in Leibethra. Even if the Muse–Orpheus–Aglaophamus–Pythagoras connection is entirely Iamblichus' invention (Edmonds 2013, 39), the inclusion of a Muse and the setting of the events in Pieria is a result of a strong tradition connecting the goddesses and Orpheus to that area of Macedonia. While very little is known about the contents of the early Orphic texts, the later writings, some associated with Neopythagoreanism, frequently referenced Orpheus, including in his role as the master of Pythagoras, and linked them both equally to Pieria and Thrace. Pimpleia and Leibethra apparently played a major role in these works, which may be interpreted either as a borrowing from the Macedonian tradition or as a continuation within the Orphic tradition.

Finally, a brief remark on the name of Orpheus' wife in the mythical tradition. As has been mentioned, her figure was anonymous in early narratives, while the

Hellenistic poet Hermesianax (fr. 3) calls her Agriope. The name Euridice is not attested until Ps.-Moschos' *Epitaphios Bionis* from the early first century. Although we do not know any details, much suggests the name had to have appeared in earlier literary works. It is still a question of why this name specifically. The most recent interesting proposal was put forth by Jan Bremmer (1991), who noted that the name 'Eurydice' was relatively popular in Macedon, especially in the Argead dynasty, and after the Classical period in the Ptolemaic royal family. In his opinion, the choice of the name may have been tied to a rise in Macedonian and Hellenistic interest in the character of Orpheus, which is visible in the source material. Bremmer's explanation fits in with other accounts clearly demonstrating the existence of a Pierian tradition and its links to Macedonia.

Conclusions

Let us recapitulate all the above arguments for the existence and relevance of the 'Pierian tradition' of Orpheus. Are the analysed accounts enough to change the traditional image of Orpheus as Thracian? If so, why? Firstly, a genealogy tracing Orpheus' ancestry from Apollo and a Muse, and therefore highlighting his musical skill rather than 'Thracian' origins, was known as early as the fifth century. Moreover, the chronology of Greek music and culture created in the fifth century placed Orpheus at the outset, and traced Homer and Hesiod to him eleven generations later. In this way, it connected the mythic era with the beginnings of the historical period, and also placed the author of Orphic theogonies many years before the mythical stories of the Trojan War and Hesiod's theogony.

As part of the discussion over the beginnings of *mousikē*, a genealogy appeared that not only linked mythical musicians to Archaic-era poets, but also merged two versions of Orpheus' lineage (from Apollo and from Oeagrus). The most interesting aspect of that genealogy was describing Oeagrus as the son of Pierus and Methone. In this arrangement, Orpheus' father would be a 'son of Pieria', as suggested by the presence of the country's eponym and of Methone, eponymous nymph of a city on the Pierian coast. This typically mythographic genealogical solution stresses the tight connection between Orpheus (as grandson of Pierus and Methone) and Pieria. The existence of such links is indirectly confirmed by the proverb of the Leibethrians' *amousia* (lack of culture) appearing in Aristotle's *Constitution of Methone*.

The following arguments tie into the popularisation of Pieria and Pierian toponyms in the stories of Orpheus and the Muses. This connection is first seen in the late fifth century in Euripides and Timotheus, two writers who were guests at the court of Archelaus I. Since the Hellenistic period, Pimpleia, a settlement in Pieria also associated with the birth of the Muses, was presented as the birthplace of the hero, while Pieria, Leibethra, or the environs of Olympus were suggested as his places of residence. In the third and second century, his ties to Macedonia became so well-known that Lycophron could arrange an erudite riddle on the basis of the stories of the Pierian hero by referencing the Macedonian geography of his life and death (Bephyra, Pimpleia, Leibethra).

Within the myth, Pieria or Leibethra became either the site of Orpheus' burial (Eratosthenes) or death (Menaechmus, proverb). Already in the fourth century that version became the basis for the spread of the proverb about the *amousia* of the Leibethrians. This demonstrates the importance of Pieria to the narrative as well as confirms the popularity of the story and its spread beyond the local area. The description of Orpheus' death in Pieria in Apollodorus' *Library* (1,14) is proof of this version's inclusion in the Imperial-era mythographic mainstream. Last but not least, the hero's links to Pieria, Leibethra and Pimpleia are also clear in Orphic, Neopythagorean and Neoplatonic writing.

The existence of a local, Pierian tradition also resulted in the appearance of Orpheus' tomb in Leibethra, or otherwise explained its presence. It remains an open question who, why and when would be interested in spreading this version of the myth. Notably, the two earliest accounts of it, by Euripides and Timotheus, authors linked to the Macedonian court of Archelaus, depict Orpheus as a hero from Pieria living 'in the valleys of Olympus'. This allows for a hypothesis that the Pierian location of the hero could be linked to Macedonian policy in the fifth century as an explanation for these elements of the portrayal. Unlike the Megarian version of the myth of Theseus and Sciron, quoted at the beginning of the chapter, the tale of Orpheus and Pieria became widespread in literature. Most importantly, this version became the foundation for some cultural and religious practices in Classical Macedonia.

6

Orpheus' Tomb in Pieria

In 1350, while travelling from Rome to Florence, Francesco Petrarca stopped in Arezzo, the town where he was born in 1304, but where he never resided. He always considered Florence to be his home city, as his parents had left Arezzo early enough that he had no memory of it. At the end of his visit, he was shown the house in which he had been born, and then he heard that the town authorities forbade its new owner from changing the building in any way. It was to remain unchanged as the 'home of Petrarca', an important place of memory on the map of the city. Apparently, the poet had been completely unaware of that fact and greatly embarrassed by how his fame as the *poeta laureatus* had become a source of local pride for the people of Arezzo. It was of no importance that most residents had never met Petrarca; he was real to them because of the story and its ties to a place in the space around them. The house and the associated tale of the birth of the poetic genius had thus become an important part of the Arezzo identity and part of the cultural capital of its residents.[1]

The other end of the commemorative spectrum, naturally, are the tombs. After Petrarca's death, his burial place in Arquà quickly became a tourist destination. The figure of the poet, the places, items and tales associated with him are some of the earliest examples of the modern phenomenon of cultural sainthood.[2] The phenomenon of worshipping mementos and visiting sites connected to the memory of exceptional individuals and the practice of telling stories about such locations and items were also present in the ancient world.[3] Memorialising a home, as in the case of Petrarca, was also not unheard of; homes of famous poets or philosophers were already venerated in Antiquity. This is demonstrated by the stories of the houses of Pythagoras and Pindar, or of Euripides' cave on Salamis.[4]

However, the most famous category of the places of memory always consisted of the graves of poets.[5] This group includes the tombs of Orpheus in

Leibethra and Dion. The cult of the mythical musician and poet was in many ways similar to the phenomena encountered by Petrarca in his life and after his death, with the minor difference that Petrarca was a real figure, while Orpheus was mythical. This begs the question: could a mythical figure have a real grave? The answer is: yes. It was not a rare occurrence in ancient culture.[6]

The gesture of the people of Arezzo and the poet's surprise suggest that the weight of such sites is only partly embedded in historical reality. As long as the stories of the homes or graves of such 'cultural saints' function in the life of the community by expressing something socially important, Petrarca and Orpheus continue to exist – regardless of how real the former or how invented the latter. Research into Orpheus has so far not focused on the matters of his tomb and worship. However, these issues were raised at times, as it was involved in the analysis of important *testimonia*, especially those of Conon and Pausanias.[7] No far-reaching conclusions were drawn from it, in part because of the late origins of the source material and due to difficulties in finding the proper cultural framing for the texts. This approach has changed in recent years as a result of research into biographical tradition and the cult of poets.[8] This chapter will analyse and evaluate surviving ancient accounts indicating the presence of a tomb, statues and cult of Orpheus in Pieria. As many of those *testimonia* are late, the information will be placed in the broader cultural context of the period between the fifth and the third century. This will allow for a verification of the possible chronological range of the phenomenon and for the centring of the mythical musician's grave within the cultural context of Classical Greece.

Lesbos and Kitharodia

However, before analysing accounts indicating the presence of a tomb of Orpheus in Pieria, we need to examine the case of the tomb of Orpheus on Lesbos.[9] The stories of the musician's head and lyre, carried to the island by the sea, were most likely used as explanations of the musicality of the islanders, including the many musicians and poets in Lesbos' history.[10] This version of the story is known mostly from late sources, which complicates the dating and analysis of the phenomenon.[11] The two earliest accounts indicating the presence of the tomb of Orpheus are fragments from a work by Myrsilus, a paradoxographer from Methymna (BNJ 477 F2 = OF 1065T), and a passage from the poet Phanocles (OF 1054T). Both were written in the early third century. Phanocles describes the still-singing head and the lyre being buried on Lesbos without assigning them to a specific location. Myrsilus, meanwhile, speaks about a tomb of Orpheus' head in Antissa, where 'nightingales sing more sweetly than elsewhere'. Other *testimonia* only date to the Imperial period, not allowing for a cohesive image of the tomb and worship of Orpheus on Lesbos. Surviving descriptions either indicate numerous changes in the organisation of the cult over the centuries or are literary inventions about it. An interesting fact in these late mentions is that at some point, the tomb was linked to another Lesbian city: Methymna, and not Antissa, as relayed by Myrsilus. It is possible it was a parallel phenomenon to the transfer of the Pierian tomb from the ruined Leibethra to Dion, as extensively described by Pausanias. We know that Antissa was destroyed and that its residents moved to Methymna in 167 BC, taking apparently the tomb with them.[12] The change in the location may have severely impacted later narratives about the head of Orpheus and resulted in the many divergences seen in the sources.

It remains unresolved why the tomb was originally specifically in Antissa, why the head itself (and the lyre) were worshipped, and when this phenomenon began. Some researchers allow the possibility that the grave on Lesbos represented an exceptionally ancient tradition, supporting that claim with the depiction of Orpheus' head on late-fifth-century pottery (Figure 4).[13] However, a detailed analysis of iconography suggests those items are more probably associated with Orphism.[14] The narrative of the soothsaying head is undoubtedly much older than even the oldest mentions of the tomb on Lesbos. It is also independent of the Lesbian legend and tied more to Thrace than to the island.[15] Other researchers consider the entire story of the tomb in Antissa and Methymna an invention intended to explain the musicality of the Lesbians.[16] In that case, the Lesbian narrative, considered by many to be one of the five most important in the myth of Orpheus, would have originated as an entirely local tradition.

What are the indicators of a local provenance and limited significance of this version? Firstly, Lesbos never features as the scene of Orpheus' actions. This is different from Pieria or Thrace, as it is there that he was supposed to be born, to rule, to charm animals and trees, and to die. Lesbos only appears in later mythical tradition like a *deus ex machina*, which is, at best, the result of local mythographic practice. Secondly, the presence of the head itself follows from earlier narratives of the dismemberment of Orpheus. The idea is already attested in Aeschylus' *Bassarids* (Eratosth. *Catast.* 24), and in that earlier tradition it is tied to Thrace or Pieria, not Lesbos. Eratosthenes' Hellenistic-era story does not mention the island and clearly claims the remains were buried in Pieria. The lack of any information about the head suggests this refers to all of the body parts. Thirdly, the tale about the fate of the kithara was quite important to the mythical tradition of Orpheus, particularly after the hero was linked to the instrument invented by Hermes.[17] Again, this line of the myth is older than the tomb in Antissa and represents a reflection over the birth or invention of *mousikē*. Moreover, explanations placing the lyre in the grave or in a local temple, characteristic of the Lesbian tradition, are just one of the several known descriptions of the history of the instrument. Based on the accounts of Eratosthenes and Hyginus, we can surmise that the version in which Zeus places the first instrument in the sky after Orpheus' death (OF 1074–5T) was far more popular in the Hellenistic period. The popularisation of the tomb on Lesbos and of the colourful story of the head and the lyre was most likely an Imperial-period phenomenon.[18]

What, then, were the origins of the idea that Orpheus' tomb was on Lesbos? To start with, the island of Lesbos was factually an important place on the Greek musical and poetical map. Many Archaic-period kitharodes, especially Terpander, as well as other musicians (Arion, Phrynis of Mytilene) and poets (Sappho, Alcaeus) were either born or active on the island.[19] The attempt to link this Lesbian musical and poetical tradition to Orpheus, the first musician, appears understandable. The phenomenon might be connected to the late fifth century, when the Greeks began to analyse earlier literary and musical traditions, as propagated by figures such as Glaucus of Region or Hellanicus of Lesbos.[20] This resulted in attempts to describe the beginnings and explain the relationships between the original inventors and the historical innovators. Kitharodes may have played an important role in the process of connecting Orpheus to Lesbos, as during the Classical period they began citing the hero as their predecessor.[21] One of the most popular representatives of that group at the end of the fifth century was Timotheus of Miletus, whose work provides a testimonium placing Orpheus at the outset of the kitharodic tradition. In his *sphragis* ('seal') to the kitharodic nomos *The Persians* (fr. 791, 221–33), the poet includes a description of the *diadoche* ('succession'), a sort of intellectual genealogy of himself within the history of music.[22] Timotheus associates the origins of kitharodia with Orpheus, Pieria and Orpheus' lyre; he then describes an intermediate stage linked to Terpander of Antissa, who introduced further musical innovation, and places the peak of musical development in his own activity.

What does this mean for the circumstances of the emergence of the tomb of Orpheus of Lesbos? Considering the absence of the island in the stories of the hero himself, it follows that the motif of burial on Lesbos was not an original part of the Orpheus tradition, but a secondary, most probably local phenomenon. The popularity of the motif of the singing head in association with the island is attested relatively lately (early third century). The Lesbian plot is preceded by stories of the dismemberment of the hero (Aeschylus), the Orphic narratives of the singing and prophesying head (Euripides and iconography), and the beginnings of the analysis of the prehistory of music and literature, where Orpheus headed many a list.

Known accounts allow us to conclude that the crucial link between Orpheus and Lesbos was Terpander. It is irrelevant if Timotheus was the first to form such a pairing, or if it was an older phenomenon, already widespread among kitharodes. Of crucial importance is the linking of Terpander and Lesbos to Orpheus as the predecessor of kitharodia. It bears mentioning that Terpander's key role in the affair is particularly highlighted by the original placement of the tomb of Orpheus in Antissa, the musician's home city. Only after the fall of Antissa in the second century was the tomb tied to Methymna and Lesbos in general, and the entire tradition gained a different, broader dimension. Furthermore, one of the late stories has the lyre of Orpheus go directly into the hands of Terpander as his successor: 'After Orpheus was killed by the Thracian women his lyre was hurled into the sea and washed up at Antissa, a city of Lesbos. Fisherman found the lyre and brought it to Terpander, and he brought it to Egypt.'[23] Taking into account the exceptional popularity of Timotheus's poetry in the fourth and third-centuries it is possible that the kitharodic nomos *The Persians* may have been the point of origin for the entire innovation in question.[24]

If, then, even the earliest accounts of the tomb and of the ties between Lesbos and Orpheus only appear by the early third century, the tomb in Antissa should be dated to a period not earlier than the fourth century, or even the second half of it. Such an innovation fits patterns characteristic for the late Classical period and could be linked to a need to create places of memory associated with great creators of the past to build the cultural capital of the local community.[25] Moreover, the story of the dismemberment of the hero's body and the burial of his head on Lesbos allow for the existence of several 'graves' and for various body parts to have been buried in different locations. As Ovid says in his description of the death of Orpheus (*Met.* 11, 50): *membra iacent diversa locis* ('his limbs were scattered to diverse places'). In this way, the Lesbian tradition inadvertently confirms the existence of another tomb of the hero, placed in Pieria by most sources.

Pieria: Tomb, statues and cult

The Pierian tomb is one of the most important elements of the ancient narratives of Orpheus, but it has failed to attract commensurate attention from researchers. This is in part due to the extraordinary spread of accounts that need to be painstakingly rearranged into a cohesive picture. However, it is a picture that is possible to recreate, and the results are of remarkable importance to our knowledge of the hero, ancient mythographic practices and Macedonian cultural policy. Therefore, we shall now examine the sources depicting the tomb, statues and worship of Orpheus in Pieria.

Epitaphs, tomb

Let us begin by recalling the *testimonium* of Eratosthenes, who, in *Catasterismoi*, placed the burial of the pieces of the hero's torn body in Pieria. This geographical choice does not appear to be his own invention, but rather a result of extensive reading, and thus the entry of Orpheus' Macedonian tradition into the mythographic mainstream. Since the Hellenistic period, if not earlier, it was clear that the hero was buried in Macedonia. The hero's burial and grave are also associated with the epitaphs, starting with the oldest one, quoted by Alcidamas and already discussed in Chapter 2.[26] Although that inscription contains no information about the place of burial, Diogenes Laertius (1,5) introduces a very similar epitaph with the following: 'According to the epitaph at Dium in Macedonia, he was slain by a bolt of lightning; it says as follows etc.' The epitaph quoted by Diogenes repeats two lines from Alcidamas' epigram and both include the same motif of punishment from Zeus. It is therefore possible that the epigram quoted by Alcidamas was connected to the Pierian tradition in some way, or, at least, proved its existence. This burial site is also suggested by the epigram by Damagetus, a third-century poet, who placed the death of the hero near Olympus (παρὰ προμολῇσιν Ὀλύμπου), and therefore in Pieria.[27] The same area can be inferred whenever tradition mentions the remains being buried by the Muses, as usually they are present there as Pierides.[28] Although the grave epigrams related to Orpheus have a clearly literary character, they also indicate broader mythographic tendencies and the spread of certain ideas on the geography and narrative of the myth in the fourth and third-centuries. They allow for the cautious conclusion that the tradition of Orpheus' burial in Pieria dates at least to the fourth century.

The broadest descriptions of Orpheus' tomb in Pieria come from late authors, however; especially Conon and Pausanias. Conon (45) not only presents the tomb, but also gives us a story of a plague, of a travelling head, and of the establishment of the hero's cult. The tale draws on other narratives, merging plots (head on Lesbos), characters (Orpheus and Homer, Thracians and Macedonians), and places (Pieria–Meles River). We shall return to his account when discussing the cult of Orpheus.

The most informative story of the Pierian tomb is found in Pausanias (9,30) when he describes the statue of Orpheus in the sanctuary of the Muses at the foot of Helicon. In his erudite narration, the writer provides four distinct versions of the hero's death, two of which are connected to Pieria. The first is introduced by the clause 'The Macedonians who dwell in the district below Mount Pieria and the city of Dium say'. The other tale, meanwhile, is attributed to a 'friend from Larisa', that is, from nearby Thessaly. Both versions indicate a strong local tradition known beyond the borders of Macedon.

The first account (9,30,7–8) connects the tomb to the territory of the Macedonian polis of Dion; it probably originated in the Imperial period, after the destruction of Leibethra.[29] This story is probably a reprocessed legend from Leibethra, adapted to new circumstances surrounding the emergence of the tomb. The narrative regarding Dion is very detailed and we can see how the myth was placed in the particular features of the natural environment of the city (the rivers Bephyra and Helicon).[30] We have already seen a similar instance of the translation of grave and cult in the case of Orpheus' grave on Lesbos (relocated from Antissa to Methymna). The second story, discussing the original tomb in Leibethra (9,30,9–11), focuses on the destruction of the city and explains the circumstances in which the remains and the grave were moved to Dion. Both accounts unequivocally indicate the existence of a tomb of Orpheus in Pieria and even make reference to its magical power.[31] We must, of course, be aware that Pausanias' *testimonium* and its details are relatively late. However, Pieria was postulated as the hero's place of rest by many other, earlier accounts. Some of them, like the proverb about Leibethrians and the passages from Eratosthenes and Conon, clearly indicate the tomb was located specifically in Leibethra. This indicates that the Pierian city was tied to the death of Orpheus and could have been the location of his grave no later than the fourth century.

The analysed accounts can finally be compared to the information of Strabo (7, fr. 10). The geographer describes Orpheus living in Pimpleia as a charlatan and religious leader, killed in a political riot. This story was undoubtedly influenced by the narrative of the fall of the Pythagorean brotherhood and the death of Pythagoras. As such, it confirms Orpheus' connection to Pieria and Macedonia. Considering the existence of the tomb of Pythagoras in Italy and the probable worship of the philosopher, it is possible that the parallelism of lives and deaths may be proof of Orpheus' tomb as well.[32]

Statues and worship

Support for the early dating of the tomb in Leibethra can be found in the information about the statue of Orpheus in the city. All known accounts of it refer to events during the reign of Alexander the Great, allowing for the dating of the phenomenon to the second half of the fourth century. Alongside epitaphs, mythographic and literary mentions of death, and late accounts of the Pierian grave, the information about the statue creates a set of arguments favouring the existence of a local Pierian tradition and a cult of Orpheus in the Classical period.

Plutarch's *Life of Alexander* (14,5) describes the miracles that took place at the beginning of the king's campaign:

Moreover, when he set out upon his expedition, it appears that there were many signs from heaven, and, among them, the image of Orpheus at Leibethra (it was made of cypress-wood) sweated profusely at about that time. Most people feared the sign, but Aristander bade Alexander be of good cheer, assured that he was to perform deeds worthy of song and story, which would cost poets and musicians much toil and sweat to celebrate.

Translated by B. Perrin

Sweating statues are a relatively frequent motif in ancient tradition and are linked with unusual events.[33] In turn, the useful explanation by the seer Aristander indicates the role of Orpheus in Leibethra as the first poet and musician, tying it into the function of literature as a means of commemoration and glorification. This reference to the hero in the context of Alexander's invasion of Asia indicates the tomb and worship were associated with *mousikē*, rather than associations of men and mysterious initiations, as Graf (1987) suggested. The same story of Orpheus' statue is presented by Arrian (*Anab.* 1,11,2) in his story of sacrifices made by Alexander on the eve of the campaign. According to him, the king also organised a competition dedicated to the Muses on that occasion, likely in Dion. During the competition, news broke that the statue of Orpheus in Pieria was sweating. This is followed by the interpretation of the event by Aristander, similar to that presented in Plutarch's work.

The third account comes from Pseudo-Callisthenes' *Historia Alexandri Magni* (1,42):

Then he went to the Pierian city of Bebrycia where there was a temple and a statue of Orpheus and standing near him the Pierian Muses and the wild beasts. And when Alexander looked at the statue of Orpheus, the wooden image sweat on the forehead and the whole body. When Alexander asked what this sign meant, the soothsayer Melampus said to him (...).

Translated by E. H. Haight

A comparison to the first two versions and basic geography suggest that either the story or the text itself have been distorted.[34] Aristander was replaced with Melampus, while the statue itself sweats in Alexander's immediate presence, making the story more dramatic. Geographic references are doubtful, as everything takes place in the 'Pierian city of Bebrycia'. In this way, the story appears to connect a reference to Macedonian Pieria with the land of the

Bebryces, a Thracian tribe inhabiting the area near Lampsacus in Asia Minor. However, a deformed narration does not necessarily imply the episode is of 'fictitious nature', as Nawotka states in his commentary, nor does it mean that in this form it does not have much in common with the information relayed by Plutarch and Arrian. Firstly, distortion of geographic references is somewhat frequent in the sources.[35] The choice of Bebrycia as the setting is justified by the region's ties to Alexander and Orpheus: the area lies on Alexander's route to Asia and is important in the story of the journey of the *Argo*, which Orpheus participated in (Apollod. 1,119). The presence of Pieria in the description of the miracle suggests that the 'Pierian city of Bebrycia' was 'Leibethra in Pieria' before the change set in. In turn, the use of the name Melampus over Aristander, mentioned by Plutarch and Arrian, is most likely a reference to the mythical Melampus (Apollod. 1,96–103), one of the most famous seers in Greek myth. The entire modification appears to be a typical case of bricolage by someone not fully in command of the text or seeking to alter it somehow, and thus making use of a set of mythical (Melampus, Orpheus, route of the *Argo*) and historical (Alexander and his route) stories known to himself and his audience.

The base of the Pseudo-Callisthenes' story matches the accounts of the miracle by Plutarch and Arrian. However, from our point of view, the problematic location is less important than the description of the statue. Unlike the other two authors, Pseudo-Callisthenes does not limit himself to a laconic remark, but presents an entire statuary group including a monument of Orpheus surrounded by animals and statues of the Muses. The collection is linked by a temple to Orpheus, which the writer mentions explicitly: 'There was a temple and a statue of Orpheus, and standing near him the Pierian Muses and the wild beasts.'

Orpheus is presented in a way that, once more, highlights his profession and unique musical ability. This is congruent with his mythical portrayal as a musician. A similar group of statues (Orpheus surrounded by animals) was also included in the descriptions of the sanctuary of the Muses near Helicon.[36] It is therefore highly likely that a portrayal of this type would also be found in Pieria, the traditional setting for the hero's musical activity. Pseudo-Callisthenes' description surrounds Orpheus with Muses as well, which perfectly fits into the presented context for the erection of the monuments. The goddesses are at home in Pieria, one of them is the hero's mother, and Orpheus was born in the same place as they were (Call. *h.* 4,7): in Pierian Pimpleia. Additionally, Arrian mentions the statue of Orpheus in the context of a festival (*Olympia*) held by Alexander and a competition dedicated to the Muses in Pieria. All this provides a solid basis for presuming the information about a statuary group in Pieria is not only acceptable, but greatly probable.

All three accounts complement each other and are not strictly contradictory. We may therefore assume that Pierian Leibethra (Plutarch) had not only a wooden (Plutarch) statue of Orpheus (Plutarch, Arrian, Ps.-Callisthenes), but an entire statuary group depicting Muses and animals surrounding the musician (Ps.-Callisthenes). This was connected to the temple of the hero which existed in the town (Ps.-Callisthenes, Conon below). The sweating of the statue was considered miraculous, requiring an explanation from a seer, as confirmed by all three sources. It is possible that Plutarch and Arrian focused on the sweating statue of Orpheus for brevity, while Ps.-Callisthenes, for some reason, perhaps even following another source, relayed more extensive information about the entire statuary group. In its basic shape, the story is almost identical in all cases, only differing in the details.

Inasmuch as the matter of the statue and its surroundings appears relatively straightforward, the issue of the temple is more difficult to assess. Neither Plutarch nor Arrian mention the sanctuary and the cult, and the statue they describe may have appeared in any context, even non-religious. However, the silence of the writers does not prove the absence of a cult of Orpheus in Pieria. Both historians abbreviate their accounts, as their focus is on Alexander and his campaign, not on the context for the placement of the statue. Naturally, the credibility of Ps.-Callisthenes may be doubtful, as some elements of his story have been distorted. Could this not also apply to the temple and worship of Orpheus? It appears, however, that the *Historia Alexandri Magni* is not the only account to mention a temple to Orpheus.

The account by Conon describes the emergence of the tomb, worship and the temple to Orpheus in Leibethra. The importance of this information demands a more in-depth look at the author himself. He is usually considered a late-first-century grammarian, paradoxographer and mythographer, but these are conclusions drawn entirely from the reading of his work, as no ancient source (except for Photius, who quotes him) provides any information about him. His *Diegeseis* (*Narrations*), dedicated to Cappadocian king

Archelaus Philopator, was a collection of erudite excerpts from the works of his predecessors, containing fifty narratives of the mythical and heroic period.[37] Most of them are obscure local myths and legends, and more than fifteen are foundational myths. Moreover, many of them contain aitiologies, and some emphasise myths set in Thrace or its environs. The work only survives in a précis by the Patriarch Photius (*Bibl.* 186), complicating the analysis of the original contents of the work. However, a papyrus of parts 46 and 47 of the work confirms that the narratives were quite brief and Photius' version was not a drastic alteration.[38]

A general assessment of the *Narrations* has to highlight the literary, compilatory nature of the collection, and a clear influence of lost Hellenistic originals on the selection and form of specific stories. Considering the author's ties to the kingdom of Cappadocia, located on the periphery of the Greek world, the versions of the myth he presents had to be very widespread. His work was written after erudite study and was intended to appeal to the ruler and Cappadocian elites. One of the stories (45) is quite detailed of Orpheus, and especially the causes and circumstances of his death. The hero was killed in Leibethra by women (Thracian and Macedonian), and in consequence an oracle orders his head to be buried. The head is found thanks to a fisherman from the mouth of the Meles River, after which:

> So they took it and buried it under a large mound, and enclosed it with a sacred precinct that for a time was a hero-shrine but later came into vogue as a temple. For it is honoured with sacrifices and all other things with which gods are honoured; but it is completely forbidden for women to enter.
>
> Translated by M. K. Brown

The level of detail in the description of the cult and its development might be surprising for a collection of excerpts of wondrous tales. A closer examination of *Narrations* as a whole reveals, however, that there are more than a dozen similar aitiological stories explaining the origins of festivals, temples or tombs. An example of a tomb that had become, like Orpheus', the starting point of a temple and worship can be found in story 17 (Heracles in Italy).[39] Apparently such details were an important part of Conon's text, allowing him to link mythical events to socioreligious institutions and the given city or place. How credible is the information from Conon? Heinrichs (1987) demonstrated some time ago that Conon's aitiologies may be based on real socioreligious phenomena. The chief example for it is the story of ritual abuse customarily exchanged between male and female worshippers of Apollo Aiglatas/Asgelatas on the island of Anaphe, as his description is corroborated by other accounts.[40] This means there is a high likelihood that the author was equally meticulous in other similar instances and his aitiologies were motivated by the reality of religious worship at a site. This presents two important conclusions for the analysis of the presence of the grave and worship of Orpheus in Pieria. Firstly, Conon, acting partly as a compiler, confirms the existence of earlier writings mentioning the existence of a local, Pierian cult tradition placing the tomb and worship of Orpheus in Leibethra. Its source may have been, for instance, Nicomedes of Acanthus, author of *About Orpheus* (OF 1130T), known from Athenaeus (14,637a). Secondly, Conons narrative is congruent with Pseudo-Callisthenes' description of the temple of Orpheus in Pieria. Considering that the worship on Anaphe was corroborated by other source material, it appears likely that Conon's information on Leibethra may have been rooted in Macedonian religious practice.

When contrasted with the *testimonium* of Pausanias (9,30), Conon's account differs in some details, giving reason for confusion. The Periegete describes a column with an urn in the tomb site and mentions a shepherd who, having fallen asleep against the grave, began to sing the songs of Orpheus. There is no great tomb, no temenos or heroon, no temple or statues. Were they removed since Conon's time? It would be somewhat surprising, as Orpheus was a popular character in the Imperial period. This discrepancy could be explained by the fall of Leibethra (late first century) and the move of the tomb to Dion, which Pausanias himself mentions (9,30,11). His description may be merely a distant echo of the Leibethran cult, and the details he describes could be the result of the appearance of another grave in the Macedonian city of Dion. In any event, the story clearly confirms the existence of a tomb in Macedonia and does not contradict Conon or Pseudo-Callisthenes in regard to temple and worship.

In summary, there are many accounts indirectly indicating a tomb in Pieria – descriptions of death or burial of Orpheus, epitaphs or statues. Some relatively late *testimonia* with sources dating at least to the Hellenistic period explicitly mention a tomb and cult of Orpheus in Pieria (in Leibethra and later in Dion). In their totality, they make the existence of a tomb of Orpheus in Macedonia very probable.

How can this phenomenon be dated and reconstructed based on available accounts? The tradition of Orpheus' death in Leibethra, known from Menaechmus, the proverb of Leibethrians, and other sources, undoubtedly originated in the Classical period. Most *testimonia* suggest at least the fourth century, which is congruent with the information about the existence of a statue of the hero in Leibethra during Alexander's time. Incontrovertible, verified information about the tomb, temple or cult is attested relatively late, as seen above. However, considering the widespread tradition of the hero's death in Pieria, the fourth-century mention of statues, and the accounts of Conon, Pausanias and Pseudo-Callisthenes, there are grounds to believe that the phenomenon appeared early and evolved over time. This is indicated particularly well by Conon's detailed story, rooted at least in the Hellenistic period. Pausanias' mention of the destruction of Leibethra serves to explain the changes after the tomb was moved to Dion, but also proves the endurance and significance of this phenomenon for the Macedonians. In line with this data, the most likely dating for the tomb of Orpheus is between the fifth and the third century. The lower boundary is based on the assumption that religious innovation of this kind is unlikely after the fall of Macedon in the second century. Considering that the statue is attested for the fourth century makes the dating to fifth-fourth-centuries more likely. The upper boundary, meanwhile, is based on the assumption that phenomena attested in the fourth century may have appeared earlier. Moreover, early *testimonia* of Euripides and Timotheus, discussed in Chapter 3, indisputably confirm the ties of Orpheus to Pieria in the late fifth century. This matter will be discussed further in the next chapter.

These accounts and their evaluation are not the extent of the analysis. It is clear that early *testimonia* are ambiguous, and evidence for the tomb and the cult only appears at the end of the Hellenistic period. In this situation, it becomes important to look more broadly at the Classical period to find a context explaining these innovations. Could the Pierian tomb of Orpheus as the first mythical musician have any parallels in other places throughout the Greek world? What cultural needs was this socioreligious innovation an answer to? Finally, what functions can be ascribed to the introduction of worship and construction of tombs of poets and musicians?

In search of parallels, the next part of this chapter will focus on related and spatially near phenomena (the cult of Rhesus in Amphipolis), other mythical musicians (Linus, Musaeus, Thamyris) and on the so-called cult of poets in general (Archilochus, forms of worship). This will be followed with final remarks on the phenomenon of appropriating the memory of poets/musicians, as it reflects contemporaneous interest in the origins of *mousikē* and literature in Greek culture. The placement of source information in this broader cultural framing allows for connecting the investigated phenomenon to period culture and a more precise dating of Macedonian innovations related to Orpheus.

Contexts

An interesting parallel for Orpheus' tomb in Leibethra is first and foremost the tomb and cult of Rhesus in Amphipolis, a city on the fringe of Macedonian influence.[41] The hero's remains brought back from Troy were the subject of a colourful story tied to Athenian attempts at conquering the politically and economically vital Strymon valley. According to Polyaenus (*Strat.* 6,54), in 436/7 BC, faced with a troubled relationship with local Thracians, Hagnon, the leader of the Athenian colonisation effort, sent men to Troy to dig up Rhesus' remains at night and bring them to Thrace.[42] Hagnon order them buried on the banks of Strymon and within three nights he had a walled settlement built around the grave and resisting Thracian assaults.[43] Polyaenus' information about the cult of Rhesus is corroborated by late-fourth-century author Marsyas of Pella (BNJ 136 F7), who mentions a temple to Muse Clio, mother of the hero, and a tomb of Rhesus on a hill near Amphipolis. The historian's story is also supported by archaeological discoveries, as the remains of the foundations of the temple of Clio date to the fifth century.[44] The hero's tomb and worship, as well as that of his mother the Muse, is in many ways similar to what we know of Orpheus' tomb in Pieria. Without disregarding the religious aspects of the cult, it has to be said that when introduced, this innovation was clearly political and propagandistic in nature. Judging by the story, it appears to have played a key role in the consolidation of the settler group and provided justification for their actions. Of course, Orpheus was not a typical hero, like Rhesus, and his grave transcended the phenomena associated with the cult of heroes, which first appeared in the Archaic period. Orpheus was the first (although mythical) musician and poet and phenomena associated with him stood at the intersection of Archaic and Classical culture. Allusions to him also express a consideration of the beginnings of *mousikē*, and his grave is closer to the cult of poets, a phenomenon that will be examined more extensively now.[45]

Cult of poets

The most famous instances of the cult of poets include primarily the graves and worship of Homer and Hesiod.[46] Between the fifth and third-centuries, there were also cases of various forms of worship of other intellectuals, such as Socrates, Pythagoras, Plato, Euripides, Aeschylus, Sophocles, Pindar, Stesichorus, Archilochus, Sappho or Simonides.[47] Some of these examples involve tombs, others statues, and some only mementos, associated locations, or worshipped 'originals' of their works.[48] The phenomenon experienced dynamic development particularly during the Hellenistic period, as seen in the cult of Philitas on Cos or the *Homereia* present in various Greek cities, starting with Alexandria.[49] The case in question here is Archilochus' heroon (fourth-third-centuries), which is the best-attested instance and bears many similarities to the tomb of Orpheus. The famous Mnesiepes inscription (third century) informs us that during the Hellenistic period, a hero cult of Archilochus, originally dating most likely to the fourth century, was reorganised on Paros.[50] At the site considered the poet's burial place, altars were set for sacrifices to Apollo Musagetes, the Muses, Mnemosyne and Archilochus. The altars were probably flanked by the statues of those gods and a depiction of the poet, as was the case in similar locations. The existence of a statue of Archilochus is also indicated by a first-century Paros coin depicting the poet sitting.[51]

The worship arrangement in the *Archilocheion* is very similar to the descriptions of Orpheus' statue and heroon in Pieria, especially under the assumption that the cult of Orpheus there was strongly connected to the cult of the Muses. Pseudo-Callisthenes' mention (1,42) of a statuary group with animals and statues of the Muses, and the possible links between the statue of Orpheus and a festival of Zeus and the Muses in Dion, as seen in Arrian (1,11,2), are therefore very relevant here.

A similar configuration – a poet, the Muses, Apollo – can also be found in Epidauros. Importantly, this is a worship site of another mythical poet, Linus. This example dates to early fourth century and is well-attested in inscriptions and material remains, such as altars and statue bases.[52] The altar (and probably statue) of Linus was placed in the shrine of Apollo Maleatas, which in the fifth century became a part of the sanctuary of Asclepius in Epidauros. The shrine of Apollo also housed altars (and probably statues) of the Muses and Apollo Musagetes. Moreover, Plato's *Ion* (530) mentions that a local Asclepieion hosted a rhapsody agon in the late fifth century. It appears that the cult of Linus, the Muses and Apollo Musagetes was related to the aforementioned musical competitions and other such events were organised there as well, including kitharode contests.

Linus' close ties to the Muses are also attested in their Thespian shrine, where sacrifices were made to the hero before sacrifices to the Muses (Paus. 9,29,6). The cult of the Muses there dates from the fourth century at the latest, making it also chronologically parallel to the worship of Orpheus in Macedonia.

Another noteworthy case is the tomb of Musaeus on the *Mouseion* hill in Athens. The hill itself is not particularly well-researched,[53] as it is only known from a brief remark by Pausanias, which presents Imperial-period depictions and gives us more questions than it answers (1,25,8):

> After freeing the Athenians from tyrants Demetrius, the son of Antigonus did not restore the Peiraeus to them immediately after the flight of Lachares, but subsequently overcame them and brought a garrison even into the upper city, fortifying the place called the Museum. This is a hill right opposite the Acropolis within the old city boundaries, where legend says Musaeus used to sing, and, dying of old age, was buried. Afterwards a monument also was erected here to a Syrian. At the time to which I refer Demetrius fortified and held it.
>
> Translated by W. H. S. Jones

The first, crucial element is the name of the hill. In theory, considering the broad meaning of the term *mouseion*, it should mean 'a place related to the Muses' or even 'dedicated to the Muses'.[54] However, if it was the place of worship of the goddesses, and especially if there was a temple of the Muses there, Pausanias would likely have mentioned that. Instead, he only notes that the hill was associated with Musaeus, who sang and died there. A heroon of Musaeus was also shown on the hillside, meaning that *mouseion* as a 'place protected by the Muses' could also have been interpreted as a place of musical activity, and later on of the worship of the 'son of the Muses'.[55]

Another hypothesis worth considering is that the Athenian hill of the Muses was linked to the tomb of Musaeus, as the hero was considered an ancestor of Homer and Hesiod by Athenians.[56] Thus, the place may have competed with Pieria and Helicon as places related to the Muses and musicians such as Orpheus and Linus. It would therefore be the local, Athenian birthplace of *mousikē*, while Musaeus would be the 'local Orpheus'.[57]

Besides the aforementioned instances, there are many more accounts for the existence of the cult of historical and mythical poets. Importantly, this phenomenon reaches far beyond traditionally understood religiosity and is not limited to hero worship.[58] Extant sources indicate that commemoration of exceptional individuals took many forms, from collecting mementos, as with Dionysius I and the mementos of Euripides,[59] through tombs as places of memory (*mnemeia*),[60] statues in city centres,[61] commemorative practices such as feasts on anniversaries of death[62] and pilgrimages to grave sites,[63] to hero cult and apotheosis, as in the case of Homer on the Archelaus relief.[64] The broad spectrum of commemoration and public honouring of outstanding individuals, both living and dead, is exemplified well in the following passage from Aristotle's *Rhetoric* (1,5,1361a. 34–6):

> The components of honor are sacrifices [made to the benefactor after death], memorial inscriptions in verse or prose, receipt of special awards, grants of land, front seats at festivals, burial at the public expense, statues, free food in the state dining room.
>
> Translated by G. A. Kennedy

One of the first examples of change in Greek mentality in over the fifth and fourth-centuries could be Gorgias erecting his own statue in Olympia, expressing the sophist's pride in his intellect and teaching ability.[65] The change of attitude towards the poets and philosophers between the fifth and third-centuries can only be properly described by first examining the change in the range of individuals that could be granted public honours. After the late fifth century, such distinctions were given not only to politicians and commanders, but also to exceptional intellectuals. This change, to put it briefly, was the result of an unprecedented appreciation for intellectual skill in Classical Greek culture, which would later cause the emergence of intellectuals as a new social identity in the fourth century.[66]

For example, when the famous grave epigram of the tragedian Aeschylus was originally written in the mid-fifth century, it only included references to his civic functions and the defence of the country against the Persians. The poet says that 'the famous grove of Marathon could tell his courage and the long-haired Mede knew it well' (*Vita* 11).[67] However, just two centuries later, Poseidippus demands in one of his poems (118 AB) to be given a statue of himself in the agora, at the political centre of the polis, exclusively because of his fame as a poet. The emancipation of intellectuals and their appreciation in the public sphere are also seen in iconography. Zanker (1995) has demonstrated long ago how far the Greeks went from the statue of Anacreon as the perfect citizen to the typical depiction of poet or philosopher in the third century.

An interest in Orpheus, Linus or Musaeus, the mythical musicians at the beginning of the Greek cultural tradition, expresses the same tendencies in a different way. It reflects an interest in past creators and a reflection over the origins of culture. Indirectly, it also results from the development of education in the fifth and fourth-centuries and from the Greeks' reckoning with their own mythical and literary tradition. One of the symptoms of the change, other than the cult of poets, would be the development of the biographical tradition.[68] Places, items and texts of an author would breed stories that later became an integral part of the Greek cultural tradition.[69] Bing (1993, 620) thus popularised the term 'memorialising impulse,' which expresses a tendency to commemorate and create select elements of the portrayal of the Greek cultural past. This socially important phenomenon would assume many forms, occasionally leading to the fabrication of items related to cultural heroes, discovery of the graves of mythical or legendary poets around one's city, and creation of (new) stories about them.

Stories and 'territories': appropriating mythical poets

The cult of poets also has an aspect related to the spatial appropriation and competition over the shares of the common cultural memory of the Greeks.[70] As part of the debate over the mythical tradition and because of the intensifying struggle to control it, many sixth and fifth-centuries Greek cities attempted to 'secure' various heroes. This meant modifying narratives of known figures and supplementing them with previously unheard narrative threads. The tombs of such heroes were placed within one's own polis, and sometimes were accompanied with regular worship and sacrifices. Examples of this are commonly known and there is no need to describe them in detail here.[71]

An important part of that phenomenon in the Classical period was also the worship of mythical musicians and the most ancient of poets. Its dynamic development was seen in the competition between cities to control traditions, burial sites or works of famous creators. The cities made references to mythical and literary traditions in order to redefine themselves and win as much space on the cultural map of the Greek world as possible. As phrased by Diskin Clay (2004, 94): 'desire for the autonomy of fame increased as political independence became a distant memory (...) the rivalry involved in the cult of poets and philosophers (what we would term "intellectuals") becomes intense as other forms of rivalry are excluded. Cities honor themselves by honoring the great men and women of their distant past.'

Alterations to the ethnic and spatial allegiance of these 'cultural heroes' made according to the shifting cultural needs and political circumstances can be seen particularly clearly in the cases of mythical musicians. The following will highlight such cases of appropriating memory, as they involve a cultural context very similar to the 'Pierisation' of Orpheus. To quote the famous epigram about the dispute over Homer's origins (*AP* 16,297):[72]

> Seven cities contend for the birth of Homer:
> Kyme, Smyrna, Chios, Kolophon, Pylos, Argos and Athens.

This brief text is not only a good example of biographical difficulty, but also evidence for many contradictory local traditions.[73] The multitude of places related to Homer stems from the complete lack of knowledge about his life on the one hand, and from the process of spatial appropriation and use of his 'biography' for ideological and political aims on the other. The situation of mythical musicians, such as Thamyris, Musaeus or Linus, was very similar.

Thamyris has usually been viewed as simply a Thracian, as that is how Homer describes him in the *Iliad*.[74] However, one of Conon's stories (7) depicts him as originally Athenian. In this version, he was the son of Philammon, who was the grandson of Eosphorus and Cleoboa from the Athenian deme of

Thoricus. His mother, according to the story, was a local nymph; embarrassed by her pregnancy, she had gone to Acte and given birth there. This journey would therefore be the only reason for his links to Thrace, which were continued in the episode that followed: 'after becoming a young man attained such skill in kithara-playing that the Scythians made him their king, even though he was a foreigner' [tr. K. Brown]. Scythia stands here for the North in general, that is, areas identified with Thrace in some way. Incidentally, Thamyris' career was remarkably similar to how Orpheus would gain power over Thracians and Macedonians in Conon's forty-fifth story. In Thamyris' case, the author stresses he was a foreigner when becoming king, not a Thracian or Scythian.

Musaeus may be another case of a 'localised' hero. While we cannot be certain due to the state of sources, there are many indications that he was a regional Athenian copy of Orpheus or Linus, only appearing in the late sixth century.[75] His name is generic and links him more closely to the Muses than in the case of his 'older colleagues'; he is 'musical' or 'coming from the Muses' by nature, and those qualifications are only reinforced by his tomb on the *Mouseion* hill in the centre of Athens. Although later sources present various, frequently surprising explanations for his origins, his ties to Athens are the earliest and strongest tradition (see [Eur.] *Rhes.* 945–7). Additionally, Gorgias (82 B25 DK) believed that Homer's and Hesiod's lineage should have been traced from Musaeus (and so, in a way, from Athens).

The third and most interesting case is that of Linus. For various reasons, the hero was never given as much attention as Orpheus was, but it appears that in Antiquity he may have been more popular than the Pierian musician, especially in certain parts of the Greek world. This is indicated by the many traditions tying him to Euboea, Boeotia or Argos, as well as his cult in Epidauros and the Valley of the Muses, which have been discussed already.[76] Of note is also that he was never depicted as Thracian, directly contradicting Strabo's argumentation and the claims of Graf that the Thracianness of mythical musicians was inherently tied to the perception of *mousikē* and poetry in Greek culture.

The most famous tradition has Linus educating Heracles and dying at the hand of his wrathful student. However, it appears that his inclusion in this story also served to link him to Thebes, Heracles' home city. Apparently the ties between Linus and Boeotia were not entirely obvious. As explained by Apollodorus in *Library* (2,63):

Heracles was taught (...) and to play the lyre by Linos, who was Orpheus' brother. After Linos had come to Thebes and become a Theban, he was slain by Heracles, who hit him with his lyre (Heracles killed him in a fit of rage because Linos had punished him by striking him).

Translated by R. S. Smith and S. M. Trzaskoma

This version of the myth presents Linus as the brother of Orpheus in an easy-to-miss detail. The genealogy is also present in another passage from Apollodorus (1,14) and in the writings of Asclepiades of Tragilus (schol. Eur. *Rhes*. 895). The latter instance indicates that links between the musicians had appeared in Athenian theatre (Asclepiades' work was a collection of mythical narratives featured in tragedies) probably as early as the late fifth century. Considering that Orpheus had already been a hero from Pieria at the time, as demonstrated by passages from Euripides and Timotheus, it should be assumed his brother had a similar background.

Another *testimonium* ties Linus to Macedonia and Orpheus more clearly. In the genealogy of Homer and Hesiod discussed in Chapter 5, 'Genealogies of Orpheus', Linus was the son of Apollo and father of Pierus, eponym of Pieria, making him the great-grandfather of Orpheus. The analysis attempted to demonstrate that this version of his lineage may have originated in the late fifth century and be related to the activity of Hellanicus of Lesbos. Both accounts suggests that a pro-Macedonian, or perhaps local Pierian version of the story of the birth of *mousikē* in Pieria appeared in the fifth to fourth-centuries. It tied the so-called 'sons of the Muses' (Paus. 9,29,4), or at least Orpheus and Linus, to the region.

This information may shed some light on a mysterious testimony by Pausanias. When describing the sanctuary in the Valley of the Muses near Helicon, he mentions a somewhat unique depiction of Linus and sacrifices to him (9,29,6):

So her portrait is here (sc. Eupheme), and after it is Linus on a small rock worked into the shape of a cave.[77] To Linus every year they sacrifice as to a hero before they sacrifice to the Muses. It is said that this Linus was a son of Urania and Amphimarus, a son of Poseidon, that he won a reputation for music greater than that of any contemporary or predecessor, and that Apollo killed him for being his rival in singing.

Translated by W. H. S. Jones

The Valley of the Muses also had a statue of Orpheus, but it does not seem to have played a significant role in the worship of the Heliconian goddesses. The local hierarchy of mythical poets considered Linus, as 'Boeotian', to have been the son of the Muse(s) *par excellence*. As explained by Pausanias, the hero had 'won a reputation for music greater than that of any contemporary or predecessor'. Betsy Robinson (2012) interprets that information as proof of a rivalry between the centres of Muse worship in Helicon and in Dion in Pieria. The tension between the two traditions (Boeotian/Heliconian and Macedonian/Pierian) is also visible in other Ancient sources.

At the same time, as seen above, some *testimonia* indicate a familial relationship between Linus and Orpheus. This implies a mythical tradition where Linus was as Pierian (and Macedonian) by birth as Orpheus was. This thread, meanwhile, would explain the further part of the passage from Pausanias, where the Periegete complements the basic information about Linus with a detail related to his tomb in Boeotia (9,29,8–9):

> The Thebans assert that Linus was buried among them, and that after the Greek defeat at Chaeroneia, Philip the son of Amyntas, in obedience to a vision in a dream, took up the bones of Linus and conveyed them to Macedonia; other visions induced him to send the bones of Linus back to Thebes. But all that was over the grave, and whatever marks were on it, vanished, they say, with the lapse of time.[78]
>
> Translated by W. H. S. Jones

Pausanias' story has many similarities to other such narrations, such as supernatural signs (dreams, droughts, oracles)[79] and the translation and burial of the corpse of a hero in a new location.[80] Nevertheless, it is commonly considered completely fictitious. As noted by Schachter, 'This story is not to be taken seriously: it depends on the literary tradition of Linos as the unfortunate music teacher of Herakles. There is no evidence for a cult.'[81] The scholars assume that the story of Linus' death at the hand of Heracles appeared first, and only later was it followed by the stories of his grave, potentially before the actual tomb site that was later exhibited near Thebes came to exist. It is true that there is little clear evidence in favour of a cult of Linus in Thebes, but it is well-attested in Epidauros and the Valley of the Muses near Thespiae. Considering the extensive mythical tradition[82] and the ties of Linus to Theban heroes (Heracles or Ismenius), the existence of a tomb and cult of the hero in Thebes appears nearly certain, especially in a period when Orpheus or Musaeus, not to mention Homer, Hesiod and other poets, also had such tombs.

Naturally, this does not mean that the events described by Pausanias must be straightforwardly true. However, there are grounds to consider them likely, chiefly because of the cult of Linus in Boeotia and similar cases of worship of other mythical musicians. The tale may be true on another level: it expresses an interest in Linus and mythical musicians by Macedonian rulers. In both cases, the story fits well into the reconstructed depiction of Macedonia as the land of the Muses, Orpheus and the cultural and religious cradle of Hellas. Philip II's decisions can be interpreted as propaganda and appear politically motivated, particularly when considering the Athenian case of the retrieval of the body of Rhesus from Troy to Amphipolis. Taken together, all of this renders the core of Pausanias' story probable: Macedonians made claims to 'Boeotian' Linus, whom they apparently considered their hero and the brother of Pierian Orpheus, and attempted to move his body back to Macedon.

So, there is not enough data to precisely reconstruct the circumstances in which Linus was linked to Boeotia and Thebes, or his ties to Macedonia. Evidently, however, the former are not as clear, nor the latter as vague, as has been thought. In neither case can there be talk of any natural ties of the hero to an area, as genealogies and tombs of mythical musicians result from ideological practice. They appear in a place only to change geographic coordinates and be altered as circumstances evolve. What can be followed in the sources is mostly the situations in which those changes happen, and for what reason. In ancient culture, the geographic appropriation of heroes and modifications of their narratives were a daily occurrence. Honouring the great men and women of the distant past allowed Greek cities to honour themselves and create a 'memory' of their origins (Clay 2004, 94).

Summary

As is often stressed, the Greeks saw a continuity between the mythical age and the historical times. This is also evidenced by the genealogy of Homer and Hesiod traced from Orpheus or Musaeus. Mythical musicians were considered primeval heroes, but also similar to early authors. Thus, the founding of the tomb of Orpheus or worship of Musaeus or Linus could be viewed as phenomena somewhere between the cult of heroes and the cult of poets such as Homer, Pindar or Aeschylus. In many ways, they answered the same questions about the origins of *mousikē* and the development of literary tradition.

The *testimonia* analysed in this chapter suggest that there was a grave and cult of Orpheus in Macedonia, and its endurance into the Imperial period demonstrates its significance to the people of Pieria. Late origins of some data points complicate dating, as early sources only indicate Pieria and Leibethra as the hero's place of death (proverb, Menaechmus). The earliest indication that these represent more than merely local stories are the mentions of the statue of Orpheus in Leibethra. Does this imply a real tomb and actual worship?

Reconstruction from sources is supported by the comparative material about the worship of Rhesus in Amphipolis, Linus in Epidauros and Thespiae, the tomb of Musaeus in Athens, and about the cult of poets/intellectuals in general, including the best-known case of the worship of Archilochus. The cult of poets appears in the second half of the fifth century and flourishes in the fourth and third-centuries, becoming one of the most important expressions of cultural rivalry between the Greek cities. An important aspect of this phenomenon was the spatial appropriation of poets, visible in alterations to biographies, as well as the appearance of tombs, statues and other material traces of a link between a distinguished individual and a specific location. One of the most interesting examples of the political and ideological role of mythical musicians may be the story of the attempted transfer of the remains of Linus to Macedonia. This obscure case of rivalry over a 'cultural saint' took place in the same area as the activity surrounding Orpheus' tomb. Indirectly, this is evidence of sizeable cultural activity by the Macedonians and of their participation in the Greek debate over the origins of *mousikē*.

These examples create a context that lends credibility to the entire informational construct regarding the tomb and worship of Orpheus in Pieria. What may have appeared an isolated and irrelevant case when supported by only a few accounts and the Pierian connections of Orpheus, when examined with this contextual knowledge seems to be a phenomenon characteristic of the period and attested in Macedon, even more so if taking into consideration credible information about the tombs and worship of other mythical musicians in Epidauros, Orchomenos, Thebes, and Athens. From this point of view, the dating of Orpheus' tomb to the fifth-fourth-centuries no longer seems like an unfounded hypothesis.

Coda: The two graves of Saint Adalbert

The mythical Orpheus had no less than three graves: one in Leibethra, one in Dion and one of his head on Lesbos. Petrarca, as befits an historical poet, only had one. However, even real figures occasionally had more than one grave and wandering body parts. One such case was Saint Adalbert of Prague, buried in both Gniezno and Prague. According to the *Vita Sancti Adalberti Pragensis*, he was murdered on 23 April 997, during a conversion mission in Prussia. His body was bought for its weight in gold by the Polish prince Boleslaus I and preserved in Gniezno. This decision helped increase Poland's political and diplomatic influence in Europe. In 1039, Duke Břetislav I of Bohemia looted the bones of Saint Adalbert from the Gniezno cathedral and moved them to Prague. However, according to Polish accounts, he stole the wrong body, and the true remains of the saint were found during the reconstruction of the cathedral in 1088. In 1127, his severed head was also found and taken to Gniezno. Today, Saint Adalbert has two elaborate shrines, one in Prague and one in Gniezno, both of which claim to possess his relics.[83]

This story is reminiscent of the history of the remains and tomb of Linus in Boeotia and the actions of Philip II, proving once more that 'invented traditions' always have a sociopolitical context and respond to vital needs of the period. Arguments over corpses and graves always implied a fight over memory and cultural capital, providing them a political and ideological dimension. However, ideology can also leave material traces, and tombs of mythical musicians surely belong in that category.

7

Mousikē, Identity and Ideology

In Book V of *Histories* (22), Herodotus describes the visit of the Macedonian king Alexander I to Olympia.¹ The ruler intended to compete in the games there, but his rivals protested his barbarian heritage. Alexander thus presented the *hellanodikai* with his genealogy, proving his house hailed from Argos and started with Temenus, the grandson of Heracles. As Herodotus presents it, 'Alexander proving himself to be an Argive, he was judged to be a Greek; so he contended in the furlong race and ran a dead heat for the first place' [tr. A. D. Godley]. This early account is interpreted as proof of Macedon's activity on the Panhellenic stage in the early fifth century and highlights the role of the myth as a political tool.

Macedon's specificity is that nearly all surviving stories about it relate to the royal house and the founding of the country. Another passage from the *Histories* (8,137–8) presents the narrative of the state's legendary founder, Perdiccas of Argos, and his two brothers, as descendants of Heracles. This genealogy is also supported by Thucydides (2,99), who writes about the origins of the Macedonian kings from the Temenids of Argos. Other versions mention the involvement of Archelaus or Caranus, but all focus on the origins of the dynasty and tie the Macedonian state to the Heraclids in one way or another.² In this way, the foundation stories highlight the role of Heracles. It appears that the relationship was important for reasons of ideology and propaganda: on the one hand, it tied the royal house to the hero's military skill; on the other, it included it in the mythical genealogy of the Greeks.³ According to these narratives, the ruler of Macedon was a legitimate descendant of the ancient royal house of Argos, personally connecting the Macedonian state to the Hellenic world.

Other explanations can be found in stories of the eponyms of Macedonian regions, who were certainly used to strengthen the sense of ethnic unity.⁴ Firstly, *The Catalogue of Women*, attributed to Hesiod (fr. 7) features Makedon, the son of Zeus and Thyia (daughter of Deucalion) and brother to Magnes.[5] Regardless of the debate over the role of the daughter of Deucalion in this genealogy, it clearly indicates the presence of the Macedonian eponym in Archaic-era mythology and his ties to the Hellenes. Moreover, the fragment from Ps.-Hesiod mentions that the two brothers lived in Pieria and near Olympus. Makedon is also mentioned by Hellanicus of Lesbos (BNJ 4 F74), who presents him as the son of Aeolus and grandson of Hellen. Both versions indicate ties to Greeks and Makedon's descent from Zeus. Other sources also feature eponyms of Emathia and Pieria.[6] The latter case is of particular interest here. Pieria already features in Homer (14,226) and in the Homeric hymns (4,71), but as no-man's land, only used by Apollo to graze his herds. However, in the fifth century, when Epicharmus (fr. 39 PCG) presents Pieria's eponym, he is tied to the Muses and *mousikē*.

Aside from the stories of the royal family and eponyms, Macedon is virtually absent from the Greek mythical and mythographical tradition. It does not feature at all in Apollodorus' *Library*, the only complete extant collection of myths; it seems removed from the Greek mythical geography, even though Apollodorus' compendium includes Epirus, Aetolia, Thrace, Egypt and even Persia and Media. Moreover, none of the important Macedonian cities, such as Dion, Aegae, Pella or Pydna, are connected to known mythical narratives. Any exceptions involve the history of the royal house, as is the case with Aegae (Iust. 7,1). In this context, the proposition of Orpheus' connection to Macedonia, and Pieria specifically, appears a promising subject of research.

The following will gather and recapitulate the conclusions of the analyses presented in previous chapters and attempt to propose a chronology for the Pierian tradition and for Orpheus' tomb and worship in Pieria. Then it will focus on the search for the cultural context and especially for the political and ideological functions of the cult of the Muses, and Orpheus in contemporaneous Macedon.

Orpheus and the Pierian tradition: A recapitulation

In the form known from textbooks, the myth of Orpheus appeared to present him as a Thracian, although this aspect of his portrayal changed over the course of the Classical, Hellenistic and Roman periods. The image of the hero and his links to Thrace was reinterpreted several times in ancient culture. Of particular note were the changes that appeared at the end of the Hellenistic period and early in Roman times. Their consequences can be seen for example in Himerius, who explains in one of his speeches that (*or.* 46,3):

> the Libethrii, who lived near Mt. Pangaeum, admired and took delight in the Thracian Orpheus, the son of Calliope, before he revealed to them the songs he had learned from his mother the Muse. But once he took up his lyre and sang a divinely inspired melody to them, the wretches were overcome by envy. Having dared to commit an act of womanly insolence against him and his melodious songs, they were subsequently turned into women in story.
>
> Translated by R. J. Penella

As seen here, the rhetor turns the citizens of the Pierian city of Leibethra, known from the proverb, into a Thracian tribe living around Mount Pangaion. Let us set aside the fantastical explanation for why Leibethrans became women in mythical narratives. Such free reinterpretations appeared late and have little to do with early accounts. Evaluated as a whole, the *testimonia* only prove that the perceptions of Orpheus were diverse and his Thracian aspect was usually not a simple declaration of ethnic origins. This invites caution about drawing far-reaching diachronic conclusions. Orpheus was not Thracian, except for when there was a need for him to be and when that part of his portrayal allowed a poet to express a meaning important for themselves and their audiences. As an aside to Himerius' explanations, Ancient authors had great freedom to modify stories, which led to creative changes in mythical plot lines. A myth known from late sources, especially commentaries and scholia, had already become a literary phenomenon. This should be kept in mind when attempting to 'reconstruct' any given story.[7]

Of course, questioning the Thracian roots of Orpheus does not by itself make him 'Macedonian'. However, frequent references to Pieria, Leibethra and Pimpleia (places in Macedonia) in early sources are notable and require an explanation. Chapters 3 and 4 focused on our knowledge of these toponyms and included an overview of the evolution of their geographic meaning starting in the Hellenistic period and especially during the Empire. Its key conclusion was the highlighting of how our idea of Orpheus was influenced by quasi-historical stories from

Strabo (C 410 [9,2,25]), Pausanias (9,29,3), and Themistius (*or.* 16,209c) indicating a primeval musicality of the Thracians, and by the account of Thucydides (2,99) placing Thracians in Pieria before the arrival of Macedonians. Arguments supporting the doubtful historical reliability and late origins of most accounts suggest setting aside the assumption about the Thracian roots of Macedon and the original Thracianness of Orpheus, which in turn prompts a re-examination of his ties to Pieria and Macedonia.

The existence of such early ties is suggested by the relatively numerous accounts indicating Pieria as the place of birth, life and death of Orpheus (Chapter 5). Most interestingly, Orpheus is found in a genealogy connecting him to the eponyms of Pieria and Methone and in a proverb about Leibethrians. If that last *testimonium* comes from the Peripatetic *Constitution of Methone* and was written no later than the fourth century, it also proves the story of Orpheus' ties to Pieria was widespread in the Classical period. Accounts of Euripides, Timotheus, Menaechmus and Alcidamas have to be understood similarly, and together they prove the existence of a strong Pierian tradition of Orpheus.

However, the key argument for the hero's close connection to Macedonia is the information about his statue and tomb in Leibethra and later in Dion, as well as his probable worship in Pieria. Based on the available *testimonia* and on the context of the cult of other mythical musicians and intellectuals in general, this worship of Orpheus can be dated to the fifth to fourth-centuries.

Are these assumptions congruent with our knowledge of Macedonia in that period? Are there other arguments for the Macedonian background for such religious and cultural innovation? Aside from the examples listed above, what speaks to the activity of Macedonians in the mythical and religious sphere in the fifth and fourth-centuries? Most importantly, considering the role of Orpheus as the first musician, what indicates an interest in *mousikē*?

Macedon: *Mousikē* and Orphics

Despite the stereotype of Macedonia as an area of low cultural development, ancient sources present many indications that it had a complex relationship with the Muses and *mousikē*. Many accounts analysed below clearly support the hypothesis of a deliberate policy of, and conscious effort towards, cultural selection creating a distinctively Macedonian culture (Pownall 2017, 215). Therefore, this is also an instance of a search for narratives that could be accepted as their own and alternative from the mythographic mainstream.[8]

The first example is Heracles, who played a major role in Macedonian religiosity and in the genealogy of the royal house.[9] Known from Alcidamas (*Ulix.* 24) Orpheus' tomb epigram depicts Orpheus as the teacher of Heracles.[10] This plot is better known from stories of Linus and his death at the hands of an impatient student, which Alcidamas mentions a moment later.[11] However, for some reason, the sophist also ties Orpheus to the son of Alcmene and Zeus. One of the explanations suggests that Heracles was roughly contemporaneous to Orpheus in the mythical tradition and that they both participated in the journey of the Argonauts. According to another interpretation, if one assumes that Orpheus' links to Pieria are older than Alcidamas, and there is much evidence to suggest it, this mention may stem from Heracles' role in the genealogy of the Argeads. If so, Pierian Orpheus would be the teacher of the ancestor of the Macedonian dynasty. Such a combination would be very interesting, as the circumstances of death described in the epigram are also non-standard (Orpheus is killed by Zeus' lightning), and Diogenes Laertius (1,5) presents the text as taken from the Orpheus' tomb at Dion in Macedonia.

Linus, who in many accounts dating even to the fifth century is variously presented as Orpheus' grandfather or brother (OF 912–14T; Linus F58–59a), was also occasionally linked to Macedonia. In the genealogy featured in *Certamen* and Charax, but originating probably from the fifth century, he was the son of Apollo and father of Pierus, eponym of Pieria, and thus the great grandfather of Orpheus. Meanwhile, Tzetzes (*Chil.* 6,53) has him as the son of Pierus, who was brother of Methone. According to Apollodorus (1,14), Linus was explicitly Orpheus' brother, either by Oeagrus or from Apollo and Calliope. In all these examples he was tightly linked to Pieria. However, as has been demonstrated in Chapter 6, the most interesting account was that of the moving of his body from Boeotia to Macedon by Philip II (Paus. 9,29,6–9). Even if the propaganda action in question did not take place, the story expresses ideas coherent with other accounts that link Linus to Macedon as his homeland.[12]

Pierus, the eponym of Pieria, is first mentioned in the early fifth century in Epicharmus' comedy *The Marriage of Hebe* (fr. 39 PCG). There, Pierus and

Pimpla are the parents of seven Muses associated with rivers.[13] Even though the story appears exceptionally fantastic, and the names (loosely translating to 'Fatso and Fulla') highlight the fertility of the region, likely in conjunction with the wealth of the wedding gifts and feast, the text proves the links of Pierus and Pieria to the Muses. However, there is too little data to state if the connection was only because of the epithet 'Pierides' or if there was some justification from local religious or mythographic practices.

Pierus' links to the Muses are also important in later accounts (Ov. *Met.* 5,310 sqq.; Ant. Lib. 9), where he was the father of the false Pierides. A full analysis of this narrative, which has been briefly discussed in Chapter 4, is outside of the scope of this section. In brief, the story may be a result of the rivalry between Muse cult centres from the late fifth century, early fourth century, in Pierian Dion and Boeotian Thespiae (Helicon). This rivalry is visible, for instance, in Pausanias' explanation that only three Muses were originally worshipped at Helicon, but later 'Pierus, a Macedonian, after whom the mountain in Macedonia was named, came to Thespiae and established nine Muses, changing their names to the present ones' [tr. W. H. S. Jones].

There are also other attestations to the ties between Pierus and the Muses, indicating that the eponymous hero was involved in the ideological discussion of the origins of literature and music. Cicero (*de nat. deor.* 3,54) presents him as the father of the third generation of Muses. In Servius (in Verg. *Ecl.* 7,21 [scholia Danielis]), Pierus, the son of Apollo, founds a temple to the Leibethrian Muses. The scholia to Juvenal's *Satires* (7,8) claim that Pierus was the first to sacrifice to the Muses. Clearly, the ties of Pierus to the Muses assume various forms, and the aforementioned accounts prove the wide reach of stories about Pieria's eponym.

An account citing Heraclides Ponticus, who lived in the late fourth century, relays that 'Pierus from Pieria' was the first to compose poems about the Muses.[14] Certain other sources also indicate that Pierus was considered one of the earliest poets.[15] In this context, it is easier to understand Pausanias' remark (9,24,4) that the people dubbed the 'children of the Muses' (Μουσῶν παῖδες) were the sons of the daughters of Pierus. This is undoubtedly a rationalisation, but also proof of the currency of the stories linking Pierus and Pieria to mythical musicians and early poets. Mythical poets as the sons of the daughters of Pierus indirectly suggest that *mousikē* originated in Pieria.

In summary, Pierus was portrayed as a poet, the first worshipper of the Muses, the builder of their temple in Leibethra, the father of the Muses or of the false Pierides, or as the ancestor of mythical poets and musicians. These associations made Pieria out to be the cradle of culture. This is most visible in the genealogy of Orpheus (and Linus) which we will refer to as the 'Hellanicus version' (see Chapter 5). It is usually presented and analysed as proof of Orpheus' links to Homer and Hesiod, his descendants in the eleventh generation, but notably, it also makes both poets descendants of Pierus. This means that according to this genealogy, Greek culture and literature were born at the foot of Olympus, in Macedonia. All these accounts refer not directly to Orpheus, but primarily to Pierus (and the Muses), indicating an alternative, Macedonian tradition of music: although Pieria existed in Greek consciousness as an area associated with the Muses, it is hard to imagine that any Greek in the fifth or fourth-centuries would claim that Greek culture was born in Macedonia.

This leads to another important aspect of Macedonia's links to *mousikē*: the Muses and their worship in Classical Macedonia. We have already quoted the *testimonium* of Epicharmus, which may have originated from something more than just metapoetic connotations and the poet's joke (Fatso and Fulla as the parents of Muses-rivers), particularly if considering that the mother of those local Muses is Pimpla, identifiable with the eponymous nymph of the Pierian village Pimpleia. Although the connotations of that name in the play suggest caution, it is worth noting that Callimachus (*h.* 4,7) presents Pimpleia as the birthplace of the Muses, parallel to Delos as the birthplace of Apollo. It is also the same Pimpleia where Orpheus was born, according to Apollonius (1,23–5).

The epithets of the Muses related to Macedonia (Leibethrides and Pimpleides) have already been discussed in Chapter 3. To recapitulate, most known accounts cite them in relation to stories of Orpheus, which is particularly clear when they appear in Orphic texts.[16]

However, the most important knowledge here is related to the cult of the Muses in Macedonian Dion. The city became the religious centre of Macedon in the fifth century (Diod. Sic. 17,16,3).[17] We have an entire range of accounts indicating that Archelaus reorganised the *Olympia* festival in Dion in the fifth century, supplementing it both with worship of the Muses and with a musical agon.[18] One of the most important sources for it is a passage from Diodorus mentioning that shortly after the destruction of Thebes, Alexander gathered his commanders and friends to discuss matters related to their expedition into Asia before holding a nine-day festival in honour of the Muses and Zeus in Dion, which involved a drama competition (17,16,3–4): 'He made lavish sacrifices to the gods at Dium in Macedonia and held the dramatic contests in honour of Zeus and the Muses which Archelaus, one of his predecessors, had instituted. He celebrated the festival for nine days, naming each day after one of the Muses' [tr. C. H. Oldfather].

Archelaus probably intended the *Olympia* to be the true festival of the Olympian Zeus, worshipped at the foot of Olympus as the traditional home of the gods.[19] Badian (1982, 35) thus goes so far as to call the festival the 'counter-Olympics'. Pownall (2017, n. 54) develops his idea by explaining that 'it seems likely, (...), that Archelaus' real goal was not simply to be accepted as Greek, but to be viewed as their cultural superior, and a "better" Olympics would therefore serve his purposes exceptionally well'. The most accurate commentary on the functions of such a broad celebration comes from Pingiatoglou (2010, 180–1):[20]

> With this festival Archelaos had probably two things in mind: On the one hand to underline his deep concern about all that the Muses represented in the ancient Greek world, i.e. intellectual life and culture, and, on the other, to remind everyone of the old Hesiodic myth which established a special link between the Olympian Muses and the area of Pieria, in other words to remind people of the myth that in Pieria Zeus gave life to the Muses after his union with Mnemosyne. We would therefore assume that with regard to the Muses the promotion of their worship was part of the propaganda launched by King Archelaos.

Two things are important for our analysis: firstly, the role of the Muses and of drama competitions in the royal plans, as they indicate a conscious intent of investing into *mousikē*; secondly, a local narrative presented in Dion, where the Muses were tied to Zeus and it was them, not Dionysus, that had the drama agons under their protection. The latter was very different from the Athenian practice.

However, our knowledge of the cult of the Muses in Macedonia does not end with the *Olympia* of Dion. We also have numerous other accounts indicating a remarkable spread of the worship of Muses in Macedon. One of them survives in Plutarch's *De liberis educandis*, where we learn of an epigram dedicated to the Muses by Eurydice, wife of Amyntas III and mother of Philip

II (*Mor.* 14b-c447). Others include a dedication to the Muses from the mid-fourth century from Macedonian Pella, a statue of a Muse from the Hellenistic period, and a dedication by the 'Mousaistai' association of Dion for King Perseus.[21] It is worth remembering in this context that Euripides has the chorus in *Bacchae* (410) describe Pieria as μούσειος ἕδρα, 'the seat of the Muses'. In terms of the number of sources documenting the worship of Muses, Macedon is seemingly only second to Athens, which is very telling.

It appears quite certain that the origins of the cult of the goddesses in the region date to the reign of Archelaus. Naturally, this does not mean an outright rejection of earlier dating, but there is simply no data that could serve as proof. Notably, *testimonia* of the cult of the Muses from neighbouring Thessaly are half a century older than that (*c*. 450).[22] Information on their worship in Syracuse under Dionysius I may also be parallel to Archelaus' decision. Interestingly, the Muses were clearly associated with theatre in Sicily as well.[23] In both instances, the narratives are local, and in many ways competitive with Athenian practice.

At this point, it becomes necessary to examine the significant role theatre played in Macedon starting with the reign of Archelaus. The *Olympia* were linked specifically to drama competitions. There are no known theatre buildings from the period, but both Pella and Dion certainly had them.[24] Tragedians from Athens were invited to the Macedonian court during this period, particularly Agathon and Euripides. Aelian (*VH* 2.21) relays an anecdote about the visit of the poet Agathon (and his beloved) to the royal court of Macedon, whereupon it is said Archelaus was interested in love as much as he was in the arts (ἐρωτικὸς οὐχ ἧττον ἢ καὶ φιλόμουσος). This, of course, means love of the Muses as the guardians of literature, including plays.

This context is also natural for the late account of Hesychius (s.v. [θούριδες]), who indicates the Muses were worshipped in Macedonia under the name or epiclesis 'Thourides'. Goukowsky (1976, 177–8) in his commentary on Strabo concludes, based on the radix of the word, that it should be translated as 'protectrices des spectacles' and ties it to the role of the goddesses as protectors of theatre in Macedonia.[25]

The presence of the tragedians is also linked to another phenomenon: the Argead patronage of arts. Some clues suggest they may have already become active in this manner under Alexander I.[26] He was interested in the *Olympia* competitions (Hdt. 5,22), and both Pindar and Bacchylides composed encomia for him.[27] Scholars differ in their interpretation of the ruler's links to these writers;[28] however, the fact that they were composed suggests Alexander was perceived as eager to enter the Greek cultural exchange. Herodotus was similarly linked to Alexander I's court, as he presents the king favourably in the *Histories*.[29]

Alexander's successor Perdiccas is linked to Hippocrates and the dithyrambic poet Melanippides.[30] However, the most intense and best attested activity was that of the third ruler in this line, Archelaus.[31] Various early and late sources confirm that the king hosted Zeuxis, Choerilus of Samos, Euripides, Agathon, and Timotheus of Miletus.[32] Later sources also mention refused invitations, like the one presented to Socrates,[33] extending the already long list of artists, writers and philosophers within the court's sphere of interest.

The Argead court especially targeted creators who were innovative for their time, like Melanippides, Timotheus, Agathon or Euripides, who may have been related to the idea of Orpheus as the first kitharode. Notably, both Melanippides and Timotheus were known for kitharodic compositions. Such links are clearly visible in *The Persians* (fr. 791, 221–4), where the poet makes reference to Orpheus as the forerunner of kitharodia.

The patronage from the ruler and an increase in theatre activity in Macedon also raised the demand for poetry. This manifested partly in commissions for plays, such as Euripides' *Archelaus*, and partly in the creation of pieces somehow related to Macedonia (e.g. *The Bacchae*).[34] Once more, it is that latter work by the Athenian tragedian (*Bacch.* 562–5) that provides us with the first account linking Orpheus to Pieria.

Biographical tradition relays that Euripides chose to affiliate himself with Pella in the final years of his life (*Vit. Eur.* Ia,6 TGrF), and even died and was buried there. Although the story of him being torn apart by dogs is clearly fiction, a Macedonian grave appears probable, despite the doubts that some occasionally profess.[35] The stories of Athenian attempts to recover the body of the tragedian are likely similarly fictitious, but the Macedonian reaction illustrates the Greeks' general belief in the Macedonian love of theatre.[36]

When considering what else could have influenced the choice of Orpheus specifically and his linking to Pieria, a case could be made for the significance of the cult of Dionysus in Macedonia and the prevalence of the so-called Orphic *testimonia* in that area.[37] Firstly, modern Derveni, where a famous papyrus of Orphic writings was found, lies in the area of Ancient Macedonia. Moreover, nine Orphic Gold Tablets were found in Macedonia (no. 30–38 in Graf and Iles Johnston 2007), some of which are dated to the fourth century. All this proves significant religious activity associated with the figure of Orpheus as an author of ritualist and theological texts in this area. Finally, an account from the Hellenistic poet Poseidippus of Pella, who ends one of his best-preserved works (118 A-B, 24–8) with a reference to 'the mystical path to Rhadamanthys'. Many scholars link these cryptic words to Orphic activity in Pella and Macedonia in general, particularly as one of the known gold leaves features the name of Poseidippus (Dickie 1995). Therefore, it appears that Orphic activity in Macedon, as well as Orpheus' and the Muses' links to Leibethra and Pimpleia in Orphic texts, may have reinforced the hero's connection to Pieria in mythical narratives and may have influenced the appearance of religious practices related to him in that area.

The final stage of the search for traces of Macedonia's connections to *mousikē* and Orpheus shall be an examination of Nicomedes of Acanthus. Today, he is nearly completely obscure. Only three things are known about him: his *ethnikon* indicates he originated from a city on the eastern coast of Chalcidice and two surviving fragments of his works (F1 and F2) prove he lived most likely during the reign of Philip II[38] (these two facts mean that Acanthus was already a part of Macedon by that time). The third fact, however, is the most interesting: Nicomedes wrote two works, *Macedonian Affairs* and *On Orpheus*. The former appears to have been a local history with elements of the mythical past, while the latter must have been a literary and mythographic monograph of Orpheus, typical of the late fourth century and especially of the school of Aristotle.

Combining all of the above paints a portrait of an artist from Macedon who dedicates one work to the history of that state and another to the figure of Orpheus. The coinciding of these two fields in the late fourth century seems more than meaningful. That Nicomedes of Acanthus decided it important in the fourth century to write not only the *Makedonika*, but also some sort of text titled *On Orpheus*, demonstrates the significance of the mythical hero at the time, indicates a wealth of narratives both available and interesting, and may corroborate the existence of various story variants that required explanation.

Crucially, however, this coincidence proves that the work was written about the 'Pierian' Orpheus we are tracking.

Macedon in context: Identity and ideology

Perhaps some information cited here appears uncertain and insignificant in isolation, but taken together it forms a clear pattern. In fifth century Macedon, especially towards the end of the period, there was an intensive growth of artistic patronage, theatre, and the cult of the Muses associated with these phenomena. As a result of literary, cultural and socioreligious activity, a supply of mythical stories about the Muses, Orpheus, Linus, Pierus or Heracles formed; these variously tied Macedonia to mythical narratives. The starting point for such stories was certainly the role of Olympus and Pieria as spaces associated with the Muses in Panhellenic literature. However, Macedonian developments derived from this idea are local and original.

What do these accounts prove? Firstly, a great interest in the field of *mousikē* in Classical Macedon, probably including its use to promote a specific image of the country. The spread of the local story of Pierus resulted in his appearance in works on the origins of *mousikē* in Greek culture. The ties of Linus, another mythical musician, to Pieria/Macedonia can now only be reconstructed from minor traces, but taken together they prove that there were attempts to link this hero to Pierus and Orpheus. Finally, the extraordinary popularity of the Muses as Leibethrides and Pimpleides in the Hellenistic and Roman periods reveals the extent to which the Macedonian version of the myth of Orpheus became common, as Leibethra and Pimpleia were closely linked to the story of his birth and death in Pieria.

All this raises the question of how to date these innovations. Considering the available data, it appears valid to point primarily to the reign of Archelaus. This is supported by his activity as patron of Greek poets and artists, his interest in theatre, and especially the linking of the Muses to the festival of Olympic Zeus and the founding of a musical competition during the king's life. Importantly, the first clear indications of a connection between Orpheus and Pieria come from this period as well and can be found in works by Euripides and Timotheus, poets affiliated with the Macedonian court. When compared with our knowledge of the worship of Linus in Epidauros, evident in archaeological findings from the early fourth century, it suggests that the assumption of a similar phenomenon in Macedonia during roughly the same period is justified. It is therefore to the last decades of the fifth century that the Leibethrian tomb and statues of Orpheus should be dated, as well as the key stage in the development of the mythographic tradition tying him to Pieria and Macedonia. Notably, this is the key stage, not the beginning, as it is impossible to rule out that ties of the story and the figure of Orpheus to Pieria had appeared earlier. It is also important to delineate between literary and mythographic activity and local religious practices. For now, there is little indisputable evidence for any earlier associations between Orpheus and Pieria, making it prudent to limit the claims to the reign of Archelaus.

There remains the question of the place of this innovation in Macedonian politics and a consideration of its propaganda and ideological functions. The actions of Archelaus can obviously be interpreted in many ways, highlighting many potential motives behind his decisions. In some instances, it is a valid approach to abandon the perspective of individual actions and focus instead on the processes, institutions and ideological content. The following remarks are only a suggestion for how the information about Orpheus, Pierus or the worship of the Muses in Pieria can be fit into a broader framework allowing for a fresh look at Classical Macedonia.

Little is known about the interactions between the royal ideology and court literature at the Ptolemaic and Seleucid courts.[39] The early Macedonian court under Archelaus I is even more obscure.[40] Thus, it is only possible to present a working hypothesis that it was the circles related to the ruler that were somehow responsible for the emergence and promotion of various versions of myths supporting the royal family and Macedonian cultural ambitions. The basic communication channels involved were royal feasts, poets patronised by the ruler or competing for that patronage, and musical contests, such as the drama competitions during the *Olympia*. Works written in these contexts have to be responsible for a major share of information regarding Orpheus' connections to Pieria, as documented by the passages from Euripides and Timotheus. The king's entourage and the Macedonian elite as a whole should also be considered involved in the foundation of the tomb in Leibethra.

What may have been the purpose of these actions? The fifth century was undoubtedly a period of increased involvement of Macedon in the events in the world of the Greek poleis. During that time, the more Macedonians were engaged with the Greeks and their culture and customs, the more they had to prove they were similar to the Greeks and not to the barbarians, especially Thracians. Nevertheless, they were sometimes accused of being uncivilised, as in Thrasymachus' speech to Larissians.[41] As Benjamin Acosta-Hughes (2012, 169) puts it:

> The fact that a century later Demosthenes could assert that Philip II was 'neither a Greek nor a remote relative of the Greeks, nor even a respectable barbarian,' but a wretched Macedonian, suggests that the kings of Macedon needed continually to assert their kinship with Greek communities. This could be the reason that Euripides began his now fragmentary play, the *Archelaus*, with this Argive genealogy.

An investment in the myth and cult of Orpheus may be seen as a signal to the Greeks that Macedonia had always been Greek and that there was no real need to prove that. Not only was the ruler a Heraclid hailing from Argos, but the core of Macedonian territory, especially Pieria and Olympus, is crucial to Greek culture as the birthplace of the Muses and Orpheus, the first mythical musician. Thus, Macedonia is the cradle of *mousikē*, a term widely understood in the fifth century as the equivalent of civilisation, close to our modern concept of culture.

Importantly, cultural innovation served not only to 'civilise' the Macedonians and prove their Hellenicity outside their borders, but perhaps also to differentiate them from the Thracians. They were similar to them in many ways: they herded mostly cattle; they assigned great importance to horses and horsemen; they had a similar way of life; they lived in a similar environment; they feasted, drank and hunted in similar ways; their rulers had similar status and practised polygamy; their funerary rites were similar, etc. From an ethnographic standpoint, they were more alike than different. Macedonians may have therefore felt the need to show they were not 'like Thracians'.

Secondly, promoting the myth and cult of Orpheus may have been part of the king's internal policy, serving to convince the elites and his subjects that the ongoing 'Hellenisation' was really a return to their roots and ancestral culture:

Macedonians would not be implementing foreign styles, since they had always been Greeks. These efforts may have therefore been an important background for the king's culture creating activity, associated particularly with spending on theatre and patronage of the arts that the Macedonian populace may have perceived as newfangled and conflicting with the 'Macedonian spirit'.[42]

The figure of Orpheus may have therefore served both to answer the accusations of barbarity and backwardness and to negotiate Macedonian cultural identity. Some *testimonia*, such as the story of the reaction to the attempts to move the remains of Euripides to Athens (Aul. Gell. 15,20), suggest that Macedonians understood and accepted the construction of an identity on the basis of references to Hellenicity, and various institutions (theatre, festivals, tomb of Orpheus, myths) supported those tendencies as important for fostering civic cohesion through the creation of an 'imagined community'.

The actions of the king may also be perceived as reverse Hellenisation, since the acceptance of (modified) Hellenic models was presented as a return to or recovery of a forgotten legacy (Pieria as the cradle of *mousikē*). Archelaus did all of this 'à la grecque', as Jonathan Hall (2002, 156) once put it; that is, through references to the language of myth, genealogy and religious gestures: a repertoire of sociocultural actions typical for the Greeks, but also fully understandable for the Macedonians. In the words of Eugene Borza (1990, 176–7): 'It was not recognition as a Hellene that Archelaus wanted, but respect.' The king's policy should therefore be seen not as a straightforward Hellenisation, but as creation of new phenomena based on Greek models.

Finally, Archelaus activity may also be interpreted as an attempt to strengthen his position and legitimise the dynasty's primacy in the nation.[43] This was potentially crucial in the face of possible disputes of Archelaus' heritage.[44] In any event, it appears that plays written by Euripides for his patron (*Archelaus, Temenus, The Temenids*) were also aimed at 'a local Macedonian audience, in order to legitimize Archelaus as the rightful king'.[45]

All of the above remarks allow for a fresh, broad look at the politics of Archelaus. While it has been suggested before that the king's aim may have been not so much a policy of Hellenisation as a search for Macedon's own way, there were few clear arguments to support this interpretation.[46] Analyses of material related to the figure of Orpheus and a new look at the worship of Muses in Dion appear to fill this gap. Due to the links of the hero and the goddesses to Pieria and Olympus, and the prototypical role of Orpheus as a musician and Muses as the protectresses of *mousikē* in Greek culture, it was possible to connect their cult in Macedonia, the stories and genealogies tying the hero and the goddesses to the area, and the idea of the inherent Hellenicity of Macedonians into a coherent message. Understood as such, the actions of the king and his court had an ideological dimension and served to build and reinforce Macedonian identity.

Epilogue: Orpheuses, not Orpheus

The first chapter of this book begins with a summary of the plot of Jacopo Peri's opera *Euridice*. Let us end it with another famous adaptation of the story of Orpheus: the Brazilian 1959 motion picture *Black Orpheus*. Here, the ending remains unchanged and tragic, but certain elements of the hero's identity and the circumstances surrounding the events are altered. Orpheus in the film is black, and first shown to the audience in a starting sequence where a Greek marble bas relief explodes to reveal a crowd of black men dancing the samba in a favela. The action is set in Rio de Janeiro during the Carnival, and the protagonists are students of a samba school that takes part in the parades. The death of Eurydice, killed accidentally by Orpheus himself when he turns a power switch and inadvertently electrocutes her, takes place at the last stop of a trolley line. Orpheus, in turn, is killed by his fiancée. In the ending scene, the children that followed him pick up his guitar, convinced that the instrument makes the sun rise every morning.

The key reason for the endurance of the Greek myth in European culture may not be the uniqueness of its story, as narratives from other cultures are no less fantastical and universal. It is distinguished rather by its exceptional literary rendition and narrative fluidity. Focusing on that last element shows that Ancient tradition has left behind many variants of every myth and encourages thinking not only of the story, but also about its margins, and to remake it anew. This provides us with a unique degree of freedom to create our own versions of the story. The exceptional vivacity of myth is proven by new generations of young people who gorge on the latest versions of it, be it Stephen Fry's books about ancient heroes and deities or Rick Riordan's *Percy Jackson* novels.

What does that say about Orpheus as a mythical figure? As Chapter 1 attempts to demonstrate, there is no single mythical tradition, but rather many tangled paths. Several of those are local traditions, and the Pierian version of the myth of Orpheus was only one of the possible depictions. There was also the Orpheus of the Athenian debate over the beginnings of *sophia*, the sage who invented writing. On the flip side, there was the Orpheus of iconography, who charmed Thracians and was killed by Thracian women. We can also talk of the Orpheus of the Orphics, the mythical mystagogue who obtained arcane knowledge of the gods, life and death; who wrote Orphic theological and mystical texts; the thaumaturge who insisted on refraining from killing. In Strabo, there is a completely different Orpheus, similar to the figure of Pythagoras as presented in pamphlets against him: a wizard, a soothsayer and a fraud, who finds a deserved death in a political riot.

Of course, there was also Orpheus the musician and poet with magical abilities, capable of charming the world of nature. It was probably he who went on the *Argo* and vanquished the power of the sirens' song. In that vein, there was also the Orpheus of Phanocles, a hero who fell in love with Calaïs and discovered homoeroticism during the quest for the Golden Fleece. As suggested later, it was the rejection of women after these events (or maybe after losing his wife?) that led to his death. Having already focused on the great journey, we should add that Apollonius, the author of the Hellenistic epic *Argonautica*, makes Orpheus his own alter ego, while the *Orphic Argonautica* tells the story from his point of view.

Finally, there was also the Orpheus of Roman poetry, whom we know best: a poet and a tragic lover who fruitlessly strove to free his wife from the clutches of death. There were also many minor Orpheuses of scholiasts and commentators, who would add to him or take away to fit him to their measure, as each wanted to have an Orpheus of their own, the way they imagined him.

It is time to ask: Who could the Pierian Orpheus be, the hero as seen locally in Macedonia? We do not know for sure, as none of the accounts is as literal as the *testimonia* of Pausanias or the poems by Phanocles or Apollonius. Some accounts suggest the hero worshipped in Pieria was Heracles' teacher and had been struck with lightning by Zeus for his extraordinary knowledge and skill, far beyond what was permitted for humans. In this version, his wife or his death by women are irrelevant elements, and his descent into Hades may have had a different reason.

The number of Orphic accounts from Macedonia and the role of Dionysus in the area beg the question of whether the Macedonian Orpheus was not the hero as imagined by the Orphics. What would that imply? Primarily the person who learned the secrets of life and death, and who perhaps attempted to conquer death themselves and return from Hades; perhaps the master of mystic initiations and a teacher of a specific lifestyle.

Most accounts, however, suggest that the Macedonian depiction of Orpheus was linked to music and the Muses. The statue of Orpheus at Leibethra sweats when Alexander marches to Asia, which the seers explain is caused by the effort needed to describe the king's achievements. The proverb about Leibethrians, although it may have originated in Athens as a biting commentary on the Pierian stories of the tomb of Orpheus in Leibethra, also suggests links to *mousikē*. Leibethrians lose their musical sensibility and aesthetic abilities as a result of Orpheus' death in their city.

The word *amousotatos*, describing that state of a lack of culture the Leibethrians were in, has a broader meaning, and thus demands a more extensive comment. The noun *amousia* is attested in the Greek language since the second half of the fifth century. It means 'a lack of the gift of the Muses for humanity, or not partaking in that gift', the gift being *mousikē*. Thus, as the meaning of the term *mousikē* changes over the fifth century, *amousos* starts to mean 'uneducated, ignorant of literature, lacking in aesthetic taste', or more broadly 'uncivilised'.[1] To quote the chorus of Euripides (fr. 1028):

ὅστις νέος ὢν μουσῶν ἀμελεῖ
τόν τε παρελθόντ' ἀπόλωλε χρόνον
καὶ τὸν μέλλοντα τέθνηκεν.
Any man who in his youth neglects the Muses has perished for the time that is past and is dead for the future. [tr. Ch. Collard and M. Cropp]

Such connotations of the term result not only from the Muses' protection of poetic inspiration and literary work, but also from their ties to education and school, beginning in the second half of the fifth century. A man who neglects the Muses (Euripidean μουσῶν ἀμελεῖ) has no part in *mousikē*. The latter term begins to mean 'education' in the fifth century, because of the role of the Muses and literature in schooling, and is more broadly an equivalent of our term 'culture'.[2] In Greek thinking, it encompasses everything that makes men civilised and sets them apart from animals or barbarians. In *Lysis* (206 b3), Plato contrasts savagery with civilisation, which he ties to *mousikē*, while the chorus of Theban elders in Euripides' *Herakles* prays that they would never have to live 'without the Muses' and for each of their days to end in song and dance (μὴ ζῴην μετ' ἀμουσίας, / αἰεὶ δ' ἐν στεφάνοισιν εἴην).

The supreme master of *mousikē* was Orpheus, who could tame the instincts of animals and force them to obey, or move rocks and trees with his magical sound. However, the proverb's use of the adjective *amousos* may lead to further associations if read in relation to the figure of Orpheus. As Orpheus was the son of a Muse (usually Calliope), a Leibethrian (as a killer of the hero or affiliated with them) not only was uneducated and tasteless, but also rejected the gifts of the goddesses, or even became their enemy. What else could be said of people less sensitive to Orpheus' music than wild beasts, rocks and trees, who all succumbed to its power? It is no accident that Zonaras' lexicon (p. 1294 Tittmann) describes Leibethrians as hapless fools (ἀνοητότεροι), while Libanius speaks of their lack of education.[3] Thus, the proverb gains an entirely new dimension when considering that all these negative traits are ascribed to the people of the realm where the Muses were supposedly born. It would therefore be unsurprising if the proverb about Leibethrians had its roots in fourth-century Athenian comedy as a reaction to Macedonian narratives of the origins of the Muses and music.

In Macedonia, Orpheus was primarily the first musician, and, as seen in Hellanicus' genealogy, the ancestor of Homer and Hesiod. The hero's tomb in Leibethra was apparently the first of its kind and may have started the phenomenon of presenting or discovering tombs of poets and founding cults of them in Greek culture.[4] Archelaus' cultural policy would therefore be not so much an imitation of Athenian customs as it was a creative transformation of Greek models and a series of proposals for innovative solutions that the Greeks themselves would soon draw on. This is not an exaggeration, as Perdiccas II and Archelaus supported primarily avant-garde, innovative creators like Melanippides, Agathon, Timotheus and Euripides. All these actions by Macedonian kings are also evidence of bold involvement in the discussion over the origins of Greek music and culture. The debate over the beginnings of *mousikē* was extremely lively in the Classical period, and it tied into attempts to confront the Greeks' own traditions and rethink the roots of culture from the beginning. But that is a very different story.[5]

Notes

Introduction

1 See OF 901+987+501+1035T. Bernabé's edition splits the source texts into subject categories (*mater, uxor, Orphica et Bacchica, mors*), which is both an advantage and a drawback. In many cases, analysing a single category (*Orpheii patria, mors*) does not provide insight into the subject matter. This book numbers the sources as per Bernabé, but the author wishes to stress he is not slavishly devoted to this numeration. At times, particularly with longer texts (which Bernabé splits), citations will reference editions of specific authors directly.
2 See e.g. Rose 1958, 210–11; March 1998 s.v.; Fry 2018.
3 See Rose 1958, 210: 'Thrace is not Greece, but must be mentioned here, not only on account of Rhesos, with whom we dealt in the last chapter, but far more because of Orpheus. (...) He was a devoted follower of Dionysos, as became a good Thracian (...).'
4 See Warden 1982.
5 More on this aspect in Segal 1988.
6 'Once and for all, / It's Orpheus when there's song' – tr. J. B. Leishman.
7 Throughout this book, the phrase 'spatial references' will be used to mean statements guiding the reader in mythical geography. For example, Apollodorus explains in the *Library* that Orpheus was 'buried near Pieria', while Apollonius claims in *Argonautica* that 'Calliope bare [Orpheus] . . . near the Pimpleian height'. Virtually all myths anchor the events and heroes in space, referencing areas around the audiences of the tale (an important characteristic of local tales) or known from second-hand accounts.
8 OF 935+951(I)+1010(I)T.
9 *Certamen* 4; Proklos, *Vita Homeri* 5,4.
10 Posidipp. 118 A–B; see Mojsik 2018.
11 On this conceptualisation of *mousikē* see Murray and Wilson 2004.
12 See Hes. *Th.* 1–115; Mimn. fr. 13 W.; Mousaios 2 B15 DK = schol. Ap. Rh. 3,1; Pind. fr. 29–35.
13 See *h. hom.* 3; Eratosth, *Cataster.* 24; Phanocles F 1 Powell.
14 See Paus. 9,29,1; 2,31,3; Ps.-Plut. *de mus.* 3 (1131F–1132C); Serv. in Verg. *Ecl.* 7,21.
15 See Pl. *Leg.* 677d; Clem. Alex. *Strom.* 1,74,1. About Ps-Plutarch see Barker 2014.

16 Tr. B. Einarson and P. H. De Lacy.
17 The accounts will be discussed further in Chapter 6.
18 See Lefkowitz 1981; Ford 2004; Kimmel-Clauzet 2013; Barker 2014; Mojsik 2019.
19 Paus. 9,30,7–11; Conon in Phot. *Bibl.* 186, 140a–b.
20 OF 1069(I)T = Zenob. Athous prov. [coll. Miller 3,1: *Mel.* p. 369]. Translations are author's unless otherwise stated.
21 'We have two traditions about Orpheus' homeland, that he was born (or lived) in Thracia or Pieria; and we find it many times mixed in our sources.'
22 In studies of the myth of Orpheus, 'early' is understood as the Classical and (occasionally) Hellenistic period.
23 On Athens, myth and ideology see recently Barbato 2020.
24 Secondary literature on Orpheus is plentiful (see Bernabé 2008, 15, n. 3). The most important studies include: Linforth 1941; Guthrie 1952; Schoeller 1969; Warden 1982; West 1983; Graf 1987; Segal 1988; Borgeaud 1991; Bremmer 1991; Masaracchia 1993; Heath 1994; Lissarague 1994; Garezou 1994; Gartziou-Tatti 1999; Bernabé 2002; Vieillefon 2003; Mund-Espín 2003; Santamaría Álvarez 2008; Bernabé et al. 2010; Burgess Watson 2013; 2014; 2015; Trzcionkowski 2015; Graziosi 2018.
25 On Heracles, Achilles, Agamemnon, or Paris/Alexander and their place in Macedonian royal ideology, see Moloney 2015.
26 See King 2017, 14; Müller 2017b, 20.
27 E.g. Hall 2001; Sourvinou-Inwood 2002.
28 Graf and Iles Johnston 2007; Bernabé and Jimenez San Cristobal 2008; Edmonds III 2011; 2013; Trzcionkowski 2013; Meisner 2018.
29 Edmonds III 2013.
30 See Graziosi 2018.

Chapter 1

1 Monteverdi's *L'Orfeo* was based on Ovid's *Metamorphoses* and written in 1607 for a court performance during the Mantua Carnival.
2 See Segal 1988, 165–6; Carter and Goldthwaite 2013.
3 Mythographic tradition may be understood in two ways: narrowly, as the work of ancient mythographers (Cameron 2004), or broadly, as all relics of a mythical tradition (available, in a sense, to the 'mythographer'). 'Mythographic analysis' or 'applied mythography' will be used throughout this book in the latter sense, as analysis of all accounts documenting the myth of Orpheus.
4 A complex analysis of *testimonia* about Orpheus may be found e.g. in Linforth (1941).

5 See LIMC 7,1,81–105 and below, 'Early iconography' Chapter 2.
6 See Ap. Rhod. 1,32–3 and scholia ad locum; but see also Eur. fr. 752g Kannicht [*Hypsipyle*].
7 Graf and Iles Johnston 2007, 165: 'In the tightly-knit network of family relations that is the hallmark of Greek heroic myth, Orpheus is an outsider. (...) there is no part of the genealogical network into which Orpheus would fit'.
8 E.g. Leos, Musaeus, Ortes and see the genealogy of Homer and Hesiod in Procl. *Vit. Hom.* 5,4.
9 West 2010, 19.
10 On early accounts, see Linforth 1941; Graf 1987; Semenzato 2016.
11 See Anderson 1982; Segal 1988; Johnson 2008.
12 On Pausanias and local stories, see Hawes 2021, 159–201, and especially 3–4: 'local stories might be those of relevance to a specific locale; they might be those told in these locales; they might be stories which existed only in oral form; stories which seem obscure or idiosyncratic; stories which project a "geographical ideal" in which toponyms are not empty references but places with independent ontological status'.
13 Of course, local mythical and religious traditions are multifaceted phenomena, and therefore difficult to define; the offered explanations have to be considered an *ad hoc* solution. For instance, some literary versions of myths never grow into any great popularity and remain considered equally idiosyncratic as local myths of Thesprotia or Syracusae, for example Phanocles' story of Orpheus' love for Calaïs. Conversely, certain literary works, like Callimachus' *Aetia* or Lycophron's *Alexandra*, may elevate very idiosyncratic and obscure local variants to the level of Panhellenic tales. The local nature of the myth could manifest in various ways, such as a regional version of known mythical plots and genealogies or completely *sui generis*, otherwise unheard of narratives of known heroes of myth. They could also be local versions of heroes only known in that specific location, such as eponyms of the polis, rivers, mountains etc. This is the case, for example, when Pausanias (2,1) explains that aside from the Corinthians themselves nobody takes the hero Corinthus seriously and does not consider him the son of Zeus.
14 Cameron 2004; Trzaskoma and Smith 2007, X–XLI; 2013; Pamias 2017; Romano and Marincola 2019.
15 See Ar. *Ran.* 1030–6; Hippias BNJ 6 F4; Pl. *Apol.* 41a; *Ion* 536a–b; Alexis fr. 140 K.-A.
16 Linforth 1941, 26; Fowler 2013, 684; see Chapter 5 below.
17 Graf 1974; West 1983, 29–33; Graf and Iles Johnston 2007, 165–84.
18 See e.g. Tzetz. *Chil.* 4,279 and schol. Eur. *Rhes.* 916: Orpheus as the son of Menippe, daughter of Thamyris. On Orphic writings and Orpheus, see e.g. Edmonds 2013, 95–194.

19 See Ar. *Ran.* 1030-6; Apollod. 1,14; Graf 1974.
20 E.g. Diod. Sic. 3,65; Iambl. *VP* 28,145-7; about Orpheus and Dionysus see Bednarek 2021.
21 Graf 1987; Burgess Watson 2013.
22 Ar. *Ran.* 1030-6; Hor. *Ars Poet.* 391-3: 'Orpheus, the priest and interpreter of the gods, deterred the savage race of men from slaughters and impure diet' [tr. B. Graziosi].
23 Herington 1991, 161-216; Power 2010 and the Italian series *Agoni poetico-musicali nella Grecia antica*.
24 Wilson 2009; Power 2010, 206; Karpati 2016.
25 Hall 2000; Sommerstein 2005; Wilson 2004; Csapo 2004. Although the kitharodes' skills were doubtlessly highly esteemed, they usually remained outside of polis structures and functioned as journeymen (Hunter 2009). The sources also stress their extravagant habits and clothing, additionally setting them apart socially and culturally.
26 Eur. fr. 183-202, and especially 199; Wilson 2004; Power 2010. See also Ar. *Thesm.* 134-45 (from Aeschylus' *Lycurgeia*, about Dionysus).
27 Ford 2002; Barker 2014. Furthermore, some mythography was most likely literary criticism, such as Asclepiades of Tragilus' *Tragodoumena*.
28 See Ford 2002, 139-46.
29 See Blum 1991, 47-52; Raffa 2018; Hadjimichael 2019, 133-70.
30 On *protoi heuretai* see Clem. Alex. *Strom.* 1,74,1 and Kleingünther 1933. Musicians and poets on the lists: Pl. *Leg.* 677d; Alcidamas *Ulix.* 23-8; Ps.-Plut. *de mus.* 5.
31 See Plutarch (*de mus.* 5) citing Herakleides Ponticus, and Chapter 6 below.
32 See Detienne 2003, 125-36.
33 Garezou 1994; 2009 (LIMC 7,1,81-105; Suppl. 1-2, 399-405).
34 Fowler 2017, 158: 'When one thinks of mythography, one thinks of variants.'
35 See Graf 1987, 80-1; Graziosi 2018, 173-8.
36 See Toepffer 1889, 181-206.
37 Another interesting Athenian thread is the history of the daughters of Leos, considered a son of Orpheus, see OF 917T.
38 See Graf 1974, 18-20.
39 See Overduin 2011, comm. ad *Theriaca* 462; OF 930T.
40 See West 2010.
41 See LIMC 7,2, fig. 6.
42 Apollod. 1,16; Paus. 4,33,3; Bremmer 1991, 15, n. 3.
43 In her review of P. Kobiliri, *A Stylistic Commentary on Hermesianax. Classical and Byzantine Monographs*, Amsterdam, 1998 (http://bmcr.brynmawr.edu/2000/2000-

04-22.html). Hermesianax's play on tradition is also visible in making Penelope and Homer a couple, see Bremmer 1991, 15.
44 See Alcidamas *Ulix.* 24; Paus. 9,30,5; Diog. Laert. 1,5.
45 See Isoc. *Bus.* 38.
46 See Apollod. 1,89; 3,99; 3,138.
47 See Alcidamas *Ulix.* 24, Diog. Laert. 1,5.
48 Trzaskoma and Smith 2007, XLII–LVII.
49 Calliope had decided Adonis would spend only half the year with Aphrodite, his mother, and the rest with Persephone in the underworld.
50 See Apollod. 1,16; 1,27; 2,53; 3,182–3.

Chapter 2

1 Graf 1987, 86: 'Orpheus is also always a Thracian.' The question of Orpheus' ties to Thrace has been raised before, but the answers were more focused on the place of *mousikē* in Greek polis or links to Dionysus – see Graf 1987, 86–7, 99–100; Marcaccini 1995. The matter is more complex than that and worth revisiting.
2 Hammond 1972, 416–18; Brown 2002, 304.
3 King 2017, 14; Müller 2016, 20.
4 See Garezou 1994; 2009; Lissarrague 1994; Tsiafakis 2002; Isler-Kerényi 2009; Galoin 2017. List of fifth-century depictions of Orpheus: Garezou 1994; Isler-Kerényi 2009.
5 Paus. 10,30,6 (Lesche of the Cnidians in Delphi); Lissarague 2002; Nippel 2002; Cohen 2012; Burges Watson 2013.
6 On the supposed Thracian kithara in fifth-century iconography, see Tsiafakis 2016, 272.
7 Garezou 1994; Lissarague 2002, 121–2; Tsiafakis 2016, 271–2.
8 On *mousikē* and musicians in iconography, see Bundrick 2005; 2020.
9 Tsiafakis 2016; Sears 2013.
10 See Zeitlin 1996; James and Dillon 2012.
11 Wolicki 2015.
12 See Eur. *Suppl.* 881–3; fr. 183–202; TGrF 39 Test. 11–12 (effeminate Agathon); Pl. *Symp.* 179d; see Wilson 1999/2000, and esp. 442, n. 52; Csapo 2004, 230–5 (about New Music practitioners as effeminate and barbarians).
13 See Garezou 2009, Isler-Kerenyi 2009.
14 We know next to nothing of Aristias' contemporary *Orpheus* (see TGrFT1–4 and F5).

15 *Catasterismoi* have not survived outside of later summaries, see Pamias and Geus, 2007, 31–4. On the reconstruction of Aeschylean *Lycurgeia*, see Bednarek 2021.
16 Alcidamas *Ulix*. 24 [p. 32 Avezzu = 30 Muir] = OF 1073T.
17 Harding 1994, 180.
18 We are already told in the fifth century of this version of the chronology of origins of Greek music/literature, with Musaeus as the ancestor of Homer and Hesiod, by Gorgias and Damastes (Procl. *Vita Homeri* 5,4; 7).
19 Arist. *Veterum heroum epitaphia* 48 (fr. 640 Rose); see De Jesus 2015.
20 OF 895–9T. It is occasionally suggested that Oeagrus is more frequently presented as father of Orpheus. However, it appears that early sources have a visible balance between the two versions, and Oeagrus pulls ahead only in late accounts, as an effect of Orpheus' portrayal as Thracian solidified. It is that late depiction that suggests Apollo's role was marginal.
21 Bassino 2018, 48: 'The claim that he fathered Orpheus is found in all versions of this genealogy and seems to be the only fixed feature of this character.'
22 Trzcionkowski 2013; Graziosi 2018; Bednarek 2021.
23 OF 894T; Servius in *Georg*. 4,523 (III 358, 14 Thilo-Hagen): 'Oeagrius Hebrus] Oeagrus fluvius est, pater Orphei, de quo Hebros nascitur, unde eum appellavit Oeagrium.' See Guthrie 1952, 63, n. 2: 'a river in Thrace'; Semenzato 2016, 298: 'but for most people Orpheus is the son of Oeagrus, the Thracian river god'.
24 On Rhesus as the son of a Muse and a river god, see Ps.-Euripides *Rhesos* and scholia; Liapis 2011.
25 Verg. *Georg*. 4,523; *Culex* 117–18; Ov. *Met*. 2,219. On Hebrus, see OF 952T; 1054T; Hor. *Epist*. 1,3,3.
26 Parker 1996, 174: 'a savage country and home of a savage people, but one with which it was indispensable for economic and strategic reasons constantly to grapple ... a land of promise and peril'; see Sears 2013.
27 Hall 1989; Dowden 1992, 60–2; Vlassopoulos 2013.
28 Thuc. 2,29; see Dowden 1992, 61; Vlassopoulos 2013, 127; Graninger 2015, 29.
29 See Isoc. *Paneg*. 68; Strabo 7,7,1 [C 321].
30 See Troezenian myths about Ardalus and the Muses as local stories about the origins of music – Paus. 2,31,3; Steph. Byz. *Ethnica* (epitome), p. 115, 13–14.
31 E.g. Linforth 1941, 28, 165; Graf and Iles Johnston 2007, 167.
32 Henrichs 1985; Wilson 2009; Karpati 2016. On the Thracisation of Musaeus (and Eumolpus), see Graf 1974, 18–19.
33 Vlassopoulos 2013; Gruen 2020.
34 Hartog 1988; Campbell 2006; Skinner 2012.
35 Simon. fr. 567 PMG: 'Numberless birds flew about over his head, and the fish leapt straight up from the darkling water at his lovely singing' [tr. M. L. West].

36 Shapiro 1983.
37 Sears 2013; Psoma 2014.
38 According to Hammond (1972, 417), Classical-era Athenians used the term Thrace as a geographic, not ethnic, descriptor of all peoples living north of them.
39 Marcaccini 1995; Bednarek 2021.
40 Eur. *Alc.* 967–9; Ar. *Ran.* 1032; see [Eur.] *Rhes.* 943.
41 Iambl. *VP* 145 (*Hieros logos*).
42 Incidentally, Thracian identities were received and conceptualised differently in the fifth century (in Athens), in the Augustan period (Conon: Thrace as a new Roman province), or in Pausanias' time (second century, Thrace as an integral part of the imperial *oikumene*).
43 Strabo 7, fr. 10: Orpheus gains power as musician, sorcerer and religious leader; see Paus. 9,29,3.

Chapter 3

1 See Soph. *OT* 1098–1109.
2 See Dueck 2021.
3 On spatiality in the myth, see Buxton 1994; Cohen 2007; Hawes 2017; 2021.
4 See e.g. Bing 1988, 37–8.
5 Said 1978.
6 *The Dictionary of Human Geography*, 369–71.
7 Lévi-Strauss 1966, 16–36. Recently, D. Meisner (2018) has used bricolage successfully to analyse the Orphic theogonic myth.
8 Rosch and Lloyds 1978.
9 Plassart 1921.
10 Based on this information, Hatzopoulos and Paschidis have described Leibethra as follows in the *Inventory of Archaic and Classical Poleis* (2004, 803): 'The territory of Leibethra probably extended from the mountainous area of Lower Olympos to the valley of Sys (Helly (1973) 35–6; Gonnoi 5). The city bordered on Gonnoi to the south-west, presumably on Herakleion to the south, and Dion to the north.'
11 See https://www.leivithrapark.gr/en/leivithra/archaeological-site-of-leivithra/.
12 Transformation into a star, constellation, comet or other celestial body.
13 Hatzopoulos and Paschidis 2004, 797: 'Possibly at Ag. Paraskevi near Litochoron.'
14 See Olson 2007, 42.
15 See LSJ s.v. Λείβηθρον, τό: 'mountain district of Thrace inhabited by Orpheus'; Schmidt 1950, 1387; Bing 1988, 37–8; Celoria 1992, 132; Montanari 2015 s.v. τό Λείβηθρον.

16 Schol. Danielis 21: 'a fonte Boeotiae [Libethro uel a] Libethro poeta, qui primus harmoniam tradidit et aram Musis consecrauit. alii [Libethron] locum, in quo Hesiodus natus est, alii templum Libethridum musarum dicunt, quod a Piero, Apollinis filio, consecratum est'; schol. Bern. ad Verg. *Ecl.* 7,21: 'Nymphae Libethrides, a monte Boeotiae Libethro qui est Musis sacer, vel Libethrus fluvius in Thracia, ubi Orpheus laniatus est, ubi se Musae lavabant. Alii fontem in Boeotia dicunt.'

17 See e.g. Clausen 1994, ad loc.; Coleman 1977, ad loc.; Lipka 2001, 100–1; Canetta 2008.

18 Translated by D. R. Shackleton Bailey. See Stat. *Silv.* 1,4,25.

19 See Merrill 1893, comm. ad Catullus 105 ('Pipleum montem'); Schubart 1932; Hornblower 2015 ad Lyc. *Alex.* 275.

20 See schol. Ap. Rhod. 1,23–5: Πίμπλεια χωρίον κατὰ Πιερίαν· οἱ δὲ ὄρος Θράκης, οἱ δὲ κρήνην καὶ κώμην τῆς Πιερίας ('Pimpleia, a place in Pieria; some say it is a mountain in Thrace, others that it is a spring and a village in Pieria'); schol. Lycoph. *Alex.* 275: Πίμπλεια δὲ καὶ πόλις καὶ ὄρος καὶ κρήνη Μακεδονίας ('Pimpleia is a polis, a mountain, and a spring in Macedonia'); Acron. ad Horat. *carm.* 1,26,9: Pipleae Musae dictae aut a Pipleo fonte Macedoniae, vel vico, aut a monte Pipleo Orchomenorum ('Pipleian Muses are [so] called either from the spring Piplea in Macedonia, or from Mount Pipleum [in the land] of the Orchomenians'); Porphyrius, comm. ad Hor. *carm.* 1,26,9 (Nisbet and Hubbard 1970, 306): Piplea dulcis: Pipleides Musae dicuntur a Pipleo fonte Macedoniae ('Pipleian Muses, [so] called after the spring Pipleum in Macedonia'); Festus s.v. *Pimplides*: Musae a fonte Macedoniae dictae propter liquoris eius unicam subtilitatem ('Muses called [so] after a spring in Macedonia due to the unique pleasantness of its waters').

21 The existence of real ties between Pieria and Boeotia is considered in the commentary ad Lycoph. *Alex.* 274–5 by Hurst and Kolde, 2008, ad loc.: 'Il se répand par la suite en Béotie, sur l'Hélicon; l'attestation des mêmes toponymes dans les deux régions témoigne de cette oscilation; cf. Strabo 9,2,25; 10,3,17.'

22 See Montanari 2015 s.v. Pimpleia: 'mountain in Pieria – Call. 4,7; Strabo 9,2,25'; Merrill 1893, ad loc.; Bing 1988, 37–8.

23 In his commentary to Apollonius, as published by Loeb, Mooney (1912, ad loc.) explained the text thus: 'σκοπιῆς: here, as in Hom., of a mountain peak, literally "a look-out place," specula; cf. 999. Πιμπληΐδος: Pimpleia in Pieria, a mountain (in later times a fountain) sacred to the Muses, who were hence called Πιμπληΐδες, cf. Hor. C. 1,26, 9, Pimplei dulcis.'

24 See Apollod. 1,24; Posidipp. 118,8–9 A.–B.

25 Schol. in. Ap. Rhod. 31–34a [Πιερίηθεν]: Πιερία ὄρος Θράκης, ἐν ᾗ διέτριβεν Ὀρφεύς.

26 See Hor. *carm.* 1,26,9: Muses as Pipleides.
27 Apollod. 1,24; Lyc. *Alex.* 275; Poseidipp. 118,8–9 A.-B.
28 Buxton 1994; Petridou 2015.
29 See Callimachus (fr. 2 Pf. and scholia Florentina ad fr. 1–2); Ennius (*Ann.* I fr. I–XII; VII, fr. I–II Vahlen); Propertius (3,1); Quintus Smyrneus (12,306–13).
30 See Kambylis 1965. Another contribution to the popularity of Hesiod's description was the creation of a sanctuary of the Muses in the Valley of the Muses below Helicon and the rise of a heroic cult of Hesiod; see Beaulieu 2004; Robinson 2012; 2013; Mojsik 2019.
31 This might be how Parnassus became the mountain of Muses in Roman literature, see Enn. *Ann.* I fr. I–XII; VII, fr. I–II Vahlen; Pers. *prol.* 1–3; von Geisau 1919; Schmidt 1949.
32 See Varro, *Rust.* 3,5,9 about a *mouseion* situated over a stream; Plin. *HN* 37,6,2 on *mouseion* as an artificial grotto; Plin. *HN* 36,154 on *mouseion* as a grotto in a Roman home; on Cicero's villa see McCracken 1935; on grottos in Roman villas see Neumann 2016, 127–36; on *locus amoenus* in ancient culture, see Hass 1998.
33 On the category of 'road' in the metapoetic language, see Nünlist 1998, 228–83; Gundlach 2019, 23–60.
34 See Call. *h.* 4,7; Euphorion 416 SH; fr. 988, 993 SH; Varro, *Ling.* 7,20.
35 See Iambl. *VP* 145; Burgess Watson 2013.
36 Kimmel-Clauzet, 2013: 207, 251.
37 On grottoes in Greek culture and *theia mania*, see in particular Ustinova 2009; 2017.
38 On nympholepsy: Connor 1988; on epiphany: Petridou 2015.
39 Kimmel-Clauzet, 2013: 251–3.
40 On the role of grottoes on Parnassus and Helicon, and their ties to nymphs and Muses, see Robinson 2013.
41 Plin. *HN* 37,14: 'musaeum ex margaritis, in cuius fastigio horologium'. On artificial grottoes in Roman culture, see Lavagne 1998. On their possible role in a garden and as part of a manufactured *locus amoenus*, or simply a place for intellectual work, see also Varro, *Rust.* 3,5,9 and commentary in Tilly 1973 ad loc.
42 See e.g. Moschos 3,76 sqq.; Kambylis 1965, 113–16; Crowther 1979.
43 Linking springs and water in general to poetic inspiration is not seen until the Hellenistic period, see Theocr. 7,148: Castalian nymphs as Muses; see Crowther 1979; Rutherford 1990, 199 and n. 106; Mojsik 2023 (forthcoming).
44 On nymphs and natural terrain features, see Larson 2001.
45 About Camenae see Waszink 1956 and Hardie 2016, which contains sources and further reading.
46 See Hardie 2016, 54.

47 See e.g. Cat. 105; Hor. *c.* 1,26,9; Stat. *Silv.* 1,4,25; 2,2,37; Mart. 12,11,3; Aus. *Ep.* 14,9.
48 Thesleff 1965: 104–5; Centrone 2014; Betegh 2014; Brisson 2016.
49 Schol. Eurip. *Rhes.* 346.
50 Schol. Ap. Rhod. 23–25b ((σκοπιῆς) Πιμπληίδος ἄγχι τεκ(έσθαι):) Πίμπλεια χωρίον κατὰ Πιερίαν· οἱ δὲ ὄρος Θράκης, οἱ δὲ κρήνην καὶ κώμην τῆς Πιερίας.
51 *AP* 7,8 (Antipater of Sydon); 7,9 (Damagetos).
52 Hom. *Il.* 2,846; 17,73. On Cicones and Orpheus, see Ps.-Arist. fr. 641,48; Verg. *Georg.* 4,520; Ov. *Met.* 11,4.
53 Cicones: Hom. *Il.* 9,164–8; Pangaion: Aeschylus [Eratosth. *Catast.* 24]. The broadest description of Thracian tribes in a story of Orpheus can be found in the Suda lexicon. Its mythographical entries feature Orpheus from Leibethra in Thrace, a city at the foot of Pieria (*o* 654); Orpheus the Cicone or Arcadian from Bizaltia in Thrace, an epic writer (*o* 655); Orpheus from the tribe of Odrysians, an epic writer (*o* 656); or Orpheus, king of Thrace, in whose time the Amazons forced the Phrygians to pay tribute (*o* 659).
54 Conon 45; Philostr. *Her.* 704; Val. Flacc. *Arg.* 1,470; 5,99; 5,439; Stat. *Silv.* 5,1,203; 5,3,271; *Theb.* 8,57.
55 Sears 2013; 2015; Psoma 2014.
56 Ov. *Met.* 11,69.
57 Tzetz. *Chil.* 1,306; 8,9.
58 Considering the role of Mount Pangaion in Orpheus' geography, the complete absence of the tribe of 'Pieres' in known narratives may be surprising. Considering the account of Thucydides (2,99) and the ties of the tribe to lands south of the Pangaion, their territory appears best suited to be the cradle of Orpheus. However, we do not encounter them in sources and this omission is greatly significant.
59 About Thracian interest in Asclepiades see Asirvatham 2011.
60 Phanocles fr. 1 Powell; Ap. Rhod. 1,34; Nicander *Ther.* 461; Ps.-Mosch. 3,17–18; see *AP* 7,10.
61 On Rhodopes and Hebrus, see Luc. *adv. ind.* 11; Ov. *Met.* 11,50–5. Terrain features became an important part of the narrative of Orpheus and his death: the river explained how the body or the head was able to move and why the graves were not at the Thracian site where he had supposedly died.
62 *Arg. orph.* 76; Nonnus, *Dion.* 13,428–31.
63 See Myrsilus of Methymna (OF 1065T) and Chapter 4 below.
64 See e.g. Burges Watson 2013, 455; Heslin 2018, 91; Graf 1987, n. 35: '*Pieriē Bistonis* in Ap. Rhod I 34 is a poetical way of saying Thracian Pieria.'
65 See Bernabé 2005, 416; Hunter 2009, 141.

66 Examples of such topographic compounds in Hellenistic literature include: Ap. Rhod. 4,260: Θήβης Τριτωνίδος, similarly 1311 (see Lycoph. *Alex*. 119 and 576); Posidippus 128: Παφίη Κυθέρεια (see *AP* 16,160 ['Plato']); Posidippus 118,8–9 A.-B. (Θήβης Πιμπλείης); Meleager, *AP* 7,417 (Ἀτθὶς ἐν Ἀσσυρίοις [...] Γαδάροις).
67 Polyb. 5,34,2–9; OGIS 54.
68 On the links between Alexandrian poets and Ptolemaic court and politics, see Asper 2011; Strootman 2017.
69 Marcaccini 1995: 241: 'in un periodo di tempo ben determinato e relativamente tardo, l'associazione tra Orfeo e la Tracia abbia assunto nell'immaginario greco un ruolo preponderante e decisivo'.
70 On scholia in general, see Wilson 2007.

Chapter 4

1 See Hammond 1972, 416–18; Graf 1987, 87 and n. 26; Brown 2002, 303–4; Graf, and Iles Johnston 2007, 167.
2 Translated by D. W. Roller; Strabo C 471 [10,3,17]: Ἀπὸ δὲ τοῦ μέλους καὶ τοῦ ῥυθμοῦ καὶ τῶν ὀργάνων καὶ ἡ μουσικὴ πᾶσα Θρακία καὶ Ἀσιᾶτις νενόμισται. δῆλον δ' ἔκ τε τῶν τόπων ἐν οἷς αἱ Μοῦσαι τετίμηνται· Πιερία γὰρ καὶ Ὄλυμπος καὶ Πίμπλα καὶ Λείβηθρον τὸ παλαιὸν ἦν Θρᾴκια χωρία καὶ ὄρη, νῦν δὲ ἔχουσι Μακεδόνες· τόν τε Ἑλικῶνα καθιέρωσαν ταῖς Μούσαις Θρᾷκες οἱ τὴν Βοιωτίαν ἐποικήσαντες, οἵπερ καὶ τὸ τῶν Λειβηθριάδων νυμφῶν ἄντρον καθιέρωσαν. οἵ τ' ἐπιμεληθέντες τῆς ἀρχαίας μουσικῆς Θρᾷκες λέγονται, Ὀρφεύς τε καὶ Μουσαῖος καὶ Θάμυρις (...).
3 Strabo's comments on Pieria are formulated in a way that leaves it unclear whether the word 'mountains' in the phrase 'places and mountains' (χωρία καὶ ὄρη) refers to all these toponyms (Pieria, Olympus, Pimpla and Leibethron) or only some (certainly Olympus; additionally, Pieria is a territory largely covered by the Olympus massif). This created an impression that Pimpleia and Leibethra could be mountains as well, although elsewhere (book 7, fr. 10) Strabo clarified that they are a village and a town in Pieria, respectively. This ambiguity caused even some modern scholars to read Strabo's information as a suggestion that the toponyms are or might refer to mountains. Montanari (2015) understood Pimpleia as a mountain based on a parallel passage from Strabo (C 471 [9,2,25]), while Hatzopoulos and Paschidis (2004, 803) note in their *Inventory* that Leibethra may be classified differently in various sources, including as 'χωρίον or ὄρος' and quote the aforementioned fragment of *Geography* (C 410 [10,3,17]). Therefore, they assume that the

geographer considered Leibethra a mountain. On the imagery of mountains in Strabo, see König 2016; on the writer himself, see Dueck 2017; on the depictions of barbarians in Strabo and his ethnographic interests, see Almagor 2005 and Dandrow 2017; on Thracians in Strabo's writing, see Boshnakov 2003.

4 Paus. 9,34,4: Κορωνείας δὲ σταδίους ὡς τεσσαράκοντα ὄρος ἀπέχει τὸ Λιβήθριον, ἀγάλματα δὲ ἐν αὐτῷ Μουσῶν τε καὶ νυμφῶν ἐπίκλησίν ἐστι Λιβηθρίων· καὶ πηγαὶ – τὴν μὲν Λιβηθριάδα ὀνομάζουσιν, ἡ δὲ ἑτέρα † Πέτρα – γυναικὸς μαστοῖς εἰσιν εἰκασμέναι, καὶ ὅμοιον γάλακτι ὕδωρ ἀπ' αὐτῶν ἄνεισιν. One of the noteworthy accounts linking Pieria to Boeotia is a passage from a work by Melisseus (BNJ 402 F1 [Rzepka] = Schol. Tzetz. Hesiod. Opp. 1 p. 32, 17 Gaisf. 2 (cf. Tzetz. Chil. 6, 931ff.): καὶ πραγματικῶς μὲν Πιερία καὶ Ἑλικὼν ὄρη καὶ πόλεις Βοιωτίας ('In fact, Pieria and Helicon are Boeotian cities and mountains'). Remarkably, the author continues on about Pieria, suggesting that the above is a result of a misunderstanding, quoting from memory, or the author's imagination. Moreover, we can say nothing about the author with certainty; Jacek Rzepka, the editor of his fragments in BNJ, believes that Melisseus is 'an invented author of the *Delphic Questions*, must have been identified as a Cretan king, known also as Melissos'.

5 Kimmel-Clauzet 2013; Higbie 2017.

6 On Ilissus, see Mojsik 2023 (forthcoming). A similar example may have been the cult of the nymphs on Cithaeron known as 'Sphragitides': Paus. 9,3,9; Plut. *Arist.* 11,3,1–51. On the Muses of Cithaeron: schol. Eur. *Phoen.* 801, see Corinn. fr. 654 PMG; Berman 2015, 73.

7 See Euphorion fr. 416 SH; fr. 988 and 993 SH; Varro, *Ling.* 7,20; and especially: Verg. *Ecl.* 7,21.

8 See SEG 58,438 [Knoepfler].

9 On the excavation, see Vasilopoulou 2000; 2001; 2013.

10 See Vasilopoulou 2013, 321: 'Classic and later figurines from the cave can be more safely identified with specific deities of the Greek mythology.' Vasilopoulou and another participant of the excavation both confirmed over e-mail that the material lacks any trace of the Muses.

11 On statues of Muses and their reuse, see Ridgway 1990; Taback 2002.

12 For a critique of Strabo's accounts see Schachter 1986, 188: 'Both are valueless'; Lipka 2001, 100–1.

13 See Schachter 1986, 188 n. 2. The matter of Strabo's sources for this passage is somewhat more complex and there is no consensus, see Kühr 2006; Prakken 1943, 422–3; Larson 2001, 139, n. 40; and V. Parker in his commentary ad loc. in BNJ.

14 On the Boeotian–Thracian conflict, see Polyaen. *Strat.* 7,43; see also V. Parker BNJ F119 ad loc.

15 On the presence of Thracians in Attica, see Strabo 7,7,1; on Eumolpus as Thracian: 10,3,17.
16 On Strabo as a historian, see Malinowski 2017.
17 Sprawski 2010.
18 On the ties between myth and the political context and history, see Fowler 2015, 195–210; Graf 1993, 121–41.
19 Hall 1996.
20 On autochthony, see Hes. fr. 160; Roy 2014.
21 On allochthony, see Fowler 2013, 84–96; on Boeotia and Thebes see Ganter 2014; Berman 2015.
22 Fowler 2013, 84–96; McInerney 2014a.
23 Call. *h.* 4,75; Paus. 9,5,1; see Ganter 2014, 229–30; Berman 2015.
24 Sears 2013.
25 Dowden 1992, 60–1.
26 V. Parker in the commentary to Ephorus (BNJ 70 F119): 'Presumably these Thracians are the ones said to inhabit the Phocian town of Daulis (e.g. Thucydides 2,29,3).' For other attempts to explain stories of 'Thracians' in Phocis/Boeotia, see McInerney 1999.
27 Pl. *Leg.* 1,637d–e; Athen. 10,442f; 10,432a.
28 Strabo C 410 (9,2,25): 'The Thracians used to be called Pieres, but, now that they have disappeared, the Macedonians hold these places'; see Strabo 7 fr. 7a: 'Regarding the Thracians, the Pieres inhabited Pieria and the region around Olympos'; see Paus. 9,29,3.
29 Hammond 1972, 416–18; see e.g. Graf 1987, 87; Papazoglou 1988, 103, n. 5; King 2017, n. 102; Vasilev 2011.
30 Vasilev 2009 also adds little to the debate.
31 This passage inspired scholars to create fantastic visions that had little to do with Thucydides' actual information. Two examples: Hammond 1995, 123: 'The Macedones over whom the first Temenid king, Perdiccas, ruled, when they were living "around Pieria and Olympus," were mountaineers who, like their counterparts today, *were engaged in transhumant pastoralism and rented some of their winter pastures from the Thracian "Pieres" who occupied the Pierian coastland* (Thuc. 2.99)'; Vasilev 2015, 150: 'This conclusion is also valid for the Pieres, whose lands, probably, were the first conquered by the Macedonians. The conquest of Pieria belongs to the first stage of the Argead invasion, *characterized by the slaughter and expulsion of the local people. It is possible the Macedonians let a small number of the Pieres remain in their homes*, though they were hardly so significant in number as to be, about one hundred and fifty years later and in spite of their

being an integral part of Macedonia, separately mobilized in the Persian army.' [emphasis mine].

32 See *Etym. Magn.* s.v. [Πιερία]: Ὄνομα τόπου, ἔνθα αἱ Μοῦσαι ἐγεννήθησαν. Παρὰ τὸ Πίηρ γέγονεν· ἢ ἀπὸ τοῦ Πιεροῦ ἀδελφοῦ τῆς Μεθώνης· ἢ ἀπὸ Πιερίας νύμφης. Τὸ δὲ Πίηρ, παρὰ τὸ πίω ῥῆμα· ἢ παρὰ τὸ πῖον, ὃ σημαίνει τὸ λιπαρόν· ἔστι δὲ ὄνομα κύριον.

33 Examples of toponyms and proper names with that root: Paus 5,16,8 (Piera, spring in Elis); 7,22,1 (Pieros, river in Achaea). The radix πίηρ also appears in first names: Apollod. 3,133 (Pieris, concubine of Menelaus, Aetolian slave); Apollod. 2,20 (Pieria, mother to some Danaids); *Etym. Magn.* s.v.; Eustath. comm. ad *Il.* 14,226,970 (nymph, eponym of Pieria); Paus. 9,30 (Pieria, wife of Oxylus); see Hammond 1972, 139, n. 1.

34 Hammond 1972, 417: 'The Thracians of Pieria took their name from that of the country.'

35 Sprawski 2010, 133–4.

36 See Bingen 2007, 83 (on Thracians in Hellenistic Egypt): 'We know how embarrassing for nonspecialists the ambiguities surrounding the notion of "Thrace/Thracian" can be: is this an ethnic expression, a geographic expression (with the Bithynian onomastics creating one more problem), a political expression (as for instance in Lysimachus' short-lived kingdom of Thrace), or simply the denomination of a military unit with servicemen from heterogeneous origins?'

37 Sprawski 2010, 143.

38 Sprawski 2010, 134; Hatzopoulos 2020.

39 Hammond 1972, 417: 'It seems that the Thracian occupation of Pieria dated from c. 1300 BC, let us say, to c. 650 BC and it was during this long time that Thracian influences in music and in religion percolated into Greece from Pieria and not from what was later known as Thrace.'

40 Hammond 1972, 418: 'It is important to make this definition, because ancient and modern writers tend to include Phrygians, Mysians, Teucrians, Illyrians, and Paeonians under the general umbrella of Thracians.'

41 Sprawski 2010, 133–4; on hybrid identity, see Reger 2014.

42 Hom. *Il.* 14,226; cf. *h. hom.* 3, 70–3; see Mari 2011, 79: 'The Homeric poems mention Pieria as a purely geographical point of reference and ignore the lands and populations beyond its northern boundaries, the remaining parts of historical Macedonia. The whole area between Pieria and the Thessalian ethnē, to the south, and the area close to the river Axios which was inhabited by the Paionians, to the north-east, is in the Homeric poems a "no man's land".'

43 Mari 2011, 464: *Corpus des inscriptions de Delphes* I, 1.

44 Eur. *Bacch.* 409–11; see Menaichmos of Sikyon (BNJ 131 F2).

45 Hellanicus BNJ 4 F74; see Hall 2002, 165; Hatzopoulos 2011, 57.
46 Epicharmus fr. 39 PCG; Hellanicus BNJ 4 F74; Marsyas BNJ 135–6 F13; Certamen 4.
47 *Certamen* 4; Melisseus BNJ 402 F1 and chapter 5 below.
48 Ps.-Scymnus 620, possibly after Ephorus.
49 For similar examples from Boeotia, see Ganter 2014.
50 On the uneasy relations between Athens and Perdiccas during the Peloponnesian War, see Zahrnt 2010; Müller 2017a. On argumentation based on previous occupation of an area, see Sprawski 2012, 169–70.
51 Considering the 'polemic' between Alcidamas (Orpheus as the inventor of writing and wisdom) and Androtion (Thracians are illiterate barbarians, thus, Orpheus must have been an illiterate barbarian), it is impossible to rule out that Strabo's notions were rooted in the fourth century and tied into the discussion on the role of Orpheus in the development of Greek culture, as well as his possible primacy (as the author of Orphic texts) over Homer and Hesiod. However, it was not until Strabo that all the arguments (including references to Boeotian Libethrion) were assembled and the hypothesis formulated.
52 See Linforth 1941, 28, 165; Graf and Iles Johnston 2007, 167.
53 See e.g. Long 1986, 63–8; Larson 2001, 169.
54 There are other accounts suggesting a narrative of seniority of the three Boeotian/Heliconian Muses, see Paus. 9,30,1 and Aug. *de doctr. christ.* 2,68–70.
55 Ov. *Met.* 5,310 sqq.; see Antoninus Liberalis 9; Paus. 9,29,4. The duel saw the false Muses turned into birds.
56 See Xen. *Anab.* 7,3; Athen. 4,130b–c; 4,151; Baralis 2015. This form of Thracian feasts must have been perceived by the Greeks as similar to those of Macedonian rulers, see Pownall 2017.
57 Tsiafaki 2016, 272.
58 See however Cowan 2021 (Oeagrus as a metonym for outmoded poetry in Ar. *Vesp.* 579–80).

Chapter 5

1 See Wickersham 1991.
2 On the local and the Panhellenic, see Graf 2011; about the need to transcend that duality see Kindt 2012, 123–54.
3 Bernabé 2005, 416. Graf 1987 postulates a Macedonian tradition, but ties it to Conon's story of associations of men.
4 E.g. Hes. *Th.* 53; *Op.* 1; Ps.-Hes. *Scut.* 206; Sa. fr. 103.

5 Revermann 1999/2000; Scullion 2003; Hardie 2006; Moloney 2014; Hecht 2017, 19–27 and 40–78; Euripides' *Archelaus*: Hyg. *Fab.* 219; Harder 1985; Pownall 2017; Stewart 2017, 118–38; on *The Bacchae*, see Dodds 1960, XXXIX–XL.
6 Csapo 2004; Wilson 2004.
7 On general editorial problems with the reconstruction of Timotheus' text, see Hordern 2002, 241–2; Budelmann 2018 (ad loc.).
8 Hordern 2002 accepts Hutchinson's supplement <τέχν>αν (sc. ποικιλόμουσον) in v. 222; Bernabé also proposes such in OF 883T. I leave Wilamowitz's emendation that was accepted by LeVen 2014, 97 and Budelmann 2018. In any event, the choice of version has no consequences for our interpretation.
9 Πιερίαθεν is Page's emendation (see PMG ad loc), papyrus says πιεριασενι ('in Pieria').
10 See Heraclides Ponticus fr. 157 Wehrli.
11 Plut. *Mor.* 117 B F 24; Hecht 2016, 32–3 and 127–54.
12 Strabo 7, fr. 10; 7, fr. 17; Conon 45; Paus. 10,5; see also OF 937T.
13 See Santamaría Álvarez 2008.
14 See Psoma 2014; Sprawski 2010, 142; Müller 2017a.
15 McNellis and Sens 2016.
16 *Aethiopis Arg.* p. 112 (4) West; Eur. *Rhes.* 973.
17 Varro, *Ling.* 7,20.
18 But see Lipka 2001, 100–1.
19 See Athen. 7,326d (Archestratus of Gela); Liv. 44,6; Claud. Ptol. 3,12,12,1; schol. in Lycoph. *Alex.* 275.
20 For evidence of its spread in ancient literature, see OF 1064T (Lib. *Decl.* 1,182, Himer. *or.* 46,3 [185 s. Colonna]).
21 There are no complete works on the manuscriptal tradition (see, however, Bühler 1987; Spirydonidou-Skarsouli 1995) or modern editions of proverbs based on all known manuscripts.
22 Suda ζ 73 s.v. Ζηνόβιος.
23 This manuscript version is only known from M. E. Miller's 1868 edition *Mélanges de littérature Grecque*. On the proverb, see Romero 2011.
24 On *amousia*, see Halliwell 2012 and Epilogue, below.
25 Long 1986, 143, probably after Himer. *or.* 46,3: 'Libethrii, who lived near Mt. Pangaeum'.
26 On 'ethnos', also meaning 'people of a polis', see McInerney 2001, 64; Gruen 2013.
27 Zonaras p. 1294 Tittmann: Λειβήθριοι· ἔθνος μωρόν· ἀπὸ τόπου Λείβηθρα καλουμένου, ἐν ᾧ κατοικοῦσιν ἀνόητοι ἄνθρωποι· Θουγενίδης. Λειβηθρίων ἀνοητότεροι. In manuscripts it is only Θουκιδίδης.
28 Bühler 1987; Spirydonidou-Skarsouli 1995.

29 Arist. fr. 487 (*Constitution of Delphi*); fr. 571; fr. 576; *Constitution of Athens* (28,3: Zenob. 1,474).
30 Natali 2013, 26: 'Popular sayings and proverbs are frequently used by Aristotle in his works (for a list of passages, see Bonitz 1870, s.v. *paroimiai*). He gathered them not out of ethnological interest but as a collection of information to be used in the physical sciences as well, for instance, astronomy'.
31 Charax's version is relayed in the Suda lexicon (*omi*. 251), which cites him in its entry on Homer. Charax's presentation of the genealogy of Homer may tie into his interest in the history of Illion and Troas (see BNJ 103 F33, F54, F59, F63).
32 Richardson 1981; Bassino 2019.
33 See 4 F5a, cf. schol. Hes. *Opp*. 631, p. 361,6 Gaisford, which only mentions Hesiod's descent from Orpheus. See Fowler 2013, 609: 'The genealogy quoted in Hellan. fr 5b, which is replicated with minimal differences in the "Contest of Homer and Hesiod" 4 (p. 322 West) and Charax BNJ 103 F62 = OF 872T, is surely that of Hellanikos'.
34 The details are provided in the commentary in BNJ 4 F5b (F. Pownall) and Bassino 2019 ad loc.
35 Hippias BNJ 6 F13; Ephor BNJ 70 F99; see Kivilo 2010, 12–17.
36 See F. Pownall in the commentary to BNJ 4 F5b.
37 Hdt. 2,53.
38 See Kivilo 2010.
39 Schol. Pind. *Pyth*. 4,313a (Asclepiades, Menaechmus, Chaeris); this genealogy is also possible in the case of Aeschylus' *Bassarids*: see Eratosth. *Cat*. 24, where Apollo gives the lyre to Orpheus.
40 Schol. Tzetz. Hesiod. *Opp*. 1 p. 32, 17 Gaisf. 2.
41 Papazoglou 1988, 105–6.
42 Pierus as the eponymous hero of Pieria, son of Makedon, son of Zeus and Thyia: Marsyas BNJ 135–6 F13; schol. Hom. Il. 14,226c,1 ex. Pierus, son of Magnes (brother of Makedon?), see Apollod. 1,16. Pierus, son of Eleuther, see schol. Hom. *Il*. 14,226c,1 ex.
43 On the ties of genealogy to oral culture, the socio-political context, on modifying stories and a gradual disappearance of the genealogical tradition, see Fowler 1999.
44 Notably, a version portraying Linus as Theban and the teacher of Heracles would gain currency in a later period. It appears that our genealogy precedes (or is an answer to) Boeotian actions related to the tomb of the musician in that region.
45 Hall 2002, 165.
46 Suda s.v. Ἑλλάνικος (*epsilon*, 739): διέτριψε δὲ Ἑλλάνικος σὺν Ἡροδότῳ παρὰ Ἀμύντᾳ τῷ Μακεδόνων βασιλεῖ.
47 Linforth 1941, 26.

48 Eur. *Bacch.* 410: καλλιστευομένα / Πιερία, μούσειος ἕδρα, / σεμνὰ κλειτὺς Ὀλύμπου ('fairest Pieria, the Muses' haunt, holy slope of Mount Olympus' [tr. D. Kovacs]).
49 Commentary in Gow-Page, vol. 2, 353–4.
50 See Magnelli 2010.
51 Fr. 988 and 993 SH; Magnelli 2010, Canetta 2008.
52 E.g. Catull. 105; *c.* 1,26,9; Opp. *Cyn.* 2,157; Statius *Silv.* 1,4,25; Mart. 12,11,3; Aus. *Ep.* 14,9. See also Nonnus, *Dion.* 13,428
53 OF 771 F: Tzetz. schol. Lycoph. 409 = Exeges. in *Iliad.* 30,12 Herm.; Maximus Astrol., Περὶ καταρχῶν 6,141; Tzetz. *Chil.* 6, 941–3.

Chapter 6

1 Hendrix 2007, 16.
2 On 'cultural saints', see Dović and Helgason 2016.
3 See Cic. *de fin.* 5,1–6; *Tusc.* 5,64–6; on ancient collections, see Gahtan and Pegazzano 2015; Higbie 2017.
4 See Timaeus BNJ 566 F133; Cic. *de fin.* 5,2,4; Paus. 9,23,2; Kimmel-Clauzet 2013, 230–3.
5 Interest in the graves of poets in Ancient and European culture has remarkably increased in recent years. One of the products of such a state of affairs has been the 'Living Poets' research project headed by B. Graziosi, and the *Tomb of the Ancient Poets* research conference with its assorted publication of the same title (Goldschmidt and Graziosi 2018).
6 On hero worship, see Antonaccio 1995 (esp. 145–98); Ekroth 2002; 2015.
7 Graf 1987, Bremmer 1991, Graziosi 2018.
8 Biographical tradition: Lefkowitz 1981; Graziosi 2002. Cult of the poets: Zanker 1995; Clay 2004; Kimmel-Clauzet 2013.
9 On the tomb of Orpheus in general, see lately Santamaría Álvarez 2008. Most researchers believe the Lesbos tomb to be a relatively early, perhaps even original part of the myth of Orpheus, see Robert 1917; Linforth 1941, 132 sqq.; Robbins 1982, 15; Jackson 1995, 70; Burges Watson 2013, 444.
10 Hyg. *Poet. astr.* 2,7: 'His head, which fell down the mountain into the sea, was washed ashore by the waves on the island of Lesbos, where it was gathered up and buried by the local people. As a result of this good deed, they are thought to be exceptionally gifted in the art of music' [tr. R. Hard]; Ael. Aristid. *or.* 24,5; Himer. *or.* 26.
11 See Hyg. *Poet. astr.* 2,7; Philostr. *Vit. Apoll.* 4,14; *Heroïc.* 28,8; Nikomachos, *Exc.* 1 (p. 266 Jan); Luc. *Adv. indoct.* 11, *de salt.* 51; Himer. *or.* 26; Procl. in Plat. *Remp.* II

315,2; Schol. German. Arat. BP (84,12 Breysig = 140 Rob.); schol. Aesch. *Pers.* 885 (240 Daehnhardt). On the *caput loquens* and Lesbos, see OF 1052–61

12 Destruction of Leibethra and transfer of the tomb to Dion: Paus. 9,30,7–11; destruction of Antissa: Liv. 43,31,14.
13 Guthrie 1952, 35–6. For examples of the head in iconography, see LIMC 7,1 (*Orpheus*), 68–9 (Garezou 1994).
14 Graf 1987, 95; Burges Watson 2013, 447: 'The principal purpose of the story about Orpheus' head was surely to account for writings ascribed to him'; Graziosi 2018.
15 See Eur. *Alc.* 969–71; schol. Eur. *Alc.* 968 (= Heracleides 'physikos').
16 Wilamowitz-Möllendorf 1903, 84; Linforth 1941, 133–4.
17 See Hyg. *Poet. astr.* 2,7; Nikomach. *Exc.* 1 [p. 266 Jan].
18 See especially Philostr. *Vit. Apoll.* 4,14; *Heroic.* 28,8; Luc. *Adv. indoct.* 11, *de salt.* 51.
19 Gostoli 1990, XVI; on the pre-eminence of kitharodes from Lesbos, see Arist fr. 545 Rose; Hsch. s.v. μετὰ Λέσβιον ᾠδόν [proverbial expression] = T 60 Gostoli; on Terpander as a kitharodos, see Ps.-Plut. *de mus.* 1132d, 1133b–d; on his victory in the first Carneia, see Hellanicus FGH 4 F 85; Athenaeus 635e–f; on Arion, see Hdt. 1,23; on kitharodia in general and Terpander, see Power 2010, 317–424.
20 See Barker 2014.
21 Pl. *Ion* 533 (kitharodes 'perform explanations about Orpheus'); Power 2010, 350–5.
22 Csapo and Wilson 2009; Power 2010, 336–45; LeVen 2014, 90–101 and 219–20.
23 See Nikomachos, *Exc.* 1 (p. 266 Jan) = Terpander T53b; translation by T. Power.
24 See Csapo and Wilson 2009, 279–80.
25 Clay 2004, 94.
26 On the epitaphs and graves of the poets, see Rossi 2001; Goldschmidt and Graziosi 2018.
27 Other epitaphs: OF 1073T; AP 7,8–10. On the epitaph of Damagetus (AP 7,9), see Graziosi 2018, 177–8.
28 SH 508 = AP 7,617; Eratosth. *Catast.* 24.
29 Only one other author mentions the burial of Orpheus in Dion: Diogenes Laertius (1,5).
30 On Bephyra and Orpheus, see Lyc. *Alex.* 274 and the discussion of the passage in Chapter 5.
31 Paus. 9,30,10; see Graziosi 2018.
32 Timaios BNJ 566 F131; Dikaiarchos fr. 35 Wehrli; and especially Iust. 20,40: 'Pythagoras autem cum annos XX Crotone egisset, Metapontum emigravit ibique decessit; cuius tanta admiratio fuit, ut ex domo eius templum facerent eumque pro deo colerent.' See Boyancé 1937; Mojsik 2015; 2017.

33 Plut. *Tim.* 12; Ap. Rhod. 4,1284–5 and scholia ad loc.; Diod. Sic. 17,10,4; Arr. *Anab.* 1,11,2; Quint. Smyrn. 12,507–9; see Bremmer 2013.
34 Nawotka 2017, *comm.* ad loc.: 'The story related in this chapter does not have much in common with historical events. The impossible geography of this passage underscores its fictitious nature, further strengthened by including the mythological seer Melampus in this episode.'
35 A similar case of corrupting the proper name in a late text is found in Hyginus (*Fab.* 14,44).
36 Callistr. *Desc.* 7; see Paus. 9,30,4.
37 Henrichs 1987, 244–7; Brown 2002; S. Blakely in BNJ; Hawes 2014, 133–47.
38 Brown 2002, 317–20; Cameron 2004, 72.
39 Henrichs 1987, 244–7; Brown 2002, 19–20.
40 Heinrichs 1987, 245–7, nn. 11 and 20.
41 Leaf 1915; Liapis 2011.
42 Similar situations: Plut. *Thes.* 36; *Cim.* 8 (Theseus); Hdt. 1,67–8; Paus. 8,54,4 (Orestes).
43 On the founding of the city, see Thuc. 4,102. On Hagnon's actions, see Mari 2012; on hero worship in Thrace, see Pavlopoulou 1994.
44 See Daux 1960; Theodossiev 2000.
45 Hanink 2018, 244–8.
46 On the problematic nature of the term 'cult' with regards to such phenomena and a need for interpretation transcending religious gestures, see Mojsik 2015.
47 On the usefulness of the term 'intellectual' as a collective noun for participants in various forms of ancient Greek intellectual activity (poets, philosophers, rhetors, etc.), see Zanker 1995, 2; Clay 2004, 94; Mojsik 2015.
48 Clay 2004; Kimmel-Clauzet 2013; Goldschimdt and Graziosi 2018.
49 About the cult of Homer: Ael. *VH* 13,22; see Kimmel-Clauzet 2013, 285–318; Zanker 1995, 171–3; about Philitas see Hardie 1997 and 2003.
50 Kondoleon 1952; Clay 2004, 9–39; latest discussion of the *testimonia*: Kimmel-Clauzet 2013, 223–9 (*testimonia* themselves: 340–52).
51 Zanker 1995, 142–5; Rossi 2001, 323–8.
52 Lamprinoudakis 1986.
53 See, however, Clinton 2022 and new published inscription *I.Rhamnous* 404.
54 On the early history of the *mouseion*, see Mojsik 2023 (forthcoming). Rutledge's conclusions (2012, 22) that Pausanias talks about the existence of a temple of the Muses on the hill, have to be considered overly reaching. Nesselrath's remarks (2013, 65, n. 2), which conclude that the altar of the Muses was on the slopes of the hill, are similarly imprecise and confusing.

55 On the heroon of Musaeus in this location, see Greco 2011, 359–67.
56 Gorgias 82 B25 DK; Ar. *Ran.* 1032–6.
57 Bremmer 1991, 26: 'When sixth-century Athens (Eleusis?) created a fictitious poet in order to enhance the credibility of oracles, it still invented the name Musaeus. Later times could do without the immediate invocation of the Muses.'
58 See Haake 2020 (on philosophers); Diog. Laert. 5,91 (a story about Heraclides Ponticus, a philosopher who sought to have himself worshipped as a hero in his home polis).
59 The art of collecting is not religious; however, if the collection is later placed in a shrine as a votive offering, it becomes sacred. See Hermippos frg. 84 Bollanseé = fr. 94 Wehrli = *Vita Euripidis* 5,80–90; see Lefkowitz 1981, 96–7, 167; Mojsik 2017.
60 See Diog. Laert. 5,64; 5,71; Cic. *de finibus* 5,2,4. The term appears in some sources, in the form *mnemeion* or *mneme*, in the descriptions of objects, places or actions associated with the commemoration of a poet, a philosopher or an orator. While not all honours bestowed upon poets or intellectuals required a religious setting (or at least it is not obvious in available sources), every action of this kind stems from a desire to pay homage to the achievements of a given individual and 'improve' them, which, in turn, refers to remembrance.
61 E.g. the statue of Stesichorus in the Himera agora, see Cic. *Verr.* 2,35; statue of Hesiod in the Thespiae agora, see Paus. 9,27,5; statue of Poseidippus in Pella, see Posidipp. 118 AB. On the statues of intellectuals in general, see Zanker 1995; Dillon 2006, 40.
62 On the anniversaries of the birth of Epicurus, see Cic. *de fin.* 2,103; Diog. Laert. 10,18. On associations linked to these practices, such as the 'Hesiodic synthytai', Platonists, Timotheastai or Hegesiastai, see Jones 2010, 44.
63 Tragedians travel to the tomb of Aeschylus, see *Vita* A 11; the poet Nossis (*AP* 7,718=11 G.-P.) assumes people travel to Mytilene to draw inspiration where Sappho lived (see Bing 1988, 39, n. 60); Call. *Iamb.* 13: Hipponax and following a poet's footsteps.
64 On the Archelaus relief, see Pinkwart 1965. On the various forms of worship of exceptional individuals of the past, see Arist. *Rhet.* 2,23, 1398b; Mojsik 2015.
65 See Paus. 6,17,7; 10,18,7; *CEG* 830; Cic. *de orat.* 3,32,129.
66 This process and the cultural circumstances surrounding the emergence of intellectuals are matters deserving of a separate book.
67 Sommerstein 2010; Palladini 2013, 296–302.
68 See Bing 1993; Lefkowitz 1981; Kivilo 2010; Hägg 2012. On the biographies of mythical poets, see Platthy 1985.
69 Knobl 2008, 85.

70 On appropriating mythical poets in Hellenistic Alexandria, see Klooster 2011, 75–113.
71 Tomb of Oedipus in Athens: Paus. 1,2,8 (see Hanink 2018, 241); tomb of Eurystheus in Attica: Apollod. 2,168; Paus. 1,44,10; tomb of Deucalion in Athens: Paus. 1,18,8.
72 See *AP* 16, 296 and 298, and the mentions of the statuary group in the Serapeum (Zanker 1995, 172).
73 Graziosi 2002.
74 Hom. *Il.* 2,595; see Wilson 2009; Karpati 2016.
75 Heinrichs 1985; Bremmer 1991, 26; Kauffmann-Samaras 1992.
76 Argos: Propert. 2,13,3–8; Paus. 2,19,8; Euboea: Diog. Laert. 1,4; Boeotia: Paus. 9,29,7.
77 Robinson 2012, 242 and n. 106: the researcher mentions parallels, such as the Archelaus relief or the cave-shaped Nymphaeum of Arsinoe (Posidipp. 113 AB).
78 Further on, Pausanias also explains the existence of alternative mythographic narrative lines (9,29,9): 'Other tales are told by the Thebans, how that later than this Linus there was born another, called the son of Ismenius, a teacher of music, and how Heracles, while still a child, killed him. But hexameter poetry was written neither by Linus the son of Amphimarus nor by the later Linus; or if it was, it has not survived for posterity.' [tr. W. H. S. Jones].
79 A dream in the story of the tomb of Sophocles, see TGrF 4, Test. 1,15. On the oracle bidding the Orchomenians find the grave of Hesiod, see Paus. 9,38,3–4; Plut. *Mor.* 162E; Procl. ad Hes. *Op.* 631; Kimmel-Clauzet 2013, 321–6; 135–41.
80 See the instances of moving the body of Orestes (Hdt. 1,66–8), Theseus (Plut. *Thes.* 36,1–2) or Hesiod (Paus. 9,38).
81 Schachter 1986, 123.
82 Paus. 9,29,9; Diod. Sic. 3,67,1.
83 See Labuda 2000, 259–73; Sitek 2016.

Chapter 7

1 See Hall 2002, 156; Sprawski 2010, 129–30; Koulakiotis 2017.
2 On Archelaus: Euripides' play *Archelaus* (fr. 228–64); on Caranus: Just. *Epitome* 7,1,7; Satyrus, BNJ 631 F1; Theopompus (BNJ 115 F393); Marsyas (BNJ 135–6 F14); for further reading and discussion, see Sprawski 2010.
3 On myth as a propaganda tool, see Bremmer 1997; on Heracles and Argeads see Huttner 1997 and Moloney 2015.
4 Fowler 1999; Hall 1997, 64.

5 Ps.-Hes. fr. 7 = Const. Porph. *de them.* 2 (p. 86 Pertusi); see Steph. Byz. s.v. [Μακεδονία]; Eust. in Dion. Per. 427.
6 On Emathia, see Marsyas BNJ 135-6 F13; Solinus IX.1; Iust. 7,1; schol. in Dion. Per. 427; schol. in Hom. *Il.* 14,225-6; schol. Hesiod. *Th.* 985.
7 A case similar to Himerius' free interpretation: Tzetz. *Chil.* 6.53: 'Pieria is a mountain in Boeotia / But also a town that was built by Pierus, / Who was brother to Methone and father of Linus. / (...) And truly, Pieria is a mountain like Helicon / And a town, as I have already said' [tr. K. Ramiotis].
8 Borza 1990, 176-7; Roisman, Worthington 2010; Lane Fox 2011.
9 Huttner 1997; Moloney 2015.
10 On the authenticity of *Ulixes*, see O'Sullivan 2008 and a reasonable assessment in Graziosi 2018, n. 49.
11 Linus OF 61-3.
12 See Melisseus BNJ 402 F1.
13 Olson 2007, 42-7.
14 Fr. 157,7 Wehrli = Ps.-Plut. *de mus.* 3, 1131F-1132C.
15 Schol. Iuv. *Sat.* 7.8: '[Nam si Pieria]: Pieria locus sub radicibus Olympi montis, cui Pierus poeta nomen dedit.'
16 OF 771 = Tzetz. *Chil.* 6,945.
17 Pingiatoglou 2010, 190.
18 Diod. Sic. 17,16,3-4; 16,55; schol. Dem. 19,192; D. Chr. 2,2; Arr. 1,11,1; see Pandermalis 1997; Mari 1998; 2002.
19 Pandermalis 1997; Mari 2002, 51-60; Voutiras 2006; Pingiatoglou 2010, 190.
20 Similarly, see Hardie 2006, 59-60.
21 See SEG 53, 2003, 619; 49, 1999, 697. Other *testimonia*: Theophr. *Hist. plant.* 4,16,3,6; Polyb. 37,1,1; Poseidippos 118 AB (Μοῦσαι πολιήτιδες) – see Mojsik (forthcoming 2). Statues: see Pandermalis 1977, 338; Karamitrou-Mentessidi 1983; Pingiatoglou 2010, 180.
22 A. Tziafalias, AD 52 (1997) [2003], 523, no. 19: "Ἀπλονι Μονσαγέ[τ]αις; see Santin and Tziafalias 2020. On the relations between Macedon and Thessaly, see Graninger 2010.
23 Mojsik 2017.
24 Karadedos 1986; Pandermalis 1997; Moloney 2014.
25 See Hammond and Griffith 1979, 48, n. 5.
26 Borza 1990; Sprawski 2010; Pownall 2017.
27 Pind. fr. 120-1; Bacchyl. fr. 20b; see Solinus 9,13; Fearn 2007, 27-86; Sprawski 2010, 142.
28 See Engels 2010; Carney 2015, 193; Pownall 2017.

29 Suda s.v. Ἡρόδοτος: τινὲς δὲ ἐν Πέλλαις αὐτὸν τελευτῆσαί φασιν; see Xydopoulos 2016.
30 Ps.-Sor. *Vit.* 5, CMG 4,176; see Luc. *Hist. conscr.* 35; Tzetz. 7,155; Suda s.v. Ἱπποκράτης; Suda s.v. Μελανιππίδης; see Pownall 2017.
31 On Archelaus' so-called philhellenism and his patronage, see Borza 1990, 171–7; Revermann 2000, 451–67; Scullion 2003, 389–400.
32 Weber 1993, 44–51; Moloney 2014, 234–40; Pownall 2017; Hecht 2017.
33 Arist. *Rhet.* 2,1398; Diog. Laert. 2,25; Dio Chrys. *Or.* 13,30.
34 Pownall 2017.
35 Ael. *VH* 2,21; Aul. Gell. *NA* 25,20,9; see Lefkowitz 1981, 97; Revermann 1999; Scullion 2003; Kimmel-Clauzet 2013, 154–60. On the similar case of the grave of Aeschylus in Gela, see Bakkola 2018.
36 Aul. Gell. *NA* 15,20; Liapis 2011, 72.
37 Hatzopoulos 1994; Graf and Iles Johnston 2007, 137–64; Fulińska 2014.
38 See Sprawski in BNJ.
39 Recently Visscher 2020.
40 On the Macedonian court and patronage in general, see Weber 1993, Strootman 2017; D'Agostini et al. 2021; Pownall et al. 2022.
41 DK 85 B2: Ἀρχελάῳ δουλεύσομεν Ἕλληνες ὄντες βαρβάρῳ.
42 On the opposition to the actions of Archelaus, see Greenwalt 2003, 151–3.
43 Müller 2017b.
44 Pl. *Gorg.* 471a–d; Borza 1990, 161–2; Pownall 2017, 220–1; for a critique of the accusations of Polus in Plato's *Gorgias*, see Müller 2017b, 190–1.
45 Pownall 2017, 220–1.
46 Borza 1990, 176–7; Pownall 2017.

Epilogue: Orpheuses, not Orpheus

1 Halliwell 2012.
2 Murray and Wilson 2004 [Introduction].
3 Lib. *or.* 1,1,182: σημεῖον δέ, Λειβήθριοι μετὰ τὸν Ὀρφέως φόνον δι' ἀμουσίας ἔδοσαν δίκην καὶ κατέχεται τὸ χωρίον ἀπαιδευσίᾳ συχνῇ.
4 Goldschmidt and Graziosi 2018.
5 See Ford 2004; Barker 2014; LeVen 2020.

Bibliography

Acosta-Hughes B. and Stephens S. 2012, *Callimachus in Context. From Plato to the Augustan Poets*, Cambridge: Cambridge University Press.

Almagor, E. 2005, 'Who is a Barbarian? The Barbarians in the Ethnological and Cultural taxonomies of Strabo', in Dueck et al. 2005, 42–55.

Anderson W. S. 1982, 'The Orpheus of Virgil and Ovid: flebile nescio quid', in Warden 1982, 25–50.

Antonaccio C. 1995, *Archaeology of Ancestors. Tomb Cult and Hero Cult in Early Greece*, Lanham/London: Rowman & Littlefield Publishers.

Archibald Z. 1998, *The Odrysian Kingdom of Thrace: Orpheus Unmasked*, Oxford: Oxford University Press.

Asirvatham S. 2011, 'Hints of Local Influence in the *Tragoidoumena* of Asclepiades of Tragilos?', in J. Pamias ed., *Parva Mythographica*, Oberhaid: Utopica Verlag, 145–51.

Asper M. 2011, 'Dimensions of Power: Callimachean "Geopoetics" and the Ptolemaic Empire', in B. Acosta-Hughes, L. Lehnus and S. Stephens (eds), *The Brill Companion to Callimachus*, Leiden: Brill, 155–77.

Badian E. 1982, 'Greeks and Macedonians', in B. Barr-Sharrar and E. N Borza (eds), *Macedonia and Greece in Late Classical and Early Hellenistic Times*, Washington: National Gallery of Art, 33–51.

Bakkola E. 2018, 'Earth, Nature, and the Cult of the Tomb: The Posthumous Reception of Aeschylus Heros', in Goldschmidt and Graziosi 2018, 123–46.

Baralis A. 2015, 'Le banquet en Thrace', in A. Esposito (ed.) *Autour du 'banquet'. Modèles de consommation et usages sociaux*, Dijon: Éditions universitaires de Dijon, 253–73.

Barbato M. 2020, *The Ideology of Democratic Athens. Institutions, Orators and Mythical Past*, Edinburgh: Edinburgh University Press.

Barker A. 2014, *Ancient Greek Writers on Their Musical Past. Studies in Greek Musical Historiography*, Pisa/Rome: Fabrizio Serra editore.

Barth F. 2002, 'Towards a Richer Description and Analysis of Cultural Phenomena', in R. G. Fox and B. J. King (eds), *Anthropology Beyond Culture*, Oxford: Oxford University Press, 23–36.

Bassino P. 2019, *The 'Certamen Homeri et Hesiodi'*, Leiden: Brill.

Beaulieu M.-C. 2004, 'L'héroïsation du poète Hésiode en Grèce ancienne', *Kernos* 17 [URL: http://journals.openedition.org/kernos/1403; DOI: https://doi.org/10.4000/kernos.1403].

Bell C. M. 1992, *Ritual Theory, Ritual Practice*, Oxford: Oxford University Press.
Bednarek B. 2021, *The Myth of Lycurgus in Aeschylus, Naevius, and Beyond*, Leiden: Brill.
Berlinzani F. 2004, 'Aspetti della musica tracia nelle antiche fonti greche', in P. Schirippa (ed.), *I Traci. Tra l'Egeo e il Mar Nero*, Milan, 47–64.
Berman D. W. 2015, *Myth, Literature, and the Creation of the Topography of Thebes*, Cambridge: Cambridge University Press.
Bernabé A. 2002, 'Orfeo. De personaje del mito a autor literario', *Itaca* 18, 61–78.
Bernabé A. 2004–2007, *Poetae epici Graeci. Testimonia et fragmenta*, vol. 2.1–3, Leiden: Brill.
Bernabé A. 2005, *Poetae epici Graeci. Testimonia et fragmenta*, Pars 2: *Orphicorum et Orphicis similium testimonia et fragmenta*, fasciculus 2, Leiden: Brill.
Bernabé A. 2008, 'Orfeo, una "biografía" compleja', in Bernabé and Casadesús 2008, 15–32.
Bernabé A. 2017, 'Orpheus in Apollodorus', in Pamias 2017, 113–25.
Bernabé A. and Jimenez San Cristobal A. I. 2008, *Instruction to the Netherworld. The Orphic Gold Tablets*, Leiden/Boston: Brill.
Bernabé A. and Casadesús F. (eds) 2008, *Orfeo y la tradición órfica. Un reencuentro*, vol. 1–2, Madrid: Akal.
Bernabé A., Casadesús F. and Santamaria M. A. (eds) 2010, *Orfeo y el Orfismo: Nuevas perspectivas*, Alicante.
Betegh G. 2014, 'Pythagoreanism, Orphism, and Greek Religion', in Huffman 2014, 149–66.
Bing P. 1988, *The Well-Read Muse: Present and Past in Callimachus and the Hellenistic Poets*, Göttingen: Vandenhoeck & Ruprecht.
Bing, P. 1993, 'The Bios-Tradition and the Poets' Lives in Hellenistic Poetry', in R. Rosen and J. Farrell (eds), *Nomodeiktes. Greek Studies in Honor of Martin Ostwald*, Michigan: University of Michigan Press, 619–31.
Bingen J. 2007, *Hellenistic Egypt: Monarchy, Society, Economy, Culture*, Berkeley: University of California Press.
Blum R. 1991, *Kallimachos. The Alexandrian Library and the Origins of Bibliography*, Madison/London: University of Wisconsin Press.
Bonano-Aravantinou M. 2009, 'The Helikon and Its Environs', in A. G. Vlochopoulos (ed.), *Archaeology: Euboea and Central Greece*, Athens: Melissa Publishing House, 260–8.
Borgeaud P. (ed.) 1991, *Orphisme et Orphée en l'honneur de Jean Rudhardt*, Genève: Librairie Droz.
Borza E. 1990, *In the Shadow of Olympus. The Emergnece of Macedon*, Princeton: Princeton University Press.

Boshnakov K. 2003, *Die Thraker südlich vom Balkan in den Geographika Strabos: Quellenkritische Untersuchungen*, Stuttgart: Franz Steiner Verlag.
Boyancé P. 1937, *Le culte des Muses chez les Philosophes Grecs. Études d'Histoire et de psychologie religieuses*, Paris: de Boccard.
Braswell B. K. 1988, *A Commentary on the Fourth Pythian Ode of Pindar*, Berlin: Walter de Gruyter.
Bremmer J. N. (ed.) 1987, *Interpretations of Greek Mythology*, London: Routledge.
Bremmer J. N. 1987, 'What is a Greek Myth', in Bremmer (ed.) 1987, 1-9.
Bremmer J. N. 1991, 'Orpheus: From Gay to Guru', in Borgeaud 1991, 13-30.
Bremmer J. N. 1997, 'Myth as Propaganda: Athens and Sparta', *Zeitschrift für Papyrologie und Epigraphik* 117, 9-17.
Bremmer J. N. 2013, 'The agency of Greek and Roman statues: from Homer to Constantine', *Opuscula* 6, 7-21.
Brisson L. 2016, 'The Making of Pythagoreanism: Orpheus, Aglaophamus, Pythagoras, Plato', in A.-B. Renger and A. Stavru (eds) *Pythagorean Knowledge from the Ancient to the Modern World: Askesis, Religion, Science*, Wiesbaden: Harrassowitz Verlag, 45-59.
Brown M. K. 2002, *The Narratives of Konon*, München/Leipzig: K.G. Saur Verlag.
Bruegger C. and others 2010, *Homers Ilias. Gesamtkommentar, Band II, Fasz. 2: Kommentar*, Leiden: Brill.
Brun P. 1991, 'Les Lagides à Lesbos: Essai de Chronologie', *Zeitschrift für Papyrologie und Epigraphik* 85, 99-113.
Budelmann F. 2018, *Greek Lyric: A Selection*, Cambridge: Cambridge University Press.
Budelmann F. (ed.) 2009, *The Cambridge Companion to Greek Lyric*, Cambridge: Cambridge University Press.
Bühler W. 1987-99, *Zenobii Athoi proverbia. Vulgari ceteraque memoria aucta*, vols 1, 4, 5, Göttingen: Vandenhoeck & Ruprecht.
Bühler W. 1987, *Zenobii Athoi proverbia. Vulgari ceteraque memoria aucta edidit et enarravit. Vol. 1: Prolegomena complexum, in quibus codices describuntur*, Göttingen: Vandenhoeck & Ruprecht.
Bundrick S. 2005, *Music and Image in Classical Athens*, Cambridge: Cambridge University Press.
Bundrick S. 2020, 'Visualizing Music', in E. Rocconi and T. Lynch (eds), *The Blackwell Companion to Greek and Roman Music*, London: Wiley-Blackwell, 17-30.
Burgess Watson S. 2013, 'Muses of Lesbos or (Aeschylean) Muses of Pieria? Orpheus' Head on a Fifth-century Hydria', *Greek, Roman, and Byzantine Studies* 53, 441-60.
Burgess Watson S. 2014, 'Orpheus' Erotic Mysteries. Plato, Pederasty and Zagreus' Myth in Phanocles 1', *Bulletin of the Institute of Classical Studies* 57.2, 47-71.
Burgess Watson S. 2015, '*Mousikê* and Mysteries: A Nietzschean Reading of Aeschylus' *Bassarides*', *Classical Quarterly* 65.2, 455-75.

Burkert W. 1994, 'Orpheus, Dionysos und die Euneiden in Athen: Das Zeugnis von Euripides' Hypsipyle', in A. Bierl and P. V. Möllendorf (eds), *Orchestra. Drama, Mythos, Bühne*, Stuttgart: Vieweg and Teubner Verlag, 44–9.

Buxton R. G. 1994, *Imaginary Greece. The Contexts of Mythology*, Cambridge: Cambridge University Press.

Calame C. 2009, *Greek Mythology. Poetics, Pragmatics and Fiction*, Cambridge: Cambridge University Press.

Cameron A. 2004, *Greek Mythography in the Roman World*, Oxford: Oxford University Press.

Campbell G. L. 2006, *Strange Creatures: Anthropology in Antiquity*, Bristol: Bristol Classical Press.

Canetta 2008, 'Muse e ninfe nella settima ecloga di Virgilio', *Eikasmos* 19, 209–24.

Capra A. 2014, *Plato's Four Muses: the Phaedrus and the Poetics of Philosophy*, Cambridge MA: Harvard University Press.

Cardin M. and Tribulato O. 2018, 'Enumerating the Muses: Tzetzes in Hes. *Op.* 1 and the Parody of Catalogic Poetry in Epicharmus', in M. Ercoles et al. (eds), *Approaches to Greek Poetry*, Berlin: Walter de Gruyter, 161–92.

Carney E. D. 2003, 'Elite Education and High Culture in Macedonia', in W. Heckel and L. A. Tritle (eds), *Crossroads of History: The Age of Alexander*, Claremont: Regina Books, 47–63.

Carney E. D. 2015, *King and Court in Ancient Macedonia: Rivalry, Treason and Conspiracy*, Swansea: The Classical Press of Wales.

Carter T. and Goldthwaite R. A. 2013, *Orpheus in the Marketplace. Jacopo Peri and the Economy of Late Renaissance Florence*, Cambridge MA: Harvard University Press.

Celoria F. 1992, *The Metamorphoses of Antoninus Liberalis*, London/New York: Routledge.

Centrone B. 2014, 'The Pseudo-Pythagorean Writings', in Huffman 2014, 315–40.

Christesen P. and Murray S. C. 2010, 'Macedonian Religion', in Roisman and Worthington 2010, 428–45.

Clausen W. 1994, *A Commentary on Virgil Eclogues*, Oxford: Oxford University Press.

Clay D. 2004, *Archilochos Heros: The Cult of Poets in the Greek Polis*, Cambridge MA: Harvard University Press.

Clinton K. 2022, 'The Reunion of the Athenian Asty with the Piraeus, 280–279 B.C.', *Grammateion* 11, 7–16.

Cohen A. 2007, 'Mythic Landscapes of Greece', in Woodard (ed.) 2007, 305–30.

Cohen B. (ed.) 2000, *Not the Classical Ideal: Athens and the Construction of the Other in Greek Art*, Leiden: Brill.

Cohen B. 2012, 'The Non-Greek in Greek Art', in T. J. Smith (ed.), *A Companion to Greek Art*, Malden, MA: Wiley-Blackwell, 456–79.

Coleman R. 1977, *Vergil Eclogues*, Cambridge: Cambridge University Press.
Connor W. R. 1988, 'Seized by the Nymphs: Nympholepsy and Symbolic Expression in Classical Greece', *Classical Antiquity* 7.2, 155–89.
Cowan R. 2021, 'Since Orpheus Was in Short Pants: Reassessing Oeagrus at Aristophanes, *Wasps* 579-80', *Classical Quarterly* 71.1, 89–94.
Crowther N. B. 1979, 'Water and Wine as Symbols of Inspiration', *Mnemosyne* 32.1-2, 1–11.
Csapo E. 2004, 'The Politics of the New Music', in Murray and Wilson 2004, 207–48.
Csapo E. and Wilson P. 2009, 'Timotheus the New Musician', in Budelmann 2009, 277–93.
D'Agostini M., Anson E. M. and Pownall F. (eds) 2021, *Affective Relations and Personal Bonds in Hellenistic Antiquity. Studies in Honor of Elizabeth D. Carney*, Oxford: Oxford University Press.
D'Agostino H. 2007, *Onomacriti Testimonia et Fragmenta*, Pisa: Istituti editoriali e poligrafici internazionali.
Dandrow E. 2017, 'Ethnography and Identity in Strabo's *Geography*', in Dueck et al. 2005, 113–24.
Daux G. 1960, 'Chronique des Fouilles', *Bulletin de Correspondance Hellénique* 84, 793–7.
De Jesus C. M. A. 2015, *Pseudo-Aristotle: Epitaphs for the Heoroes*, Berlin: Logos Verlag.
Delattre Ch. 2006, 'L'ordre généalogique, entre mythographie et doxographie', *Kernos* 19, 145–59.
Delattre Ch. 2017, 'Islands of Knowlege. Space and Names in Imperial Mythography', in Hawes (ed.) 2017, 261–80.
Desbals M.-A. 1997, *La Thrace et les thraces dans l'imaginaire Grec aux epoques archaique et classique* I-11, Paris [http://www.theses.fr/1997PA100157].
Detienne M. 2003, *The Writing of Orpheus: Greek Myth in Cultural Context*, Baltimore: Johns Hopkins University Press (fr. orig.: *L'écriture d'Orphée*, Paris 1989).
Dickie M. W. 1995, 'The Dionysiac mysteries in Pella', *Zeitschrift für Papyrologie und Epigraphik* 109, 81–6.
Dillon S. 2006, *Ancient Greek Portrait Sculpture*, Cambridge: Cambridge University Press.
Di Marco M. 1993, 'Dioniso ed Orfeo nelle *Bassaridi* di Eschilo', in Masaracchia 1993, 101–53.
Dodds E. 1960, *Euripides: Bacchae*, edited with Introduction and Commentary, Oxford: Oxford University Press.
Dović M. and Helgason J. K. 2016, *National Poets, Cultural Saints: Canonization and Commemorative Cults of Writers in Europe*, Leiden: Brill.
Dowden K. 1992, *The Uses of Greek Mythology*, London/New York: Routledge.
Dowden K. and Livingstone N. (eds) 2011, *A Companion to Greek Mythology*, London: Wiley-Blackwell.

Dueck D. (ed.) 2017, *Routledge Companion to Strabo*, London: Routledge.
Dueck D. 2021, *Illiterate Geography in Classical Athens and Rome*, London/New York: Routledge.
Dueck D., Lindsay H. and Pothecary S. (eds) 2005, *Strabo's Cultural Geography*, Cambridge: Cambridge University Press.
Edmonds III R. G. 2011, *The 'Orphic' Gold Tablets and Greek Religion: Further Along the Path*, Cambridge/New York: Cambridge University Press.
Edmonds III R. G. 2013, *Redefining Ancient Orphism. A Study in Greek Religion*, Cambridge: Cambridge University Press.
Eidinow E. and Kindt J. (eds) 2015, *The Oxford Handbook of Ancient Greek Religion*, Oxford: Oxford University Press.
Ekroth G. 2002, *The Sacrificial Rituals of Greek Hero-Cults in the Archaic to the Early Hellenistic Period*, Liège: Presses universitaires de Liège.
Ekroth G. 2015, 'Heroes – Living or Dead?', in Eidinow and Kindt 2015, 383–96.
Engels J. 2010, 'Macedonians and Greeks', in Roisman and Worthington 2010, 81–98.
Fearn D. 2007, *Bacchylides. Politics, Performance, Poetic Tradition*, Oxford: Oxford University Press.
Ford A. 2002, *The Origins of Criticism: Literary Culture and Poetic Theory in Classical Greece*, Princeton: Princeton University Press.
Fowler R. L. 1999, 'Genealogical Thinking, Hesiod's *Catalogue*, and the Creation of the Hellenes', *Proceedings of the Cambridge Philological Society* 44, 1–19.
Fowler R. L. 2000, *Early Greek Mythography*, vol. I, *Texts*, Oxford: Oxford University Press.
Fowler R. L. 2013, *Early Greek Mythography*, vol. II, *Commentary*, Oxford: Oxford University Press.
Fowler R. L. 2015, 'History', in Eidinow and Kindt 2015, 195–209.
Fowler R. L. 2017, 'Apollodorus and the Art of the Variant', in Pamias 2017, 158–75.
Freiert W. K. 1991, 'Orpheus: a Fugue on the Polis', in D. C. Pozzi and J. M. Wickersham (eds), *Myth and the Polis*, Ithaca: Cornell University Press, 32–48.
Fry S. 2018, *Heroes: Mortals and Monsters, Quests and Adventures*, London: Penguin Books.
Fulińska A. 2014, 'Dionysos, Orpheus and Argead Macedonia. Overview and Perspectives', *Classica Cracoviensia* 17, 43–67.
Gahtan M. W. and Pegazzano D. (eds) 2015, *Museum Archetypes and Collecting in the Ancient World*, Leiden: Brill.
Galoin A. 2017, *L'iconographie d'Orphée dans la céramique attique au Vè siècle av. J.-C.*, (accessible in https://www.academia.edu/34608326/Liconographie_dOrphée_dans_la_céramique_attique_au_Vè_siècle_av_J_C_pdf).
Ganter A. (née Kühr) 2014, 'Ethnicity and Local Myth', in McInerney (ed.) 2014, 228–40.

Garezou M.-X. 1994, 'Orpheus', in LIMC 7.1, 81–105.
Garezou M.-X. 2009, 'Orpheus', in LIMC, Suppl. 1–2, 399–405.
Gartziou-Tatti, A. 1999, 'Θάνατος και ταφή του Ορφέα στη Μακεδονία και τη Θράκη', *Ancient Macedonia* 6, 439–51.
Geisau H. von 1919, 'Kastalia', in RE, vol. 20, col. 2336–8.
Goldschmidt S. and Graziosi B. (eds) 2018, *Tombs of the Ancient Poets*, Oxford: Oxford University Press.
Gostoli A. 1990, *Terpander*, Rome: Edizioni dell'Ateneo.
Goukowsky P. 1976, *Diodore de Sicile: Bibliothèque historique. Livre XVII*, Paris: Les Belles Lettres.
Graf F. 1974, *Eleusis und die orphische Dichtung Athens in vorhellenistischer Zeit*, Leiden: Brill.
Graf F. 1987, 'Orpheus. A Poet Among Men', in Bremmer (ed.) 1987, 80–106.
Graf F. 1993, *Greek Mythology: An Introduction*, transl. T. Marier, Baltimore/London: Johns Hopkins University Press.
Graf F. 2011, 'Myth and Hellenic Identities', in Dowden and Livingstone (eds) 2011, 211–26.
Graf F. and Iles Johnston S. 2007, *Ritual Texts for the Afterlife. Orpheus and the Bacchic Gold Tablets*, London: Routledge.
Graninger D. 2010, 'Macedonia and Thessaly', in Roisman and Worthington 2010, 306–25.
Graninger D. 2015, 'Ethnicity and Ethne', in Valeva et al. 2015, 22–32.
Graziosi B. 2002, *Inventing Homer. The Early Reception of Epic*, Cambridge: Cambridge University Press.
Graziosi B. 2018, 'Still Singing: The Case of Orpheus', in Goldschmidt and Graziosi 2018, 171–96.
Greco E. (ed.) 2011, *Topografia di Atene*, vol. 2, *Colline sud-occidentali, Valle dell'Illisso*, Atene: Scuola archeologica italiana; Paestum, Salerno: Pandemos.
Greenwalt W. S. 2003, 'Archelaus the Philhellene', *Ancient World* 34, 131–53.
Greenwalt W. S. 2015, 'Thracian and Macedonian Kingship', in Valeva et al. 2015, 337–51.
Griffiths A. 2011, 'Myth in History', in Dowden and Livingstone 2011, 195–208.
Gruen E. 2013, 'Did Ancient Identity Depend on Ethnicity? A Preliminary Probe', *Phoenix* 67.1-2, 1–22.
Gruen E. 2020, *Ethnicity in the Ancient World – Did it Matter?* Berlin/Boston: Martin de Gruyter.
Gundlach I. 2019, *Poetologische Bildersprache in der Zeit des Augustus*, Hildesheim/Zürich/New York: Olms.
Guthrie W. K. C. 1952, *Orpheus and Greek Religion*, Princeton: Princeton University Press.

Haake M. 2020, 'Städtische Philosophenkulte in der griechischen Welt zwischen Archaik und Hellenismus – Fakten und Fiktionen', *Mythos. Rivista di Storia delle Religioni*, 14 (URL: http://journals.openedition.org/mythos/1901).

Hadjimichael T. A. 2019, *The Emergence of the Lyric Canon*, Oxford: Oxford University Press.

Hägg T. 2012, *The Art of Biography in Antiquity*, Cambridge: Cambridge University Press.

Hall E. 1989, *Inventing the Barbarian. Greek Self-Definition Through Tragedy*, Oxford: Oxford University Press.

Hall E. 1996, 'When is a Myth not a Myth? Bernal's *Ancient Model*', in M. Lefkowitz (ed.), *Black Athena Revisited*, Chapel Hill, NC: The University of North Carolina Press, 333–48.

Hall E. 2000, 'Female Figures and Metapoetry in Old Comedy', in D. Harvey and J. Wilkins (eds), *The Rivals of Aristophanes. Studies in Athenian Old Comedy*, London: Classical Press of Wales, 407–18.

Hall J. 1997, *Ethnic Identity in Greek Antiquity*, Cambridge: Cambridge University Press.

Hall J. 2001, 'Contested Ethnicities: Perceptions of Macedonia within Evolving Definitions of Greek Identity', in Malkin 2001, 159–86.

Hall J. 2002, *Hellenicity: Between Ethnicity and Culture*, Chicago/London: University of Chicago Press.

Halliwell S. 2012, '*Amousia*: Living without the Muses', in I. Sluiter and R. M. Rosen (eds), *Aesthetic Value in Classical Antiquity*, Leiden: Brill, 15–46.

Hammond N. G. L. 1972, *A History of Macedonia*, vol. 1, *Historical Geography and Prehistory*, Oxford: Oxford University Press.

Hammond N. G. L. 1995, 'Connotations of "Macedonia" and of "Macedones" Until 323 B. C.', *Classical Quarterly* 45.1, 120–8.

Hammond N. G. L. and Griffith G. T. 1979, *A History of Macedonia*, vol. 2, Oxford: Oxford University Press.

Hanink J. 2018, 'Pausanias' Dead Poets Society', in Goldschmidt and Graziosi 2018, 235–52.

Harder A. 1985, *Euripides' Kresphontes and Archelaus*, Leiden: Brill.

Hardie A. 1997, 'Philitas and the Plane Tree', *Zeitschrift für Papyrologie und Epigraphik* 119, 21–36.

Hardie A. 2003, 'The Statue(s) of Philitas (*P. Mil. Vogl.* VIII 309 col. X. 16–25 and Hermesianax fr. 7.75-78 P.)', *Zeitschrift für Papyrologie und Epigraphik* 143, 27–36.

Hardie A. 2006, 'The Aloades on Helicon. Music, Territory and Cosmic Order', *Antike und Abendland* 52, 42–71.

Hardie A. 2016, 'The Camenae in Cult, History, and Song', *Classical Antiquity* 35.1, 45–85.

Harding P. 1994, *Androtion and the Atthis*, Oxford: Oxford University Press.

Harrison Th. (ed.) 2002, *Greeks and Barbarians*, New York: Routledge.
Hartog F. 1988, *The Mirror of Herodotus. The Representation of the Other in the Writing of History*. Berkeley, LA/London: University of California Press.
Harvey D. 2000, 'Phrynichus and his Muses', in D. Harvey and J. Wilkins (eds), *The Rivals of Aristophanes*, London: Classical Press of Wales, 91–113.
Hass P. 1998, *Der locus amoenus in der antiken Literatur: Zu Theorie und Geschichte eines literarischen Motivs*, Erlangen/Nürnberg.
Hatzopoulos M. B. 1994, *Cultes et rites de passage en Macedoine*, Athens.
Hatzopoulos M. B. 2011, 'Macedonia and Macedonians', in Lane Fox 2011, 43–50.
Hatzopoulos M. B. 2011a, 'Macedonians and Other Greeks', in Lane Fox 2011, 51–78.
Hatzopoulos M. B. 2020, *Ancient Macedonia*, Berlin/Boston: Martin de Gruyter.
Hatzopoulos M. B. and Paschidis P. 2004, 'Makedonia', in H. Hansen (ed.), *Inventory of Archaic and Classical Poleis*, Oxford: Oxford University Press, 794–809.
Hawes G. 2014, *Rationalizing Myth in Antiquity*, Oxford: Oxford University Press.
Hawes G. (ed.) 2017, *Myths on the Map. The Storied Landscapes of Ancient Greece*, Oxford: Oxford University Press.
Hawes G. 2021, *Pausanias in the World of Greek Myth*, Oxford: Oxford University Press.
Heath J. 1994, 'The Failure of Orpheus', *Transactions of the American Philological Association* 124, 163–96.
Hecht Ch. 2017, *Zwischen Athen und Alexandria: Dichter und Künstler beim makedonischer König Archelaos*, Wiesbaden: Harrassowitz Verlag.
Hendrix H. 2007, 'The Early Modern Invention of Literary Tourism. Petrarch's Houses in France and Italy', in H. Hendrix (ed.), *Writers' Houses and the Making of Memory*, London: Routledge, 15–29.
Henrichs, A. 1985, 'Zur Genealogie des Musaios', *Zeitschrift für Papyrologie und Epigraphik* 58, 1–8.
Henrichs A. 1987, 'Three Approaches to Greek Mythography', in Bremmer (ed.) 1987, 242–77.
Herington J. 1991, *Poetry into Drama: Early Tragedy and the Greek Poetic Tradition*, Berkeley: University of California Press.
Heslin P. 2018, *Propertius, Greek Myth, and Virgil*, Oxford: Oxford University Press.
Higbie C. 2017, *Collectors, Scholars, and Forgers in the Ancient World*, Oxford: Oxford University Press.
Hordern J. H. 2002, *The Fragments of Timotheus of Miletus*, Oxford: Oxford University Press.
Hornblower S. (ed. transl. and comm.) 2015, *Lykophron: Alexandra*, Oxford: Oxford University Press.
Huffman C. A. (ed.) 2014, *A History of Pythagoreanism*, Oxford: Oxford University Press.

Hunter R. (transl., introduction and notes) 2009, *Apollonius of Rhodes, Jason and the Golden Fleece (The Argonautica)*, Oxford: Oxford University Press.

Hunter R. and Rutherord I. (eds) 2009, *Wandering Poets in Ancient Greek Culture*, Cambridge: Cambridge University Press.

Hurst A. and Kolde A. (ed. transl. and comm.) 2008, *Lycophron. Alexandra*, Paris: Les Belles Lettres.

Huttner U. 1997, *Die politische Rolle der Heraklesgestalt im griechischen Herrschertum*, Stuttgart: Franz Steiner Verlag.

Isler-Kerényi C. 2009, 'Orfeo nella ceramografia greca', *Mythos. Rivista di Storia delle Religioni* 3, 13–32.

Jackson S. 1995, *Myrsilus of Methymna: Hellenistic Paradoxographer*, Amsterdam: Adolf M. Hakkert.

James, S. L. and Dillon, S. (eds) 2012, *A Companion to Women in the Ancient World*, Malden, MA: Wiley-Blackwell.

de Jáuregui M. H., Jiménez san Cristóbal A. I and Santamaria M. A. (eds) 2011, *Tracing Orpheus. Studies of Orphic Fragments*, Berlin/Boston: Walter de Gruyter.

Johnson P. J. 2008, *Ovid Before Exile. Art and Punishment in the Metamorphoses*, Madison: University of Wisconsin Press.

Jones C. P. 2010, *New Heroes in Antiquity: From Achilles to Antinoos*, Cambridge MA: Harvard University Press.

Kambylis A. 1965, *Die Dichterweihe und ihre Symbolik. Untersuchungen zu Hesiodos, Kallimachos, Properz und Ennius*, Heidelberg: C. Winter Verlag.

Kania R. 2012, 'Orpheus and the Reinvention of Bucolic Poetry', *American Journal of Philology* 133.4, 657–85.

Karadedos, G. 1986, 'To ellenistiko teatro tou Diou', in *Ancient Macedonia 4. Papers Read at the Fourth International Symposium Held in Thessaloniki*, Thessalonika, 325–40.

Karamitrou-Mentessidi G. 1983, Άγαλμα καθισμένης γυναικείας μορφής στο μουσείο της Πέλλας, *Makedonika* 23.1, 273–84.

Karpati A. 2016, 'Thamyras' Song Contest and the Muse Figures', in L. Bravi, L. Lomiento, A. Meriani and G. Pace (eds), *Tra lyra e aulos. Tradizioni musicali e generi poetici*, Pisa: Fabrizio Serra, 167–98.

Kauffmann-Samaras A. 1992, 'Mousaios', in LIMC vol. VI.1, 685–7.

Kimmel-Clauzet F. 2013, *Morts, tombeaux et cultes des poetes grecs*, Bordeaux: Ausonius.

Kindt J. 2012, *Rethinking Greek Religion*, Cambridge: Cambridge University Press.

King C. J. 2017, *Ancient Macedonia*, New York: Routledge.

Kivilo M. 2010, *Early Greek Poets' Lives*, Leiden: Brill.

Kleingünther A. 1933, *ΠΡΩΤΟΣ ΕΥΡΕΤΗΣ. Untersuchungen zur Geschichte einer Fragestellung*. Leipzig.

Klooster J. 2011, *Poetry as Window and Mirror. Positioning Poet in Hellenistic Society*, Leiden: Brill.
Knobl R. 2008, Biographical Representations of Euripides. Some Examples of their Development from Classical Antiquity to Byzantium (PhD thesis, University of Durham).
Kondoleon N. M. 1952, 'Neai epigraphai peri tou Archilochou', *Archaiologike Ephemeris* 91, 32–95.
König J. 2016, 'Strabo's Mountains', in J. McInerney and I. Sluiter (eds), *Valuing Landscapes in Classical Antiquity: Natural Environment and Cultural Imagination*, Leiden: Brill, 46–69.
Kotzias N. 1948–9, 'Λείβηθρα, Πίμπλεια, Πιερίς, ἡ πατρίς τοῦ Ὀρφεως', *Archaiologikē Ephēmeris*, vol. 86–88, 25–40.
Koulakiotis E. 2017, 'The Hellenic Impact on Ancient Macedonia: Conceptualizing Origin and Authority', in Müller et al. (eds) 2017, 199–213.
Kühr A. 2006, *Als Kadmos nach Boiotien kam. Polis und Ethnos im Spiegel thebanischer Gründungsmythen*, Stuttgart: Franz Steiner Verlag.
Labuda G. 2000, *Święty Wojciech, biskup-męczennik, patron Polski, Czech i Węgier*, Wrocław.
Lamprinoudakis V. K. 1986, 'Anaskaphe Epidaurou', *Praktika tes en Athenais Archaiologikes Etaireias* 139, 151–59, il. 125–37.
Lane Fox R. (ed.) 2011, *Brill's Companion to Ancient Macedon: Studies in the Archaeology and History of Macedon, 650 BC-300 AD*, Leiden: Brill.
Larson J. 2001, *Greek Nymphs: Myth, Cult, Lore*, Oxford: Oxford University Press.
Lasserre F. 1995, 'Le genealogie dei musicisti mitici', in Restani 1995, 89–96.
Lavagne H. 1998, *Operosa antra. Recherches sur la grotte à Rome de Sylla à Hadrien*, Rome/Paris: de Boccard.
Leaf W. 1915, 'Rhesos of Thrace', *Journal of Hellenic Studies* 35, 1–11.
Lee M. O. 1996, *Virgil as Orpheus. A Study of the Georgics*, New York: State University of New York Press.
Lefkowitz M. 1981, *The Lives of the Greek Poets*, London: Duckworth.
LeVen P. 2014, *Many-Headed Muse, Tradition and Innovation in Late Classical Greek Lyric Poetry*, Cambridge: Cambridge University Press.
Lévi-Strauss, C. 1966, *The Savage Mind*, Chicago: University of Chicago Press.
Liapis V. 2011, 'The Thracian Cult of Rhesus and the Heros Equitans', *Kernos* 24, 95–104.
Lightfoot J. L. 1999, *Parthenius of Nicaea. The Poetical Fragments and the Ἐρωτικὰ Παθήματα*, Oxford: Oxford University Press.
Linforth I. M. 1931, 'Two Notes on the Legend of Orpheus', *Transactions and Proceedings of the American Philological Association* 62, 5–17.
Linforth I. M. 1941, *The Arts of Orpheus*, Berkeley, LA: University of California Press.

Lipka M. 2001, *Language in Vergil's Eclogues*, Berlin: Walter de Gruyter.

Lissarague F. 1994, 'Orphee mis a mort', *Musica e storia* 2, 269-307.

Lissarague F. 2002, 'The Athenian Image of the Foreigners', in Harrison 2002, 101-24.

Long T. 1986, *Barbarians in Greek Comedy*, Carbondale: Southern Illinois University Press.

Ma J. 2009, 'City as Memory', in G. Boys-Stones et al. (eds), *The Oxford Handbook of Hellenic Studies*, Oxford: Oxford University Press, 248-59.

Magnelli E. 2010, 'Libetridi in Euforione, in Virgilio e altrove', *Materiali e discussioni per l'analisi dei testi classici* 65, 167-75.

Malinowski G. 2017, 'Strabo as Historian', in Dueck et al. 2005, 337-52.

Malkin I. (ed.) 2001, *Ancient Perceptions of Greek Ethnicity*, Cambridge MA: Harvard University Press.

Marcaccini C. 1995, 'Considerazioni sulla morte di Orfeo in Tracia', *Prometheus* 21, 241-52.

March J. 1998, *Dictionary of Classical Mythology*, Oxford/Philadelphia: Oxbow Books.

Mari M. 1998, 'Le Olimpie macedoni di Dion tra Archelao e l'età romana', *Rivista di Filologia* 126, 137-69.

Mari M. 2002, *Al di là dell'Olimpo*, Atene/Paris: de Boccard.

Mari M. 2011, 'Archaic and Early Classical Macedonia', in Lane Fox 2011, 79-92.

Mari M. 2012, 'Amphipolis between Athens and Sparta. A Philological and Historical Commentary on Thuc. V 11, 1', *Mediterraneo antico* 15.1-2, 327-53.

Masaracchia A. (ed.) 1993, *Orfeo e l'Orfismo. Atti del Seminario Nazionale (Roma-Perugia 1985-1991)*, Rome: Gruppo Editoriale Intern.

McCracken G. 1935, 'Cicero's Tusculan Villa', *Classical Journal* 30.5, 261-77.

McInerney J. 1999, *The Folds of Parnassos. Land and Ethnicity in Ancient Phokis*, Austin: University of Texas Press.

McInerney J. 2001, 'Ethnos and Ethnicity in Early Greece', in Malkin 2001, 51-73.

McInerney J. 2014a, 'Pelasgians and Leleges: Using the Past to Understand the Present', in J. Ker and C. Pieper (eds), *Valuing the Past in the Greco-Roman World*, Leiden: Brill, 25-55.

McInerney J. (ed.) 2014, *A Companion to Ethnicity in the Ancient Mediterranean*, London: Wiley-Blackwell.

McNellis C. and Sens A. 2016, *The Alexandra of Lycophron*, Oxford: Oxford University Press.

Meisner D. A. 2018, *Orphic Tradition and the Birth of the Gods*, Oxford: Oxford University Press.

Merrill E. T. 1893, *Commentary on Catullus*, Cambridge: Cambridge University Press.
Miller M. E. 1868, *Mélanges de littérature Grecque*, Paris.
Mojsik T. 2011, *Antropologia metapoetyki: Muzy w kulturze greckiej od Homera do końca V w. p.n.e.*, Warsaw: Neriton.
Mojsik T. 2015, 'Arist. Rhet. 2.23.1398b and the Cult of Pythagoras', *Classica Cracoviensia* 18, 293–310.
Mojsik T. 2017, 'Hermippus FGrH 1026 F84: Dionysius I, the Theatre and the Cult of the Muses in Syracuse', *Klio* 99.2, 485–512.
Mojsik T. 2018, 'Alexandria as "Pi(m)pleian Thebes"? A Commentary on Posidippus 118 A.–B. (P. Berol. 14283)', *Zeitschrift für Papyrologie und Epigraphik* 205, 68–76.
Mojsik T. 2019, 'From Hesiod's Tripod to Thespian *Mouseia*: Archaeological Evidence and Cultural Contexts', *Klio* 101.2, 405–26.
Mojsik 2023 (forthcoming), 'Nymphs, Muses (and Cicadas) at Ilissos: Plato's *Phaedrus* 278b and the Early Meanings of *Mouseion*', *Hermes*.
Mojsik T. (forthcoming 2), 'Muses as "fellow-citizens"? Commentary in Posidippus 118,1 AB'.
Moloney E. 2014, 'Philippus in acie tutior quam in theatro fuit… (Curtius 9, 6, 25): The Macedonian Kings and Greek Theatre', in E. Csapo et al. (eds), *Greek Theatre in the Fourth Century B.C.*, Berlin: Walter de Gruyter, 231–48.
Moloney E. 2015, 'Neither Agamemnon nor Thersites, Achilles nor Margites: The Heraclid Kings of Ancient Macedon', *Antichthon* 49.1, 50–72.
Mooney G. W. (ed., transl. & comm.) 1912, *The Argonautica of Apollonius Rhodius*, London/New York: Longmans.
Moreno F. M. 2008, 'La música de Orfeo', in Bernabé and Casadesús (eds) 2008, 33–58.
Muir J. V. 2001, *Alcidamas. The Works & Fragments*, Bristol: Bristol Classical Press.
Müller S. 2016, *Die Argeaden: Geschichte Makedoniens bis zum Zeitalter Alexanders des Großen*, Paderborn: Brill.
Müller 2017a, *Perdikkas II. – Retter Makedoniens*, Berlin: Frank & Timme.
Müller 2017b, 'The Symbolic Capital of the Argeads', in Müller et al. (eds) 2017, 183–98.
Müller S., Howe T., Bowden H. and Rollinger R. (eds) 2017, *The History of the Argeads: New Perspectives*, Wiesbaden: Harrassowitz Verlag.
Mummprecht V. 1964, *Epitaphios Bionis*, Zurich: Juris-Verlag.
Mund-Espín Ch. (ed.) 2003, *Blick auf Orpheus. 2500 Jahre europäische Rezeptionsgeschichte eines antiken Mythos*, Tübingen/Basel: A. Francke.

Murray P. and Wilson P. (eds) 2004, *Music and the Muses. The Culture of Mousike in the Classical Athenian City*, Oxford: Oxford University Press.

Natali C. 2013, *Aristotle. His Life and School*, Princeton/Oxford: Princeton University Press.

Nawotka K. 2017, *The Alexander Romance by Ps.-Callisthenes: A Historical Commentary*, Leiden: Brill.

Nesselrath H.-G. 2013, 'Das Museion und die Große Bibliothek von Alexandria', in T. Georges, F. Albrecht and R. Feldmeier (eds), *Alexandria*, Tübingen: Mohr Siebeck, 65–88.

Neumann S. 2016, *Grotten in der hellenistischen Wohnkultur*, Marburg: Eigenverlag des Archäologischen Seminars der Philipps-Universität.

Nippel W. 2002, *The Construction of the Other*, in Harrison 2002, 278–310.

Nisbet R. G. M. and Hubbard M. 1970, *A Commentary on Horace Odes, Book I*. Oxford: Clarendon Press.

Nora P. 1984–92, *Les Lieux de mémoire*, Paris: Gallimard.

Nünlist R. 1998, *Poetologische Bildersprache in der frühgriechischen Dichtung*, Stuttgart/Leipzig: B. G. Teubner.

Olmos R. 2008, 'Las imágenes de un Orfeo fugitivo y ubicuo', in Bernabé and Casadesús (eds) 2008, 137–77.

Olson S. D. 2007, *Broken Laughter: Select Fragments of Greek Comedy*, Oxford: Oxford University Press.

O'Sullivan N. 2008, 'The Authenticity of [Alcidamas] *Odysseus*: Two New Linguistic Considerations', *Classical Quarterly* 58.2, 638–47.

Overduin F. 2011, *Nicander of Colophon, Theriaca. A Literary Commentary*, Leiden: Brill.

Palladini L. P. 2013, *Aeschylus at Gela. An Integrated Approach*, Alessandria: Edizioni dell'Orso.

Pamias J. (ed.) 2017, *Apollodoriana*, Berlin: Walter de Gruyter.

Pamias J. and Geus K. 2007, *Eratosthenes, Sternsagen (Catasterismi)*, Oberhaid: Utopica Verlag.

Pandermalis D. 1997, *Dion. The Archaeological Site and the Museum*, Athens.

Papazouglou F. 1988, 'Les Villes de Macedoine a l'Epoque Romaine', *Suppléments au Bulletin de Correspondance Hellénique* 16, Athens/Paris: de Boccard.

Parker R. 1996, *Athenian Religion. A History*, Oxford: Oxford University Press.

Pavlopoulou A. 1994, *Myth and Cult of Founder-Heroes in the Greek Colonies of Thrace*, Athens.

Petridou G. 2015, *Divine Epiphany in Greek Literature and Culture*, Oxford: Oxford University Press.

Pingiatoglou S. 2010, 'Cults of Female Deities at Dion', *Kernos* 23, 179–92.
Pinkwart D. 1965, *Das Relief des Archelaos von Priene und die "Musen des Philiskos"*, Kallmünz (üb. Regensburg) Lassleben.
Plassart A. 1921, 'Inscriptions de Delphes, la liste des Théorodoques', *Bulletin de Correspondance Hellénique* 45, 1–85.
Platthy J. 1985, *The Mythical Poets of Greece*, Washington, D.C.: Federation of International Poetry Associations.
Poulake-Pantermale E. 2007, Λείβηθρα, in AEMTH 21, Thessalonika, 161–9.
Poulake-Pantermale E. (Ε. Πουλάκη-Παντερμαλή) 2008, ΛΕΙΒΗΘΡΑ, Katerine.
Power T. 2010, *The Culture of Kitharoidia*, Cambridge MA: Harvard University Press.
Pownall F. 2017, 'The Role of Greek Literature at the Argead Court', in Müller et al. (eds) 2017, 215–32.
Pownall F., Asirvatham S. R. and Müller S. (eds) 2022, *The Courts of Philip II and Alexander the Great. Monarchy and Power in Ancient Macedonia*. Berlin: Walter de Gruyter.
Prakken D. W. 1943, *Studies in Greek Genealogical Chronology*, Lancaster: Lancaster Press.
Psoma S. 2014, 'Athens and Macedonian Kingdom from Perdikkas II to Philip II', *Revue des Etudes Anciennes* 116, 133–44.
Rabadjiev K. 2015, 'Religion', in Valeva1 et al. 2015, 443–56.
Raffa M. 2018, *Theophrastus of Eresus: Commentary*, vol. 9.1: *Sources on Music* (Texts 714–26), Leiden: Brill.
Reger G. 2014, 'Ethnic Identities, Borderlands, and Hybridity', in McInerney (ed.) 2014, 112–26.
Restani D. (ed.) 1995, *Musica e mito nella Grecia antica*, Bologna: Il Mulino.
Revermann M. 1999/2000, 'Euripides, Tragedy and Macedon: Some Conditions of Reception', *Illinois Classical Studies* 24/25, 451–67.
Richardson N. J. 1981, 'The Contest of Homer and Hesiod and Alcidamas' *Mouseion*', *Classical Quarterly* 31.1, 1–10.
Ridgway B. S. 1990, *Hellenistic Sculpture I*, Bristol: University of Wisconsin Press.
Robbins E. 1982, 'Famous Orpheus', in Warden (ed.) 1982, 3–23.
Robert, C. 1917, 'Das orakelnde Haupt des Orpheus', *Jahrbuch des Kaiserlich Deutschen Archäologischen Instituts* 32, 146–7.
Robinson B. 2012, 'Mount Helikon and the Valley of the Muses: the Production of a Sacred Space', *Journal of Roman Archaeology* 25, 227–59.
Robinson B. 2013, 'On the Rocks: Greek Mountains and Sacred Conversations', in D. Ragavan (ed.), *Heaven on Earth: Temples, Ritual, & Cosmic Symbolism in the Ancient World*, Chicago: Oriental Institute of the University of Chicago, 175–99.

Roisman J. and Worthington I. (eds) 2010, *A Companion to Ancient Macedonia*, London: Wiley-Blackwell.

Romano A. J. and Marincola J. (eds) 2019, *Host or Parasite. Mythographers and their Contemporaries in the Classical and Hellenistic Periods*, Berlin: Walter de Gruyter.

Romero F. G. 2011, 'ἀμουσότερος Λειβηθρίων (OF 1069)', in de Jáuregui et al. 2011, 339–43.

Rosch E. and Lloyds B. (eds) 1978, *Cognition and Categorization*, Hillsdale NJ.

Rose H. 1958, *A Handbook of Greek Mythology*, London/New York: Routledge (6th ed.).

Rossi L. 2001, *Epigrams Ascribed to Theocritus: A Method of Approach*, Leuven: Peeters Publishers.

Roy J. 2014, 'Autochthony in Ancient Greece', in McInerney (ed.) 2014, 241–55.

Rutherford I. 1990, *Pindar's Paeans: A Reading of the Fragments with a Survey of the Genre*, Oxford: Oxford University Press.

Rutledge S. 2012, *Ancient Rome as a Museum. Power, Identity, and the Culture of Collecting*, Oxford: Oxford University Press.

Said E. 1978, *Orientalism*, New York: Pantheon Books.

Santamaría Álvarez M. A. 2008, 'La muerte de Orfeo y la cabeza profética', in Bernabé and Casadesús (eds) 2008, 105–35.

Santin E. And Tzafalias A. 2020, Les Muses de Larissa: une nouvelle inscription votive thessalienne d'époque hellénistique sur la fondation d'un sanctuaire, *Bulletin de Correspondance Hellénique* 144,1 (online edition: https://doi.org/10.4000/bch.1090)

Schachter A. 1986, *Cults of Boeotia*, vol. II: *Herakles to Poseidon*, London: University of London.

Schirippa P. 2004, 'Il confine mobile della Tracia e la fantasia tragica. Miti traci a teatro', in P. Schirippa (ed.), *Traci tra l'Egeo e il Mar Nero*, Milan: CUEM, 65–83.

Schmidt J. 1949, 'Parnassos [1]', RE vol. 18.4, col. 1573–1663

Schmidt J. 1950, 'Pimpleia', RE vol. 20.2, Stuttgart, col. 1387–9.

Schneidewin F. G. and Leutsch E. L. von 1839, *Paroemiographi Graeci*, Göttingen: Vandenhoeck & Ruprecht.

Schoeller F. M. 1969, *Darstellungen des Orpheus in der Antike*, Freiburg.

Schubart W. 1932, *Posidippus redivivus*, in *Symbolae philologicae O. A. Danielsson octogenario dicatae*, Upsalla, 290–8.

Scullion S. 2003, 'Eurypides and Macedon, or the Silence of the Frogs', *Classical Quarterly* 53.2, 389–400.

Sears M. A. 2013, *Athens, Thrace, and the Shaping of Athenian Leadership*, Cambridge: Cambridge University Press.

Sears M. A. 2015, 'Athens', in Valeva et al. 2015, 308–19.
Segal C. 1988, *Orpheus: The Myth of the Poet*, Baltimore: Johns Hopkins University Press.
Semenzato C. 2016, 'Orpheus and *mousikê* in Greek Tragedy', *Trends in Classics* 8.2, 295–316.
Shapiro H. A. 1983, 'Amazons, Thracians, and Scythians', *Greek, Roman and Byzantine Studies* 24.1, 105–14.
Sitek, M. 2016, 'The Threefold Movement of St. Adalbert's Head', *Mediaevistik* 29.1, 143–74.
Skinner J. E. 2012, *The Invention of Greek Ethnography. From Homer to Herodotus*, Oxford: Oxford University Press.
Sommerstein A. H. 2005, 'A Lover of His Art: the Art-form as Wife and Mistress in Greek Poetic Imagery', in E. Stafford and J. Herrin (eds), *Personification in the Greek World: From Antiquity To Byzantium*, Aldershot: Routledge, 161–71.
Sommerstein A. H. 2010, 'Aeschylus' epitaph', in A. H. Sommerstein, *The Tangled Ways of Zeus and Other Studies in and Around Greek Tragedy*, Oxford: Oxford University Press, 195–201.
Sourvinou-Inwood C. 2002, 'Greek Perceptions of Ethnicity and the Ethnicity of the Macedonians', in L. M. Castelnuovo (ed.), *Identità e Prassi Storica nel Mediterraneo Greco*, Milan: Edizioni ET, 173–203.
Spirydonidou-Skarsouli M. 1995, *Der erste Teil der fünften Athos-Sammlung griechischer Sprichwörter*, Berlin: Walter de Gruyter.
Sprawski S. 2010, 'Early Temenid Kings to Alexander I', in Roisman and Worthington 2010, 127–44.
Sprawski S. 2012, 'Narodziny Macedonii: wersja Tukidydesa', in R. Kulesza et al. (eds), *Świat starożytny: państwo i społeczeństwo*, Warsaw: Wydawnictwo UW, 164–71.
Stamatopoulou M. 2007, 'Thessalian Aristocracy and Society in the Age of Epinikian', in *Pindar's Poetry, Patrons and Festivals*, ed. C. Morgan and S. Hornblower, Oxford: Oxford University Press, 309–42.
Stephens S. 2003, *Seeing Double. Intercultural Poetics in Ptolemaic Alexandria*, Berkeley/ Los Angeles/London: University of California Press.
Stewart E. 2017, *Greek Tragedy on the Move: The Birth of a Panhellenic Art Form c.500–300 BC*, Oxford: Oxford University Press.
Strootman R. 2017, *The Birdcage of the Muses: Patronage of the Arts and Sciences at the Ptolemaic Imperial Court, 305–222 BCE*, Leuven: Peeters Publishers.
Taback N. 2002, *Untangling the Muses. A Comprehensive Study of Sculptures of Muses in the Greek and Roman World*, Cambridge MA (PhD thesis, Harvard University, available as microfilm).

Thalmann W. G. 2011, *Apollonius of Rhodes and the Spaces of Hellenism*, Oxford: Oxford University Press.

Theodossiev N. 2000, 'Monumental Tombs and Hero Cults in Thrace', in V. Pirenne-Delforge and E. Suárez de la Torre (eds), *Héros et héroïnes dans les mythes et les cultes grecs*, Liège: Presses universitaires de Liège, 435–47.

Thesleff H. 1965, *Pythagorean Texts of the Hellenistic Period*, Abo.

Tilly B. 1973, *Varro the Farmer: a Selection from the Res Rusticae*, London: University Tutorial Press.

Tittmann I. A. H. 1808, *Iohannis Zonarae Lexicon*, vols 1–2, Oxford: Oxford University Press.

Toepffer J. 1889, *Attische Genealogie*, Berlin.

Trzaskoma S. and Smith R. S. 2007, *Apollodorus' Library and Hyginus' Fabulae. Two Handbooks of Greek Mythology*, Indianapolis/Cambridge: Hackett Publishing Company.

Trzaskoma S. and Smith R. S. (eds) 2013, *Writing Myth: Mythography in the Ancient World*, Leuven/Paris Walpole: Peeters Publishers.

Trzcionkowski L. 2013, *Bios – thanatos – bios. Semiofory orfickie z Olbii i kultura polis* (in polish; *Bios-thanatos-bios. Orphic Semiophors from Olbia and polis culture*), Warsaw.

Trzcionkowski L. 2015, 'The Prophetic Voice of Orpheus', in K. Bielawski (ed.), *Mantic Perspectives: Oracles, Prophecy and Performance*, Lublin/Krakow, 143–68.

Tsiafakis D. 2000, 'The Allure and Repulsion of Thracians in the Art of Classical Athens', in Cohen 2000, 364–89.

Tsiafakis D. 2002, 'Thracian Influence in Athenian Imagery of the 5th Century: The Case of Orpheus', in A. Fol (ed.), *Thrace and the Aegean*, Sofia, 727–38.

Tsiafakis D. 2016, 'Ancient Thrace and the Thracians through Athenian Eyes', *Thracia* 21, 261–82.

Ustinova Y. 2009, *Caves and the Ancient Greek Mind: Descending Underground in the Search for Ultimate Truth*, Oxford: Oxford University Press.

Ustinova Y. 2017, *Divine Mania. Alteration of Consciousness in Ancient Greece*, London: Routledge.

Valeva J., Nankov E. and Graninger D. (eds) 2015, *A Companion to Ancient Thrace*, London: Wiley-Blackwell.

Vasilev M. I. 2011, 'Thucydides II.99 and the Early Expansion of the Argeadae', *Eirene* 47.1-2, 93–105.

Vasilev M. I. 2015, *The Policy of Darius and Xerxes towards Thrace and Macedonia*, Leiden: Brill.

Vasilopoulou V. 2000. 'Από το άντρο των Λειβηθρίδων στον Ελικώνα', *Epetiris tes Etaireia Boiotikon Meleton* 3.1, 404–31.

Vasilopoulou V. 2001, *From the Cave of the Nymph Koroneia, Introduction to Diary: Ephorate of Palaeoanthropology – Speleology, Hellenic Ministry of Culture*, Athens.

Vasilopoulou V. 2013, 'The Cavern of the Libethrian Nymphs at Helicon', in F. Mavridis and J. T. Jensen (eds), *Stable Places and Changing Perceptions: Cave Archaeology in Greece and Adjacent Areas*, Oxford: Oxford University Press, 319–28.

Vergados A. 2013, *The Homeric Hymn to Hermes, Introduction, Text and Commentary*, Berlin: Walter de Gruyter.

Vieillefon L. 2003, *La figure d'Orphée dans l'Antiquité tardive*, Paris: De Boccard.

Visscher M. S. 2020, *Beyond Alexandria. Literature and Empire in the Seleucid World*, Oxford: Oxford University Press.

Vlassopoulos K. 2013, *Greeks and Barbarians*, Cambridge: Cambridge University Press.

Voutiras E. 2006, 'Cult de Zeus in Macedonie', in M. Guimier-Sorbets, M. B. Hatzopoulos and Y. Morizot (eds), *Rois, cités, nécropoles. Institutions, rites et monuments en Macédoine*, Athens: Centre de recherches de l'antiquité grecque et romaine, 333–45.

Warden J. (ed.) 1982, *Orpheus. The Metamorphoses of a Myth*, Toronto: University of Toronto Press.

Waszink J. H. 1956, 'Camena', *Classica et mediaevalia* 17, 139–48.

Weber G. 1993, *Dichtung und höfische Gesellschaft. Die Rezeption von Zeitgeschichte am Hof der ersten drei Ptolemäer*, Stuttgart: Franz Steiner Verlag.

West M. L. 1983, *The Orphic Poems*, Oxford: Oxford University Press.

West M. L. 1990, *Studies in Aeschylus*, Stuttgart: Walter de Gruyter.

West M. L. 2010, 'Orpheus and the Argonauts', in Bernabé et al. 2010, 11–23.

Wickersham J. M. 1991, 'Myth and Identity in Archaic Polis', in D. C. Pozzi and J. M. Wickersham (eds), *Myth and the Polis*, Ithaca and London: Cornell University Press, 16–31.

Wilamowitz-Möllendorf U. von 1903, *Timotheos, Die Perser*, Lepizig.

Wilson N. L. 2007, 'Scholiasts and commentators', *Greek, Roman and Byzantine Studies* 47.1, 39–70.

Wilson P. 1999/2000, 'Euripides' Tragic Muse', *Illinois Classical Studies* 24/25, 427–50.

Wilson P. 2004, 'Athenian Strings', in Murray and Wilson 2004, 269–306.

Wilson P. 2007, 'Sicilian Choruses', in P. Wilson (ed.), *The Greek Theatre and Festivals*, Oxford: Oxford University Press, 351–77.

Wilson P. 2009, 'Thamyris the Thracian: the Archetypal Wandering Poet?', in Hunter and Rutherord 2009, 46–79.

Wolicki A. 2015, 'The Education of Women in Ancient Greece', in W. M. Bloomer ed., *A Companion to Ancient Education*, Malden MA: Wiley-Blackwell, 305–20.

Woodard R. (ed.) 2007, *The Cambridge Companion to Greek Mythology*, Cambridge: Cambridge University Press.

Xydopoulos I. K. 2012, 'Anthemus and Hippias The Policy of Amyntas I', *Illinois Classical Studies* 37, 21–37.

Xydopoulos I. K. 2016, 'The Eastern Macedonian Border in Alexander I's Reign', in M. Giannopoulou and Chr. Kalline (ed.), Τιμητικός Τόμος για τη Στέλλα Δρούγου, ἡχάδιν II, Athens.

Zahrnt M. 2015, 'Early History of Thrace to the Murder of Kotys I (360 BCE)', in Valeva et al. 2015, 35–47.

Zanker P. 1995, *The Mask of Socrates. The Image of the Intellectual in Antiquity*, Berkeley: University of California Press.

Zeitlin F. 1996, *Playing the Other. Gender and Society in Classical Greek Literature*, Chicago/London: University of Chicago Press.

Ziegler, K. 1939, 'Orpheus', RE, vol. XVIII.1, col. 1200–1316.

Index

Achilles 8 n.25, 13, 54, 96–7, 105
Acronius ad Horat. *carm.* 1,26,9: 51 n.20
Aeschylus 24, 26, 45, 61, 113, 124, 126 n.63, 127, 133
   Bassarids: 33, 40, 48, 57, 64–5, 92, 94–6, 102, n.39, 112,
   Lycurgeia: 19 n.26, 33 n.15
Agathon 32 n. 12, 143–4, 154
Aglaophamus 61
Agriope 2, 24, 35, 107
Alcidamas 40, 114–15, 84 n.51, 138
   Ulixes 24: 20, 34–5, 86,
Alexander I: 78, 80, 103, 135, 144
Alexander the Great 94, 103, 116–19, 141–2, 153
Alexandria 4, 58, 66 and n.68, 124, 127 n.71
amousia 6, 98, 99 n.24, 108, 153
Amphion 19, 85
Amphipolis 40, 64, 123, 132–3
Amyntas II: 104, 131
Androtion 37, 40, 84 n.51
   BNJ 324 F54a: 34–5, 86
Antissa 16, 24, 111–14, 111 n.12, 116
Apollo 1, 4–5, 14, 20, 24, 31, 36–7, 36 n.20, 51, 81, 87, 93–4, 100–7, 130, 136, 139–40,
   Aiglatas/Asgelatas 121
   Maleatas 125
   Musagetes 125
Apollodorus 12, 21, 104, 136,
   1, 14–15: 1–2 and n.7, 95, 130, 139; 2,63: 129–30; 3,27–8: 43
Apollonius Rhodius
   1,23–34: 3–4, 22–3, 35, 37, 42, 45, 53–5, 54 n.23, 58, 61–8, 90–1, 95, 141, 152; 4,260: 66 n.66
Archelaus I: 8–9, 80, 92–3, 103, 108, 141–4, 146–9, 154
Archilochus 123–4, 133
Ardalos 5, 38 n.30, 85

Aristophanes 14
   Ranae 1030–6: 16 n.15, 19,
   Thesmophoriazusae 134–45: 19 n. 26
   Wasps 579–80: 87 n.58
Aristotle 19, 59, 94, 100 n.30, 103, 145,
   Rhetorica 1,5,1361a: 126
   fr. 7: 13
   fr. 545: 112 n.19
   fr. 552 (*Constitution of Methone*): 6, 99–100, 108,
   fr. 640 (*Veterum heroum epitaphia*): 35 n.19
Arrian
   Anabasis 1,11,2: 117–19, 124
Athenaeus
   14,632c: 4
   14,637a: 121
Athens 6, 7 n.32, 16–17, 38, 40, 63, 65–6, 83 n.50, 89, 95–6, 100, 126 n.58, 128–9, 128 n.72, 149

Bacchylides 144 and n.27
Bephyra 53, 60, 74, 96–8, 108, 116 and n.30
Boeotia 49, 51–3, 51 n.16, 52 n.20, 61, 69–77, 70 n.4, 74 n.14, 83, n.49, 84, 105, 129 and n.77, 131–2, 134, 139,
Bistones 36, 64–6
Bistonia 3–4, 22, 36–7, 54, 58, 62–8, 88, 91, 95
Bizaltia 63 and n.5

Cadmus 75–6
Callimachus 16 n.13
   hymn 4,7–8: 4, 52, 54, 106, 141
   fr. 2 Pfeiffer: 58 n.29
Calliope 1, 3, 26 and n.49, 54, 92–3, 100–6, 137, 154,
Camenae 51, 60 and n.45
Charops 36

Catullus
    105: 51 n.19, 54, 57–8,
Certamen Homeri et Hesiodi (4) 100–4, 139
Charax
    BNJ 103 F62: 100–4, 100 n.31, 139
Cicones 22, 35, 40, 63–5, 63 n.52–3
Clio 62, 123
Conon 21, 46, 110,
    7: 41, 128
    45: 6, 39, 41 and n.42, 62, 67, 90 n.3, 98, 115–16, 119–22, 129
Cyme 17, 74, 101

Damastes of Sigeum 16–7, 19, 35 n.18, 101
Dichterweihe 57, 73–4
Diodorus Siculus 39
    3,59,2: 43; 3,65,6: 36; 17,16, 3–4: 141–2
Diogenes Laertios
    1,5: 114–15, 139, 115 n.29
Diogenianus
    2,26: 53, 99
Dion 45, 47–9, 56, 87, 97–8, 110, 111 and n.12, 115–17, 115 n.29, 121–2, 124, 131, 134, 136, 138–43, 149, 161
Dionysius I 126, 143
Dionysus 1, 9, 17 and n.20, 29 n.1, 33–4, 40, 42–3, 68, 91, 95, 142, 144, 152
    Melpomenus 22
Drys 22, 62,

Edoni 64
Ephorus of Cyme 69, 73–7, 79, 88,
    BNJ 70 F99: 101 n.35,
    BNJ 70 F119: 74, 76 n.26
Epicharmus
    fr. 35 PCG: 49, 52, 78, 82, 103, 136, 139–41,
Eratosthenes 26,
    Catasterismi 24: 24, 33, 37, 65, 94–7, 102, n.39, 108, 112, 114, 116
Eumolpus 38, 74 n.15, 76, 160
Euneus 22, 92
Euneids 16
Euripides
    Alcestis 962–71: 33, 56
    Bacchae 560–5: 34, 91–2, 92 n.5, 144; 410: 104 n.48, 143

Hypsipyle 16, 22, 33, 37, 92
Rhesus 945–7 (*see* Pseudo-Euripides)
Archelaus, Temenus and Temenidai 92, 149
Eurydice (Orpheus' wife) 1–2, 14, 24–5, 107, 151
Eurydice (wife of Amyntas III) 142

Gorgias 126
    82 B25 DK: 35 n.18, 101, 129

Haemus Mt. 45, 62, 64
Hagnon 64, 123 and n. 43
Hebrus 36 and n.23 and 25, 45, 64–6, 97
Helicon 5, 51, 52 n.21, 53–4, 58, 70–4, 77, 80, 86, 97, 106, 115–16, 118, 126, 130–1, 140
Hellanicus of Lesbos 16–17, 19, 35, 82, 112, 130, 141, 154
    BNJ 4 F5: 101–4, 101 n.33
    BNJ 4 F74: 82, n.45–6, 104, 136
Heracles 1, 3, 8 and n.25, 13, 34, 103 n.43, 120, 129–32, 131 n.78, 135 and n.3, 139,
Hermesianax
    fr. 3 CA: 2, 24 and n.43, 35, 107
Herodoros
    BNJ 31 F42: 16–17
    BNJ 31 F43a: 17, 23
Hesiod 3, 14–17, 20, 34–5, 35 n.18, 37, 51, 57–9, 58 n.30, 71, 73, 91, 93, 100–4, 101 n.33, 107, 124, 126 and n. 61–2, 130, 131 n.79, 132, 135–6, 141–2, 154, 157,
    Theogony 1–8: 74; 53: 91 n.4; 1–115: 4 n.12
    Works and Days 1: 91 n.4
    fr. 7: 136 n.5
    fr. 160: 75 n.20
    Catalogue of Women (*see* Pseudo-Hesiod)
Hippias of Elis
    BNJ 6 F4: 16 n.15, 19,
    BNJ 6 F13: 101 n.35
Hieros Logos (Neopythagorean pseudepigraph) 17, 61, 106
Homer 3, 5, 13–17, 20, 23, 34–5, 35 n.18, 37, 40, 59, 63–4, 71, 78, 81 n.42, 84 n.51, 93, 100–4, 100 n.31,

101 n.33, 107, 115, 124 n.49, 126,
    128–33, 136, 141, 154
  Iliad 14,226: 78 and n.33
Hyginus
  Astronomia 2,7: 26, 112, 118 n.35
  Fabulae 14: 93

ideology 7 n.23, 8 n.25, 86, 134–5,
    147
Iamblichus 61,
  Vita Pythagorei 145–6: 41 n.41, 59 n.35,
    106
Ilissus 72 and n.6

kitharodia 18–24, 32, 94, 110–13, 112 n.19
    and 21, 125, 129, 144

Leibethra (*see* Libethra) 6, 42, 45–53,
    47 n.10, 55–62, 65–70, 70 n.3, 72–4,
    77–8, 84, 88, 93, 95–100, 104–6, 108,
    110–11, 111 n.12, 115–23, 133–4,
    137–8, 145–7, 153–4
Leleges 75
Lesbos 5, 16–17, 19, 20, 24, 64–6, 95, 101,
    110–16, 110 n.9–11, 112 n.19, 130,
    134, 136,
Libethra 48, 50, 53–4, 56, 61 (*see*
    Leibethra)
Libethrides Nymphs (*see* nymphs)
Libethrion Mt. 49, 51 and n.16, 61, 70–4,
    78, 84 n.51
Linus/Linos 1, 5, 14–15, 34, 38, 85, 100–4,
    103 n.44, 123, 125–34, 131 n.78,
    137 n.7, 139, 141, 146–7
Lycophron IX, 16 n.13
    273–275: 53–5, 58, 60, 62, 74, 96, 98,
    104–5, 108; 410: 48

Magnes 103 n.42
Magnesia 47, 50
Makedon 81–2, 103 n.42, 104, 135–6
Melanippides 144, 154
Menaechmus
  BNJ 12F2: 94–5, 108, 122, 133, 138
Metho 6, 39, 102
Methone 6, 36, 50, 82, 93, 99, 100–4, 107–8,
    138–9, 177
Methymna 111,113, n.63
Mnemosyne 4, 124, 142

Musaeus 3, 14 and n.8, 16, 22–3, 35
    and n.18, 38 and n.32, 85, 101,
    123, 125–9, 126 n.55 and 57,
    132–3
Mouseion Hill 6, 125–6, 129
mouseion/musaeum 58 n.32, 59 n.40,
    125–6 n.55
mousikē 4–6, 24, 31–2, 36, 38, 41, 61, 85–8,
    112, 117, 123, 126, 129–30, 133,
    135–54
Myrsilos
  BNJ 477 F2: 110–11
mythical geography 3 n.7, 8, 38, 40, 44–6,
    57, 62, 68, 136
mythography 12 and n.3, 14, 16–17,
    19 n.27, 20, 25, 39, 44, 77, 85, 93, 102
    applied mythography 12 n.3
Muses
  Heliconiades 52, 54, 74, 87, 105
  Libethrides 50–2, 51 n.16, 58–9, 72, 74,
    105,
  Pierides 74, 85, 87, 97, 104–5, 115,
    140–1
  Pi(m)pleides/Pipleiai 51–2, 51 n.20, 54,
    55 n.26, 58, 105, 141, 146
  Thespiades 54, 87

Neopythagorean(s) 17, 25, 41, 57, 59, 61,
    98, 106, 108
Nicander of Colophon
  Theriaca 461–2: 22, 62, 64
Nicomedes of Acanthus 16, 121, 145
Nonnus 67
  Dionysiaka 13,428–431: 22, 36
Nymphs ix, 39, 43, 50–2, 54, 58–62,
    59 n.40 and 43–4, 69–74, 72 n.6,
    96–7, 100, 107, 129, 141
  Libethrides 50–2, 51 n.16, 59, 62, 74,
    105
  Sphragitides 72 n.6
nympholepsy 59 and n.38
Nysa 43–4, 67–8, 90–1, 94

Odrysians 63–4
Odrysian kingdom 67
Oeagrus 3, 14, 22, 29, 31, 33–42, 36 n.20
    and 23, 54, 56, 62, 64, 87 and n.58,
    93, 100–7, 139
Olympia (festival) 119, 141–3, 147

Orphic Argonautica 22–3, 56, 59, 67, 106, 152
   50–1: 53, 93
   1373–6: 22, 55, 61, 90
Orphic(s) 9–10, 16–25, 17 n.18, 35–6, 40–1, 56–7, 59, 61, 101, 106–8, 113, 138, 141, 145, 152
Ovid 11 n.1, 25, 41, 87
   Metamorphoses 10,1–11,56: 15, 114, 140

Palamedes 34
Pangaion Mt. 4, 33, 40–1, 43, 45, 57, 59, 61, 63 n.53, 63–6, 79, 83, 92, 95–6, 137
Pausanias 6, 16 and n.12, 52, 56, 60, 84, 93, 152
   1,25,8: 125
   9,29–30: 39, 48–9, 69–72, 86–8, 97–8, 110–11, 115–16, 121–2, 130–2, 131 n.78, 138, 140,
   9,34,4: 70,
Pelasgus 75, 102
Pelasgians 40, 73, 75–6
Pella 100, 123, 136, 143–5
Phanocles
   fr. 1 Powell: 16 n.13, 23, 35, 64–5, 111, 152
Philammon 17, 23, 128
Pherecydes of Athens 16–17, 23, 101
Philip II: 100, 103, 131–2, 134, 139, 145, 148
Pieres 66 n.58 and 31, 67, 73, 77–81, 83, 94
Pimpleia (vel Pipleia vel Pi(m)pleia) viii, 3–4, 6, 42–3, 45–9, 51 n.19–20, 51–63, 65–9, 70 n.3, 73–4, 78, 88, 90, 93, 95–8, 103–6, 108, 116,119, 137, 141, 145, 146
Pimpleis 49, 52
Pindar 23, 71, 109, 124, 133,
   Pyth. 1,1–28: 31
   Isthm. 8,57–8: 97
   fr. 29–35: 4
   fr. 120–1: 144 and n.27
Plato
   Ion 530: 125; 533: 18, 112 n.21, 124
   Phaedrus 259b–d: 5
   Gorgias 471a–d: 149 n.44
   Lysis 206 b3: 153

   Symposion 179d: 13, 19
   Theaetet 174a: 31
Pliny
   NH 4,16: 50; 4,35: 79; 36,154: 58 n.32; 37,6,2: 58 n.32; 37,14: 59 n. 40
Plutarch
   Vita Alexandrii 14: 116–19
   Questiones convivales 11: 102
   De musica (*see* Pseudo-Plutarch)
   De liberis educandis (*see* Pseudo-Plutarch)
   Vita Thesei 1: 89
Polyaenus
   Stratagemata 6,54: 123; 7,43: 74 n.14
Pomponius Mela 50, 62
Porphyrius comm. ad Hor. *carm*. 1,26,9: 51 n.20
Posidippus of Pella
   118 AB: viii–ix, 4, 14 n.8, 127 and n.61, 145,
Proclus
   Vita Homeri 5,4: 14 n.8, 16–17, 101
Pseudo-Aristotle
   Peplos: 35
Pseudo-Callisthenes
   Historia Alexandri Magni 1,42: 117–24
Pseudo-Euripides
   Rhesus 945–7: 36 and n.24, 62 and n.49, 129
Pseudo-Hesiod 15, 104, 136
   Catalogue of Women (fr. 7) 81–2, 136 n.5
Pseudo-Moschos
   Lament for Bion: 24, 107,
Pseudo-Plutarch
   De musica 3–5: 5 and n.14–5, 112 n.19
   De liberis educandis 142
Pythagoras 25, 61, 106, 109, 116 and n.33, 124

Rhesus 36 and n.24, 62, 123, 132–3
Rhodopes Mts 62–6, 64 n.61

scholia 51–7, 62, 67–8, 101, 137, 152
Scholia in Ap. Rhod. Arg. 1, 23–5: 51 n.20, 55
Scholia in Lycoph. Alex. 275: 51 n.20, 55
Servius (Maurus Honoratus) 36 and n.23, 51, 59, 60, 62, 72, 140

Simonides 15, 40, 89, 124
Socrates 5, 18, 34, 124, 144
Sitalces 38, 40, 78–9, 83
Strabo
   C 410 [9,2,25]: 39, 48, 69–74, 70 n.3,
      73 n.12, 77, 28, 138
   C 471 [10,3,17]: 2, 38, 48, 70–4,
      70 n.2–3, 73 n.12, 79,
      7 fr. 10: 25, 49, 53–6, 98
Strymon 4, 33, 36, 40–1, 45, 56, 61–6,
   78–81, 95, 97, 123
Suda o 654–6, s.v. Ὀρφεύς: 16, 62, 63 n.53,
   67

Tereus 38, 79
Teres 38, 79
Terpander 5, 20, 24, 92, 112–13 and n.19
Thamyris 3, 5, 14, 17 n.18, 18, 24, 38–9, 41,
   64, 70, 85, 123, 128–9
Thebes 4–5, 7, 66, 75 n. 21, 85, 129–32, 134,
   141
Thessaly 43, 47–8, 50, 84, 115, 143 and n.
   22
Thespiae 5, 85–6, 126 n.61, 131, 133,
   140
Thrace 3, 6, 12–13, 17, 22–3, 29, 33–5, 3
7–43, 45, 49, 51–2, 55–6, 59, 61–9,
   85–6, 90, 92–3, 95–6, 102, 106,
   111–12, 112, 120, 123, 129, 136–7
Timotheos
   fr. 791 (*Persians*): 18, 91–3, 92 n.7, 104,
      108, 112–13, 122, 138, 144, 146–7, 154
Tzetzes 102
   Chiliades 6,53: 137 n.7, 139; 6, 931:
      70 n.4;
Thucydides 63
   2,99: 67, 69–70, 77–84, 78 n.31, 88, 135,
      138
   7,27: 76

Varro 60
   De re rustica 3,5,9: 58 n.32, 59 n.41
   De lingua latina 7,20: 50, 52, 54, 105
Vergilius/Virgil 11, 25–6, 36, 41, 59
   Georgics 4,508–527: 15, 36 n.25, 56
   Eclogue 7,21: 50–2, 50 n.16, 57–8, 60–3,
      74, 105, 140

Zenobius 6, 53, 99–102
Zeus 3–4, 25, 31, 34, 38, 43, 82, 92, 94, 112,
   115, 124, 136, 139, 142, 146, 152
Zone 3, 62

www.ingramcontent.com/pod-product-compliance
Lightning Source LLC
Chambersburg PA
CBHW062227300426
44115CB00012BA/2246